Roots of Haiti's
Vodou-Christian Faith

Roots of Haiti's Vodou-Christian Faith

African and Catholic Origins

R. MURRAY THOMAS

 PRAEGER

AN IMPRINT OF ABC-CLIO, LLC
Santa Barbara, California • Denver, Colorado • Oxford, England

Library of Congress Cataloging-in-Publication Data

Thomas, R. Murray (Robert Murray), 1921–
    Roots of Haiti's Vodou-Christian faith : African and Catholic Origins / R. Murray Thomas.
        pages cm
    Includes index.
    Includes bibliographical references.
    ISBN 978-1-4408-3203-1 (hardback) — ISBN 978-1-4408-3204-8 (ebook)
    1. Vodou—Haiti.   2. Catholic Church—Haiti.   3. Christianity and other religions—Vodou.   4. Haiti—Religion.   I. Title.
    BL2530.H3T49   2014
    299.6'75097294—dc23   2014000223

ISBN: 978-1-4408-3203-1
EISBN: 978-1-4408-3204-8

18 17 16 15 14   1 2 3 4 5

This book is also available on the World Wide Web as an eBook.
Visit www.abc-clio.com for details.

Praeger
An Imprint of ABC-CLIO, LLC

ABC-CLIO, LLC
130 Cremona Drive, P.O. Box 1911
Santa Barbara, California 93116-1911

This book is printed on acid-free paper ∞

Manufactured in the United States of America

To
Professor Claudine Michel,
distinguished scholar in the international field of Haitian studies
and assistant vice-chancellor for student affairs at the University
of California, Santa Barbara

Contents

Preface

An historical review of religions confirms the observation that belief systems are not static but are constantly changing. The rate of change can vary from one faith to another and from one aspect of a faith to another aspect. The change may be extremely slow—almost imperceptible. Or, the change may be rapid, often resulting in a traditional version of the faith splitting into separate denominations—with some denominations more radically deviant than others from the original version.

In this book, I propose that the Haiti's combined Vodou/Christian religion has identifiable roots and in recent decades has displayed an accelerating rate of change. To document this proposition, I reach back five centuries to inspect the nature of the two religious traditions that have been credited as the most influential sources of the dominant form of Haitian faith. Those sources have been: (a) traditional African religions brought by the slaves who were imported to Haiti to labor in the island nation's fields and mines and (b) the Catholicism promoted by Spanish and French colonial authorities who so affected Haitian culture from the beginning of the 16th century until the present day. Following the description of indigenous African and traditional Catholic religious practices, I describe present-day Haitian Vodou as it relates to those African and Catholic roots. I also suggest what the future may hold for religion in Haiti.

I wish to express my gratitude to Dr. Claudine Michel, a distinguished professor of Black Studies at the University of California, Santa Barbara, who inspired me to write this book and who offered valuable guidance in that endeavor.

Finally, I note that the Catholic portions of several chapters of this book have drawn liberally on portions of my earlier volume titled *Manitou and God: North-American Indian Religions and Christian Culture* (© R. Murray Thomas), published by Praeger in 2008.

R. Murray Thomas

PART I

Introduction

Two chapters comprise Part I. Chapter 1 describes the purpose and structure of *Roots of Haiti's Vodou-Christian Faith* and Chapter 2 offers a historical sketch depicting political, social, and religious developments in Haiti from the end of the 15th century until 2014.

The Nature of the Book

T his book is the result of my first attempt to seek answers to two questions:

What, precisely, is the dominant form of religion in the nation of Haiti?
From what sources has that religion evolved?

I began the search for answers by surveying the published literature, an effort that yielded the following sort of information:

It is sometimes said that Haiti is 90 percent Catholic and 100 percent voodoo; this statement is not, of course, entirely accurate, but nevertheless it does emphasize the fact that the duality in Haitian religious history has never been a confrontation between two separate groups of people. Almost all voodoo adherents would call themselves Catholics, and most Catholics practice voodoo. (Nicholls, 1970)

Haitian Voodoo is believed to have started in Haiti in 1724, in the form of a snake cult that worshipped many spirits. The practices of this cult were intermingled with many Catholic rituals and saints, forming Haitian Voodoo. (Dakwar & Wissink, 2004/2009)

According to Jules Anantua, head of the Haitian Ministry of Cults, "Voodoo has always been practiced clandestinely, first by the slaves brought here from Africa, but even after independence [in 1804], because Catholicism became the official religion in Haiti in 1860. In order for voodoo to survive, it had to borrow symbols from the officially recognized religion [Catholicism]. Most voodoo spirits have their counterparts in Christian saints." (Williams, 2003)

Today, most of the Catholic saints have been appropriated as African loa [spirits] in the minds of the Haitian peasants. Thus Legba, the Vodun god of communications, is also the Catholic Saint Peter, the one who holds the key—the one who opens barriers to communication between God and humans. His symbol is a cross, which, for the vodunsi, represents the crossroads; to the Catholic, it is the cross of Jesus. Damballah-Wedo, the serpent deity of Dahomey, is associated with Saint Patrick—the saint who walked on the snakes. Shango, the god of lightning and thunder, is Saint John the Baptist, who, according to tradition, controls the storm clouds. . . . These are only a few of the subtle borrowings or one-dimensional syncretisms that have operated whenever African religions confront other religions. Unlike Catholicism's inflexible dogma, African religion is protean, always adding to its form selective aspects of other religions without endangering its function. (Lippy & Williams, 2010)

There are some anthropologists who believe that some Voodoo rites, and especially the Petwo Voodoo rites, might have their origins in [Native-American] Arawak/Taino religion, but this is speculative. (Corbett, 1988)

In 2012, the *World Factbook* estimated the religious affiliation of Haitians to be: Roman Catholic 80%, Protestant 16% (Baptist 10%, Pentecostal 4%, Adventist 1%, other 1%, none 1%, other 3%). About half of the population also practices Vodou. (Haiti, 2012)

Although I found such observations enlightening, they failed to tell in detail what I had hoped to learn. I now had further questions to ask—ones that I would be obliged to answer by conducting an extensive investigation of the research literature about traditional African religions and Catholicism, thereby generating from the resulting information a series of principles that might account for the curious nature of Haiti's combined Vodou/Christian faith. The chapters of this book explain in detail what I have discovered.

To prepare readers for what to expect in the following pages, I offer guidance in the form of answers to three questions.

What, exactly, is the connection between indigenous African religions and Vodou?

Vodou itself is a belief system patched together from segments of different traditional African faiths that slaves brought from Africa to the Caribbean during the 16th through the 18th centuries. The slaves had been captured from various African ethnic regions where the people of each district or village subscribed to their own particular faiths. When such a potpourri of Africans settled in Haiti, their religious beliefs gradually altered, with some versions becoming more dominant than others and forming a commonly held mix. That mix assumed the title *Vodou*, a Haitian Creole term derived from the West African Ewe word *vodu* or Fon word *vodun*, meaning *spirit*.

In what ways are Vodou and Catholicism alike and different?

The detailed answer will be found in Chapters 3 through 11. However, the short answer is that while the two traditions are alike in numerous aspects, their organizational structures are dramatically different. Local Vodou groups are independent and operate on their own. In marked contrast, Catholicism has a monolithic worldwide organization that operates through a hierarchy of decision making that is headquartered in Rome. A second significant difference between Vodou and Catholicism is in their modes of conveying religious lore from one generation to the next and from one place to another. Catholicism is grounded in written documents that are formally approved, whereas African and Vodou beliefs have traditionally been passed orally; such beliefs depend for their authenticity on the memories and motives of both the religious leaders and common devotees.

By what form of logic could rational humans subscribe simultaneously to such contrasting worldviews as those of Vodou and Catholicism?

This question was at the forefront of my mind as I conducted the investigation that led to the contents of Chapters 3 through 11. As I worked through those chapters, I generated seven *principles of accommodation* that I believe help render Haiti's Vodou/Christian faith a rational belief system. It was only near the end of my study that I could complete the series of principles. However, I introduce them at this point in order to alert readers to the basis of the interpretations that close each of the chapters from 3 through 11—interpretations founded on the seven principles.

- *The in-name-only principle:* When elements of two religions have the same meanings but bear different names, those elements can compatibly coexist within a combined belief system.

Example: In both Vodou and Christianity, there is an invisible, all-powerful Supreme Being who created the universe. Therefore, the Vodou name *Bondye* and the Christian name *God* can both be accepted without conflict in Haiti's Vodou/Christian faith (Chapter 5).

- *The nonconflicting-add-ons principle:* If a novel belief from Religion A does not contradict or violate any belief of Religion B, then the novel belief can be accepted by devotees of Religion B.

Example: The notion of a virgin giving birth is not part of traditional African religions, so the Christian belief that Jesus' birth resulted from an immaculate conception does not contradict any Vodou beliefs and thus can be included within a Vodou/Christian faith (Chapter 5). Likewise, the African ceremonial tradition of engaging in dances accompanied by drumbeats is not forbidden in Christian biblical lore, so such behavior can be accepted by adherents of the juxtaposed Vodou and Christian beliefs (Chapter 7).

- *The variations-on-a-theme principle:* Religions that share the same basic belief (same theme), but manifest that theme in different practices, can exist comfortably together.

Example: A basic belief (theme) held in many religions is that a person who ingests a powerful being—such as an animal or human—acquires some of that being's power. In keeping with this theme, a familiar ritual in African religions involves killing an animal, then drinking its blood, and/or eating its flesh. A familiar Christian ritual is the Eucharist, which involves adherents drinking wine that represents Jesus' blood and eating pastry that symbolizes his flesh (Chapter 7).

- *The tolerance principle:* Religions can differ in the extent to which they accept add-on beliefs and practices. A more-tolerant tradition will permit greater importation of add-ons than will a less-tolerant tradition.

Example: During the centuries of Spanish and French colonial control of Haiti, Vodou practices were either ignored or accepted by the Catholic authorities as harmless amusements. Such tolerance has more or less continued into modern times even though there were periods when Vodou practitioners were actively persecuted by both the state and the Catholic Church. In contrast, Protestant Christians have proven to be less tolerant by systematically rejecting potential add-ons in an effort to keep their doctrine "pure" (Chapter 2).

- *The separate-compartments principle:* People can compartmentalize their lives in a way that insolates one set of beliefs or activities from another set, thereby allowing inconsistencies and conflicts between the contents of different compartments to go unrecognized.

Example: In religions, two of the forms of compartmentalization are based on place and time. As for place, an adherent of the Vodou/Christian faith can pray to the Virgin Mary at the Catholic Church, then return home to prepare a Vodou food offering at a Vodou altar to honor the spirit of a dead ancestor without being aware of any conflict between the beliefs underlying the two acts because the two occurred in separate settings (Chapter 10). As for time, a follower of Vodou/Christianity can celebrate an indigenous African religion equivalent to a summer solstice celebration of cycles of nature and body rhythms that follow patterns of the planets, then six months later celebrate Christmas with its modern consumerism—thus willingly accepting any inconsistency between the meanings of the two events because they happened at separate times (Chapter 7).

- *The availability principle:* When there are alternative versions of a religious belief or practice, adherents are apt to adopt the version that is most available, that is, most frequently encountered. This principle is supported by social-learning theory (social-cognition theory) which proposes that, to a great extent, individuals acquire their beliefs from observing the consequences that other people experience as a result of those people's actions (Bandura, 1977).

Example: Indigenous African religions offer a variety of proposals about how the universe was created. Those tales have not been a prominent part of most Vodou teachings. Therefore, it seems likely that most Haitians, because of Catholic or Protestant training, are better acquainted with the dominant Christian version of creation offered in the first two chapters of the Bible. We assume that, if asked about the world's creation, followers of Vodou would most often cite the biblical version (Chapter 6).

- *The social-pressure principle:* Individuals are likely to adopt the religious beliefs of the majority of people in their environment because they believe that doing so increases their chance of being approved by the majority.

Example: Because most Haitians apparently subscribe to some version of Vodou while also being members of the Christian religion (baptized, receiving communion and last rites, and living in Haiti), they are prone to adopt the Christian faith as well as rituals and practices of the Vodou religion.

In summary, I suggest that, when the combined Vodou-and-Christian belief system is rationalized by means of the foregoing seven principles, the system becomes a logically comprehensible worldview.

THE BOOK'S STRUCTURE

The book is divided into three parts.

Part I, *Introduction,* is composed of this initial chapter plus Chapter 2, which is a historical sketch tracing political, social, and religious developments in Haiti from the end of the 15th century until the present day.

Part II, *Religious Beliefs and Practices,* consists of nine chapters, each devoted to a separate aspect of religion:

The sources of people's religious beliefs and practices

How religions are organized

Religions' invisible spirits

The creation of the universe

Causes of events and how religious ceremonies relate to those causes

Religious sayings and tales

Symbols and sacred objects

Sacred sites

Religious societies

The contents of each of the nine chapters are presented in an identical five-part sequence that traces the evolution of Haiti's dominant present-day religion from its two most influential founding traditions—African indigenous faiths and European Catholicism. That sequence consists of the following:

A definition of the chapter's theme

The theme viewed from an African indigenous religions perspective

The theme viewed from a Christian perspective—predominantly Spanish/French versions of Roman Catholicism

A comparison of African and Catholic belief systems

The blending of African faiths and Catholicism to produce present-day versions of a Vodou/Christian faith

Part III, titled *Postscript*, consisting of a single chapter, offers my estimate of what the years ahead may hold for the Haitians' traditional religion.

THE BOOK'S RESEARCH SOURCES

Material about African indigenous religions was drawn from a broad selection of books and Internet websites focusing on African history and culture. Information about Catholicism was collected from *The Catholic Study Bible* (2006), the *Catholic Encyclopedia Online* (2008), the *Catechism of the Catholic Church* (1993), and a variety of books and websites describing Catholicism and Haitian history and culture.

To supplement the published sources of present-day Vodou/Christianity, Dr. Claudine Michel of the University of California, Santa Barbara, conducted guided interviews with a pair of university professors who have been recognized as experts on Haitian matters and, particularly, on Haitian Vodou: (a) Patrick Bellegarde-Smith, professor of Africology at the University of Wisconsin—Milwaukee and (b) Roberto Strongman, associate professor of Black Studies at the University of California, Santa Barbara.

FOUNDATIONAL ASSUMPTIONS

It is important for readers to recognize two assumptions on which the contents of this book were founded.

First, I assume that the most influential roots from which Haiti's present-day Vodou/Christian religion has grown were (a) primarily indigenous African religions, brought to the Caribbean by slaves, then adapted, evolved, and creolized in the Americas and (b) Catholicism, brought by the Spanish and French who colonized the country from the beginning of the 16th century into the 19th century. Even after Haiti became an independent nation in 1804, Catholic orders continued to determine the official religious practices of most Haitians, while vestiges of African religions were widespread as unofficial beliefs and rituals. Over recent decades, fundamentalist Protestant denominations have rapidly converted adherents of traditional Vodou/Catholicism to versions of fundamentalist Protestantism. This movement has thus created a second potential variety of Vodou/Christian faith—that of Vodou/Protestantism.

Second, I assume that the Vodou/Christian combination has not been practiced as a monolithic religion. I believe that people who can be classified to any extent as Haitian Vodou/Christian adherents will differ from each other in the degree to which their beliefs and rituals reflect African and Catholic traditions. At one extreme, some Haitians may subscribe thoroughly to Christian doctrine, yet they wear an amulet of African origin. At the opposite extreme, some Haitians' belief systems may be predominantly African based, but they also celebrate Christmas. Between these extremes are the majority of Haitians whose religious convictions represent various amounts and combinations of African-based faiths, Christianity (Catholic or Protestant), and personal insights.

CHAPTER 2

The Origins

On October 12, 1492, three sailing ships, traveling westward across the Atlantic Ocean from Spain for 70 days, chanced upon an island, which the fleet's commander, Christopher Columbus, naively assumed was part of the Indies—that is, part of the Orient's spice islands. Unaware that he had reached the earth's western hemisphere—and unaware that there even was such a hemisphere—Columbus mistakenly referred to the island's residents as Indians—a misnomer that continues today as the popular label for descendants of the hemisphere's early peoples.

Modern-day historians estimate that the island on which Columbus landed was perhaps present-day Watling Island or the Semana Cay in the Caribbean Sea's Bahamas cluster. Columbus named that island San Salvador and claimed it for Spain. Over the next few weeks, the Spaniards visited nearby Cuba (called *Juana* by Columbus) and La Isla de Española (later renamed *Hispaniola*).

Today, Hispaniola is occupied by two nations—Haiti on the western one-third and the Dominican Republic on the eastern two-thirds. On December 5, 1492, Columbus had guided the largest of his three vessels, the *Santa Maria*, into a harbor on the north coast of Hispaniola, where he was greeted by the native residents. At the time, an estimated several hundred thousand indigenous Arawak/Taino people lived on the island. The visiting Spaniards set about exploring the territory until, on Christmas morning, the *Santa Maria* ran aground and had to be abandoned. Columbus was then given permission by the reigning Taino *cacique* or chieftain, Guacanagari, to leave 40 sailors there in a fortified settlement that would be named *La Navidad* to signify that it was created on the day commemorating Jesus' birth. The Spaniards' desire to establish such a community had been whetted by Guacanagari's tales of large quantities of gold on the island. Hence, *La Navidad* was intended to be the New World's first permanent Spanish community and gold collecting center. In Columbus's daily journal, he expressed his confidence that the 40 Spanish settlers would be safe.

> I have ordered a tower and fortress to be constructed [with lumber from the wrecked Santa Maria] and a large cellar, not because I believe there is any necessity on account of [the Tainos]. I am certain the people I have with me could subjugate all of this island . . . as the population are naked and without arms and very cowardly (Columbus, 1962). The [Tainos] would make fine servants. . . . With fifty men we could subjugate them all and make them do whatever we want. (Deep look, 2008)

Columbus then departed for Spain with his two remaining ships, the *Pinta* and *Niña,* to report his discoveries to King Ferdinand and Queen Isabella and to plan a second expedition. But *La Navidad* was an ill-fated experiment. When Columbus returned to the Caribbean in 1493, he found the settlement deserted. He was told by the Tainos that his sailors had mistreated the natives, who then retaliated by slaying them all. Undeterred by the tragedy, Columbus ordered the construction of a community farther east on the island, to be called *La Isabela,* in honor of Spain's queen. Five years later, the headquarters for Spanish operations in the Caribbean would be moved to the city of Santo Domingo, the present-day capital of the Dominican Republic. From that location, the Spanish would launch the colonization of Hispaniola that proved disastrous for the native population and led to the conquerors eventually importing slaves from Africa to work the mines and fields that the colonials hoped would produce wealth for themselves and their sponsors in Spain.

And so, in late 1492, the Spanish conquest of Hispaniola set off five centuries of events that would produce Haiti's present-day political and social conditions as well as the nation's Vodou/Christian form of religion. This chapter traces the country's history since the Europeans first appeared, including events that contributed to Haitian society's present-day religion. The narrative advances through three eras: (a) the Spanish colony, (b) Haiti under French control, and (c) the independent republic.

THE SPANISH COLONY

Spain maintained colonial control of Hispaniola for more than two centuries before ceding the western third—Haiti—to France in 1697. During those

203 years, the Spanish wrested wealth from the island by exploiting its mining and agricultural potential. At the same time, the colonialists pursued a second mission that accompanied all of Spain's conquests throughout the New World—solidly planting Catholicism in the conquered territories.

The Economic Development Plan

The secular part of the Spanish endeavor—wrenching riches from the land—involved organizing gold mining operations and introducing the cultivation of such export crops as sugarcane, which Columbus introduced in 1493 during his second voyage to the New World. Indigo, tobacco, and coffee would also eventually become important export commodities. To find the thousands of laborers needed to conduct the colony's business venture, the Spanish conscripted the island's indigenous occupants, the Tainos.

The Tainos were part of a broader Arawak ethnic group whose members spoke a common language and who extended from Venezuela through the Caribbean and Central America into Florida. Corbett (1988) has portrayed the Hispaniola Tainos as a gentle people with a "lack of guile." Their culture was "characterized by happiness, friendliness, and a highly organized hierarchical, paternal society." Their occupations focused on farming, fishing, and hunting such small animals as rodents, ducks, and snakes. In easily maintained gardens, they grew cassava, maize, squash, beans, peppers, sweet potatoes, yams, peanuts, tobacco, and cotton.

The Tainos' religion featured a supreme god, Yocohuguama, and a collection of lesser gods known as *zemi,* who controlled life on earth and manifested themselves through such forces of nature as the sun, wind, and rain. These divine beings were worshipped in song and dance festivals conducted by shamans—tribe members who served as mediums between the visible world and the invisible spirit world. Shamans, when assuming the role of healer, sought the guidance of the zemi for treating the ill and infirm during public ceremonies (Meier, 1912/1992).

In 1503, Spain's Queen Isabella expressed her compassion for the native peoples of the Caribbean by ordering governors of Spain's island colonies to treat the Indians well, permit them to live in their own communities, protect their rights, tax them at only a low level, erect a church in each community to convert the inhabitants to Catholicism, and build a school where the priest would teach Indian children to read, write, and recite simple Christian prayers. But the islands' governors, such as Nicolàs de Ovando in Hispaniola, recognized that the only way the Spanish could extract the wealth they sought was to enslave the natives to perform the labor-intensive work that mining and sugarcane production required. Consequently, the queen's orders were set aside in favor of an *encomienda* system in which lands were granted to Spanish colonists, who would then exploit the natives living on those lands and would completely ignore the colonists' commitment to Christianize the Tainos.

So, the Spanish colonials proved to be hard taskmasters, forcing the Tainos to dig the mines and till the fields to the point of exhaustion. As a consequence, many indigenous islanders died from overexertion and malnutrition. Recalcitrant natives were often killed by their conquerors, and many thousands died from such imported European diseases as smallpox for which the Taino had no immunity. The rapidity with which the Tainos of Hispaniola were wiped out is reflected in estimates that the original hundreds of thousands had dwindled to 60,000 by 1507, to 600 by 1531, and to 150 by 1550 (Haggerty, 1989). "Today there are no easily discerned traces of the Arawak Tainos at all except for some of the archaeological remains that have been found. Not only on Hispaniola, but also across the Windward Passage in Cuba. Complete genocide was practiced on these natives" (Corbett, 1988).

As the supply of local laborers drastically dropped, the Spanish began importing black slaves from Africa. The first contingent that arrived in 1502 consisted mostly of *ladinos*—Spaniards of African descent. However, shiploads soon came directly from Africa. By 1520, African blacks were employed throughout Hispaniola. The African sources of Haiti's slaves were mainly west-central territories, where the nations of Togo, Benin, and Nigeria are now located—a region known as the Slave Coast, populated by more than 40 ethnic groups speaking around 250 dialects (Map 2.1).

Black Africans brought substantial economic advantages to the Spaniards' colonial ventures because

> They came from an environment where those who survived into adolescence acquired some immunity to such "Old World" diseases as smallpox, mumps, and measles, as well as to such tropical maladies as malaria and yellow fever. This meant they lived three to five times longer than white laborers under the difficult conditions on plantations, and longer still than Native Americans. Also, when Africans ran away they could neither go home nor be mistaken for members of the planters' society. Through most of the years of the Atlantic trade, prices for Africans remained favorable in relation to the price of the crops they produced. They were, thus, the best economic solution for plantation owners seeking inexpensive labor. (Atlantic Slave Trade, 2008)

The process of providing slaves for transport to the New World usually began with members of one African tribe capturing members of an enemy

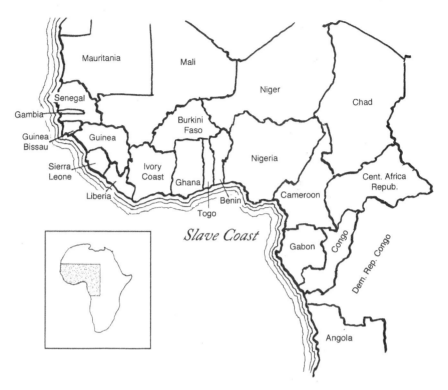

Map 2.1 Slave Coast and Environs. (Based on Lovejoy in Boddy-Evans, 2009)

tribe and sending them to the western seaports, where they were sold to European traders for firearms, liquor, and such manufactured goods as cloth. Sugarcane in Hispaniola, processed into molasses that was then converted into rum, would be sent to West Africa in exchange for slaves. As David Brion Davis explained,

> The religious and political power structure of West African states was peculiarly susceptible to the corrosive effects of the slave system. In the Niger delta, where the [African religions'] priests had traditionally imposed heavy fines on men who offended an oracle, it was relatively easy to discover an increasing number of offenses which could be expiated only by a payment of slaves, who could then be sold profitably to European traders. . . . Since tribes which captured the most slaves received the most European goods, and were thus best equipped in the struggle for survival, it was only natural that certain ones in the interior, such as the Ashantis and Dahomeans, should rise to power as specialists in the art of enslaving. (Davis, 1966, pp. 182–183)

As a result of this trading arrangement, by 1550, there were an estimated 30,000 African slaves toiling in Hispaniola's mines and fields. From the 16th century well into the 19th, between 10 million and 12 million slaves were shipped to the Americas from Africa. The regions of Africa that were the principal sources of slaves sent to South America, the Caribbean, and North America are shown in Map 2.2. Bandele (2009) estimated that the percentages of slaves from the different regions were approximately:

Bight of Biafra (Nigeria) = 25%
West-Central and South-East = 25%
Bight of Benin (Togo, Benin, Nigeria) = 15%
Gold Coast (Ghana) = 14%
Windward Coast (Ivory Coast) = 12%
Senegal/Gambia = 6%
Sierra Leone = 3%

The Spanish Missionary Effort

Paralleling the Spaniards' worldwide military/economic conquests was their commitment to spread Catholicism in the lands they captured. The priests and lay brothers who accompanied the conquistadores on their adventures were in charge of this religious mission. However, throughout the years of Spanish rule in Hispaniola, the padres' attention focused primarily on the spiritual needs of the Spanish colonists rather than on the Tainos. An exception to this neglect of the natives' souls appeared in Ramòn Panè's attempt to spread the gospel among the Indians. Panè was one of three lay brothers among the 14 members of the Catholic clergy brought to the island in late 1493 by Columbus during his second voyage to the Caribbean. Panè—after learning one of the three native languages spoken in Hispaniola—tried to convert the cacique Guarionex to Christianity. That proved to be a futile endeavor—another instance of the flawed cross-cultural communication that marred much of the interaction between the Spaniards and the Indians throughout the New World.

> The religious instruction given by Panè was very rudimentary; he had taught the people the Ave Maria and the Pater Noster and explained to them in simple words that God was the Creator of heaven and earth. The use of religious paintings for this purpose led to a major misunderstanding. The Tainos buried these religious images, since they associated

Map 2.2 Main African Sources of Slaves. (Based on Lovejoy in Boddy-Evans, 2009)

this act with a fertility ritual [that would enhance harvests]. Instead of interpreting the act as a first attempt at inculcating the Christian faith into the world of the Tainos, the Spaniards saw it as an act of desecration, and Bartolomè Columbus [Christopher's brother who governed the island] ordered them to be punished severely. (Meier, 1912/1992)

In contrast to Queen Isabella's desire to educate captured peoples in the Catholic faith, the Spanish plantation owners feared that religious education for slaves could undermine the colonists' control of both the Tainos and the blacks from Africa. As early as 1511, the diocese of Santo Domingo was established in eastern Hispaniola, with priests and brothers assigned to look after the welfare of the clergy and the spiritual needs of the faithful among the colonists, but they had no intent to convert slaves to Catholicism. However, the slaves' spiritual needs would not go wanting, for the Africans brought from their homeland their traditional gods—the *loas*—and ceremonies that featured chants and dances. These practices formed the foundation of the Vodou religion that was destined to thrive in this New-World setting.

THE FRENCH ERA

In Europe during the last decade of the 17th century, a nine-year war was fought between France and a coalition of enemies called The Grand Alliance. The Alliance consisted of Britain, Spain, the Holy Roman Empire, and the Netherlands. The conflict was finally settled in 1697 through the Treaty of Ryswick in which France yielded some districts in Europe to the Alliance but won the western third of Hispaniola from the Spanish. The French named their new colony Saint Dominigue. The Spanish retained control of the eastern two-thirds of the island, which they named Santo Domingo, a title that would be changed to The Dominican Republic in 1844.

The Economic Development Program

The French made their newly acquired colony far more successful economically than had the Spanish. The French introduced coffee to Saint Dominigue from Martinique in 1726, and soon, coffee became an important colonial commodity. By the mid-18th century, Haiti was France's wealthiest overseas colony through the export of sugar, indigo, coffee, cotton, cacao, and logwood. By the 1780s, Haiti was furnishing "about 60 percent of the world's coffee and about 40 percent of the sugar imported by France and Britain. [The Haitian colony] played a pivotal role in the French economy, accounting for almost two-thirds of French commercial interests abroad and about 40 percent of foreign trade" (Haggerty, 1989).

Because growing and processing such products was labor intensive, the demand for African slaves increased. Between 1764 and 1771, the annual importation of slaves ranged from 10,000 to 15,000. From 1787 onward, the colony received more than 40,000 slaves a year. Over time, maintaining the plantations required an estimated 790,000 African slaves. "At all times, a majority of slaves in the colony were African-born, as the brutal conditions of slavery prevented the population from experiencing growth through natural increase" (*History of Haiti*, 2006).

The Spanish had been harsh in their treatment of slaves, but the French were even more brutal. How vicious the French colonials could be was described in the memoirs of a former slave of that era.

> Have they not hung up men with heads downward, drowned them in sacks, crucified them on planks, buried them alive, crushed them in mortars? Have they not forced them to eat shit? And, having flayed them with the lash, have they not cast them alive to be devoured by worms, or onto anthills, or lashed them to stakes in the swamp to be devoured by mosquitoes? Have they not thrown them into boiling cauldrons of cane syrup? Have they not put men and women inside barrels studded with spikes and rolled them down mountainsides into the abyss? Have they not consigned these miserable blacks to man-eating dogs until the latter, sated by human flesh, left the mangled victims to be finished off with bayonet and poniard? (Heinl, 1966)

The Social Structure of Haitian Society

The three principal ethnic divisions in the French colony consisted of the white French, the black Africans, and the brown racially mixed mulattos who were referred to as "people of color" *(gens de couleur)*. First-generation people of color were usually the offspring of a white planter and a black slave woman, with such matings often assuming the form of a *plaçage*, a type of common-law marriage. The three-tiered social structure located the French colonists at the top, mulattos in the middle, and African slaves at the bottom.

In 1685, King Louis XIV of France signed an edict titled *Le Code Noir* (The Black Code) that included 59 articles specifying how slaves should be treated in the American colonies. The code included the following provisions:

- All slaves should baptized and instructed in the Roman Catholic faith.
- No religion other than Catholicism could be practiced in public.
- No Protestants would be allowed to interfere with slaves' Catholic faith.
- No one, including slaves, was to work on Sunday.

- If a free man was not married to any other woman when he had a child by a slave woman, then the man should marry the woman, she would be freed of slave status, and their children would be declared free and legitimate.
- Children born of two slaves would themselves be slaves.
- Freed slaves deserved the same rights, privileges, and immunities enjoyed by freeborn persons. (Arsenault & Rose, 2006)

By 1789, there were 500,000 slaves, 32,000 whites, and a middle class composed of 28,000 mulattos and free blacks who were accorded a variety of privileges not available to slaves (Censer & Hunt, 2008). For example, mulattos and free blacks could own property, so eventually, they controlled one-third of plantation acreage and a quarter of the colony's slaves. As their wealth grew, increasing numbers traveled to France for advanced education. However, in order to keep the members of this middle class in their place, statutes designed by the whites forbade *gens de couleur* from taking up such professions as medicine, holding public office, marrying whites, wearing European clothing, carrying swords or firearms in public, sitting among whites in church, or appearing at social functions attended by whites (Haggerty, 1989). This middle class would figure importantly in the freedom movement that ended French control of Haiti.

The French Religious Endeavor

Although Roman Catholicism was the official religion under the French, it failed to attract many of the colony's blacks, who continued to practice Vodou as a local version of traditional African faiths. The French colonists were aware of superstitions within the slave population but regarded the African dances—performed to drum beats—as simply entertainment without religious implications. Yet, the essence of Vodou was actually imbedded in those celebrations. Furthermore, Vodou was a flexible, accommodating worldview, so the slaves were willing to incorporate a variety of Christian practices into their belief system without apparent conflict. Eventually, the practice of Vodou was outlawed, as colonial authorities saw this local version of African religion as a threat to the stability of the white-dominated Saint Dominigue.

The Haitian Independence Movement

In Saint Dominigue, near the end of the 18th century, the rallying motto of the revolution back in France—*liberty, equality, fraternity*—threatened the island colony's prosperity. If liberty and equality were now the foundation of life in France, why not in French colonies as well? Should not slavery be outlawed in Haiti? And if outlawed, how could the plantation system survive without the cheap labor that slavery furnished?

Conditions in Saint Dominigue at the time were ripe for revolution. There were 10 times more slaves and mulattos than whites. Furthermore, increasing numbers of slaves had already threatened the whites' control of the colony by escaping to the mountains, where they armed themselves and attacked plantations to steal supplies and kill whites. Leaders of these runaway maroons were often Vodou priests—*houngans*—such as François Makandal, a one-armed slave from Guinea who escaped from a plantation in 1751. For six years thereafter, Makandal and his followers carried on guerilla warfare against plantations in an effort to overthrow the white regime. The French finally captured Makandal and publicly burned him at the stake. Other forms of slave resistance included mass suicides, infanticide to prevent slaves' offsprings from growing up as slaves, poisoning whites, and setting fire to French property.

In 1790, the pleas in France to grant everyone *freedom-equality-fraternity* led to the National Assembly issuing a decree ensuring equal rights for all peoples under the French flag. An envoy from France traveled to Saint Dominigue to enforce the decree, which would involve freeing all the slaves. However, the governor of the colony, at the urging of plantation owners, refused to recognize the envoy's mission. This refusal produced armed skirmishes between the governor's forces and a group of slaves who were incited by the envoy. The governor's forces defeated the rebels and executed the envoy. Hence, this first attempt to free the slaves failed.

One year later, revolution broke out in earnest as one black leader after another led the slaves in revolt. The first commander was a Vodou houngan, Dutty Boukman, who, along with fellow rebels, signed a freedom pact in August 1791, then launched attacks against plantations and whites that left an estimated 10,000 blacks and 2,000 whites dead and more than 1,000 plantations ransacked and razed. When Boukman was captured and executed by the French, a succession of other leaders took command—Jean-François, Biassou, Jeannot, and Toussaint L'Ouverture (Haggerty, 1989).

Toussaint, a self-educated former household slave, became the most renowned of the group, often portrayed as the father of Haitian independence. During the latter 1790s, Toussaint commanded a well-trained, disciplined army of former slaves to wrest control of the entire island from the French and Spanish by 1801. But he did not declare full independence from France nor did he seek vengeance on the country's former white slaveholders

because he believed the French would not restore slavery and "that a population of slaves recently landed from Africa could not attain to civilization by
'going it alone'" (James, 1990, p. 290). However, back in France, Napoleon
Bonaparte now headed the government and was intent on maintaining slavery in the Caribbean colonies. To achieve this goal, a large military force from
France managed to overwhelm Toussaint's troops and capture him. He died
of pneumonia in a French prison in 1803.

Following Toussaint's capture, Jean Jacques Dessalines took command
of the rebel forces and, in a series of bloody battles, defeated the French.
On January 1, 1804, Dessalines declared Saint Dominigue an independent
nation—the world's first black republic. To solve the problem of racial identity (mulattos and blacks) in Haitian society, Dessalines declared that all
citizens henceforth would be referred to as black, and no whites would be
allowed to own property. He also renamed the former colony Haiti, a variant
of the original Tainos label for the territory, *Ayiti*, meaning "mountainous
land." Whereas Toussaint had shown compassion for white plantation owners, Dessalines did not. He ordered 2,000 Frenchmen to be massacred at
Cap-Français, 800 in Port-au-Prince, and 400 at Jérémie. He announced that
"We have repaid these cannibals, war for war, crime for crime, outrage for
outrage" (Heinl, 1966, pp. 123, 125).

THE INDEPENDENT REPUBLIC

Over more than two centuries—1804–2014—life in Haiti has been marked
by the frequent overturn of governments, economic difficulties, and the evolution of a Creole culture that combined African and French traditions.

Political Turmoil

Problems maintaining a stable government began early in the 19th century.
After proclaiming Haiti an independent republic in 1804, Dessalines was
assassinated two years later through the complicity of a pair of his advisers,
who then divided the country into two rival regimes. That division lasted
until 1820, when Jean Pierre Boyer reunited Haiti as a single republic and
ruled as president until ousted by revolutionaries in 1843. The fate of subsequent rulers over the next 72 years has been summarized by James C. Ley-
burn (in Haggerty, 1989).

Of the twenty-two heads of state between 1843 and 1915, only one
served out his prescribed term of office, three died while serving, one

was blown up with his palace, one presumably poisoned, one hacked to pieces by a mob, one resigned. The other fourteen were deposed by revolution after incumbencies ranging in length from three months to twelve years.

In 1915, worrisome conditions in Haiti prompted United States' President Woodrow Wilson to order U.S. marines to take control of the island nation. One troubling condition was the dominant control that the Germans in Haiti wielded over the country's economic system. Another condition was the deep debts Haitians owed to American banks.

The American military presence in Haiti lasted until 1934, when the multiple troubles it faced in controlling events on the island convinced the American government to abandon the venture. The United States' 19 years' occupation produced a mixture of good and bad results. The positive influences included stabilizing the country's currency, reducing corruption, establishing a strong police force, improving public roads, promoting agricultural development, expanding education, creating a national health service, and modernizing port facilities. However, a host of negative influences outweighed the positive contributions. The Americans rewrote the country's constitution, dissolved the National Assembly, put a puppet president at the nation's head, engineered a treaty that made Haiti a U.S. protectorate, forced peasants to labor on road building projects, permitted foreigners to buy land, and responded viciously to demonstrators who objected to the occupation forces' policies and behavior. Jim-Crow laws that continued to oppress blacks in the American South were applied to all nonwhites in Haiti. Periodic insurrection by Haitians was met with immediate armed retaliation by the marines. A report to the U.S. Secretary of the Navy estimated that 3,250 Haitians had been killed in a 1919 encounter, a number that a Haitian historian placed at "five times that—somewhere in the neighborhood of 15,000 persons" (Farmer, 2003, p. 98).

> The U.S. occupation was self-interested, oppressive, sometimes brutal, caused problems that lasted past its lifetime, and never paid any reparations for its crimes. . . . All three rulers during the occupation came from the country's small mulatto minority, whom the Americans considered more "civilized", while the black majority was kept in subordination. (History of Haiti, 2006)

In the period between the Americans' departure in 1934 and the election of a medical doctor, François Duvalier, to the presidency in 1956, Haiti was ruled by a series of three heads of state, two of them ousted by military coups.

After France had lost Haiti as a colony in the 1804 revolution, the political and economic control of the country would be wielded mainly by the growing class of brown-skinned mulattos who had identified with the white French upper class and had enjoyed privileges—educational, social, occupational—not available to the blacks. Over the decades, and up to the mid-20th century, mulattos continued as political, economic, and social leaders. Their identification with French culture would sustain that culture throughout the 19th and 20th centuries, continuing with the French language, Catholicism, and French names. The Creole language that evolved among the common people grew from French and African roots.

Duvalier served as a break with the mulatto-leader tradition. He was a middle-class black—known as Papa Doc—who employed Vodou as a key instrument for frightening the populace into accepting his rule. To ensure that people adhered to his policies, Duvalier organized a paramilitary police force named the *Volontaires de la Sécurité Nationale* (Volunteers for National Security), more popularly known as *Tonton Macoutes,* in reference to a fiend in Vodou lore. To support his reputation as a Vodou aficionado, Duvalier included large numbers of Vodou practitioners—houngans—among the *Volontaires,* thereby helping endear him to the common people. The *Volontaires* combated political opposition to Duvalier's rule with intimidation, beatings, and murder. In this manner, Papa Doc established an extremely repressive and corrupt dictatorship that ruthlessly attacked his opponents. During his reign, an estimated 30,000 Haitians were killed by the *Tonton Macoutes* (Schmidt, 1995, p. 232).

Duvalier's 15-year reign ended with his death in 1971. Before he expired, he established his son, Jean-Claude Duvalier ("Baby Doc") as Haiti's next president for life. Jean-Claude turned out to be a licentious young man with neither the talent nor the inclination to govern well. He was more interested in amassing personal wealth through corruption and in pursuing a luxurious lifestyle than in combating the poverty suffered by the majority of the population. Unlike his dark-complexioned father, Jean-Claude was light-skinned. When he married a light-skinned mulatto divorcee, many of the nation's blacks considered him a traitor to their cause. The nation's economic welfare deteriorated, foreign relations worsened, and health conditions declined. In 1986, after 15 years as the nation's president, widespread riots forced Baby Doc to resign and, accompanied by his wife, seek refuge in France.

They left behind them a country economically ravaged by their avarice, a country bereft of functional political institutions and devoid of any tradition of peaceful self-rule. Although the end of the Duvalier era provoked much popular rejoicing, the transitional period . . . did not lead to any significant improvement in the lives of most Haitians. Although most citizens expressed a desire for democracy, they had no firm grasp of what the word meant or of how it might be achieved. (Haggerty, 1989)

The two decades following Jean-Claude Duvalier's departure featured desultory political turmoil that included military coups and the election of two presidents who served multiple periods in office—Jean Bertrand Aristide and René Garcia Préval.

Aristide was a former Catholic priest and social activist from a black peasant family. He gained national attention after attending Catholic schools from the primary grades though to university and becoming a priest in 1983. Assigned to a parish in the slums of Port-au-Prince, Aristide ministered to the city's destitute and soon rose to prominence defending the poor against the oppressive policies of the Duvalier family. He became more politically involved after the Duvalier regime ended in 1986. As a result, he was expelled as a priest in 1988 from the Catholic Society of Saint Francis de Sales for advocating revolution. In 1991, he was elected president of Haiti as a populist activist intent on bettering the lives of the poor, but was soon overthrown by a military coup, only to return twice for subsequent terms as president (1994–1996, 2001–2004).

René Garcia Préval was also black but from the privileged class rather than the peasantry. His father had been a government minister who, during the Duvalier years, escaped into exile. René Préval's advanced education included training as an agronomist at Belgium's State Agricultural College. When he returned to Haiti in the 1980s, he became a close friend of Aristide and would serve as the nation's prime minister under Aristide's presidency during 1990–1991. In 1996, when Aristide could not continue in office, Préval was elected president—a post he held until 2000. In 2006, he was again elected president.

Such has been the recent political history of the Haitian republic. But what has been the country's economic status in the 21st century?

Haiti is the poorest country in the Western Hemisphere, with 80% of the population living under the poverty line and 54% in abject poverty. Two-thirds of all Haitians depend on the agricultural sector, mainly small-scale subsistence farming, and remain vulnerable to damage from frequent natural disasters, exacerbated by the country's widespread deforestation. A macroeconomic program developed in 2005 with the help of the International Monetary Fund helped the economy grow

3.5% in 2007, the highest growth rate since 1999. . . . The government
relies on formal international economic assistance for fiscal sustainabil-
ity. (Haiti economy, 2008)

By the end of 2010, living conditions for the common people were dismal.
Over 60 percent of the population, primarily in rural areas, lacked access to
basic healthcare services. The nation had the highest rates of infant, under-
five, and maternal mortality in the western hemisphere, with diarrhea, respi-
ratory infections, malaria, tuberculosis, and HIV/AIDS the leading causes
of death. An estimated 5.6 percent of people aged 15–49 had HIV/AIDS,
including 19,000 children. Antiretroviral drugs have been in very short supply (At a Glance, 2008).

The literacy rate for the general population in 2002 was 54 percent for
males and 50 percent for females. The percentage of youths aged 15–24 who
could, in 2004, both read and write a short statement related to their everyday lives was 66.2 percent, up from 54.8 percent in 1990. By 2008, slightly
over half of the nation's children of primary-school age attended school, and
less than 2 percent of children finished secondary school. Many schools and
hospitals were closed because teachers, social workers, and health providers
could not go to work for fear of violence (At a Glance, 2008).

Thus, after two centuries of independence, Haiti, by 2010, suffered from
political unrest, an unstable economy, widespread violence, poor health conditions, and low rates of literacy and education. More than two-thirds of
the labor force lacked formal jobs. Consequently, the majority of the populace faced the worst prospect for a healthy, satisfying future of any nation
in the western hemisphere. Burdened by such conditions, Haitians were
ill-prepared to weather a sudden cruel blow from nature—the devastating
earthquake of 2010.

The 2010 Earthquake

In the late afternoon of January 12, 2010, a 7.0-magnitude quake erupted
10 miles west of the Haitian capital city, Port-au-Prince, to put three million
people in immediate need of emergency aid. The initial quake was followed
by more than 50 aftershocks that ranged in size between 4.2 and 5.9 on the
Richter scale (Fox News, 2010).

Estimates of the number of people killed ranged from 46,000—as reported
by a privately hired survey team—to the Haitian government's figure of
316,000. The team also estimated that 895,000 people had been moved into
temporary settlements around the capital after the quake and that no more

than 375,000 people were still living in them by mid-2011. However, the United Nations International Organization for Migration put those numbers higher, reporting that as many as 1.5 million people had been moved into the camps and that 680,000 remained there in 2011 (Trenton, 2011).

A massive relief effort by foreign governments and international philanthropic agencies was launched in early 2010 and continued over the following years. In May 2011, a newly elected president, Michel Martelly, took over the reins of state. Martelly, before officially entering politics, had been a musician—a recording artist, composer, and businessman known by the stage name Sweet Mickey. His early months in office were plagued by difficulties in forming a government acceptable to legislators, thereby making the prospects for social recovery efforts questionable (Basu, 2011).

In summary, by 2014, the people of Haiti faced an extremely bleak future. Under such conditions, a large portion of the population depended on religious convictions to sustain their willingness to live, day after day. The nature of those convictions is the subject of this book.

MATTERS RELIGIOUS

From the earliest years of the Spanish occupation of Hispaniola until the present time, Catholicism has played a highly influential public role in island society. Also, at the outset of the 16th century, the arrival of slaves in Hispaniola was accompanied by African religions that formed the Vodou core of spiritual life among the island's blacks—an influence that continues even today. Finally, in the 19th century, Protestant missionaries began arriving in Haiti to offer a Christian alternative to the dominant Roman Catholic presence. The following discussion focuses on the way these contending movements—Catholic, Vodou, and Protestant—evolved across two centuries of Haitian independence.

Catholic Dominance

Over the decades, the status of Catholicism in Haiti has varied from one political period to another. Sometimes, Catholicism has been the official state religion. Other times, it has been only one of the religions recognized by the government. However, regardless of its official status, Catholicism has always been the dominant publicly recognized faith in Haitian society. The ability of Catholicism to maintain such strength ever since the French colonialists were ousted in 1804 has been due to the nature of the island's colonial social class structure and the pervasive presence of the Catholic clergy.

As noted earlier, Haitian society in colonial times was organized into three racial tiers. At the top in privilege and power were the whites. At the bottom were the African slaves. In the middle were the growing numbers of mulattos—typically the offspring of a white father and an African mother. Because of the mulattos' half-European heritage, the French rulers afforded them greater privileges than the African slaves—such privileges as a French education, the chance to own property, favored occupations, and limited social intercourse with whites. Some blacks who became educated and freed by compassionate French planters would rise to membership in this middle class. The mulattos and freed slaves bore French names and emotionally identified themselves with French culture, including the French language and Catholic religion. They typically looked down on the slaves as their inferiors.

When independence was won in 1804, activists from the middle class were the ones prepared to lead the nation. Their French Catholic education and occupational experience equipped them to cope with problems of governance and economic development that were beyond the capacity of most black slaves. Hence, French culture continued to reign in the island society. Under the first independent government, headed by the highly literate ex-slave Toussaint L'Ouverture, Catholicism was declared the official state religion.

After the French rulers were expelled from Haiti in 1804, the Catholic pope in Rome displayed his support for the French by refusing to recognize Haiti as an independent nation. Such refusal was resented by Haitian leaders for it weakened their fledgling republic's status in the world. Although numbers of priests and lay leaders continued to ply their trade in the island, Roman Catholicism lacked any official status in Haiti until 1860, when the Haitian government signed a concordat with the Vatican. The agreement provided for the appointment of an archbishop in the Haitian capital, the establishment of dioceses, and a yearly government subsidy for the church. In addition to maintaining their own religious schools, the Catholics in 1862 were also furnished a key role in secular education through an amendment to the concordat. The priests' and nuns' educational efforts were directed chiefly at the urban elite—mulattos and blacks who had risen in the social system. Until the mid-20th century, most priests in Haiti were French-speaking Bretons with little interest in rural communities. Hence, black peasants continued to follow traditional Vodou practices, usually mixed with elements of Catholicism.

In 1864, 34 French priests tended to the spiritual needs of Catholics in 65 parishes and seven annexes. Over the next half century, additional Catholic orders served in Haiti, establishing schools and seminaries that expanded

French religious education. However, the ability of Catholic societies to maintain schools, hospitals, and hospices was continually challenged by a tropical climate that the Europeans often found difficult to tolerate. Among the 516 priests sent to Haiti from France over the 45-year period between 1864 and 1909, 200 had died, 182 were still in Haiti, and 134 had returned to Europe as invalids. Catholic orders conducting schools in 1909 included Fathers of the Holy Ghost and Holy Heart of Mary, Brothers of Christian Instruction, Sisters of Saint Joseph of Cluny, Society of Saint Vincent de Paul, the Third Order of Saint Francis, the Confraternities of the Sacred Heart, the Holy Rosary, the Children of Mary, the Christian Mothers, and La Persévérence (Haiti, Mission History, 1912, 1992).

Throughout the first half of the 20th century, Catholicism maintained a dominating presence in Haiti, particularly through the favored status accorded the religion by the ruling mulatto elite. However, educated black nationalists felt that the Catholic Church wielded too much influence over Haitian affairs, so they acted to reduce that influence. The individual who most effectively altered the Church's political role was Papa Doc Duvalier. When he became president, he ousted the Jesuit archbishop of the nation's capital, Port-au-Prince, and expelled a number of priests. The pope in Rome retaliated by excommunicating Duvalier. However, the rift between Haiti's president and the Church was mended in 1966, when Papa Doc was granted the right to appoint bishops. But amicable relations between Duvalier's government and the Catholic Church would not last long.

> The mid-1980s marked a profound change in the church's stance on issues related to peasants and the urban poor. Reflecting this change was the statement by Pope John Paul II, during a visit to Haiti in 1983, that "Things must change here." Galvanized by the Vatican's concern, Roman Catholic clergy and lay workers called for improved human rights. Lay workers helped develop a peasant-community movement, especially at a center in the Plateau Central. The Roman Catholic radio station, Radio Soleil, played a key role in disseminating news about government actions during the 1985–86 crisis and encouraging opponents of the Duvalier government. The bishops, particularly in Jérémie and Cap-Haïtien, actively denounced Duvalierist repression and human-rights violations. (Haggerty, 1989)

For the first time in its history, the Catholic Church in Haiti allied itself with the lower-class peasants and urban poor. Church officials openly endorsed the suppressed 1987 constitution, which granted all citizens human rights and officially recognized Creole as a national language equal in status to French. The constitution also stated that:

> All religions and faiths shall be freely exercised. Everyone is entitled to profess his religion and practice his faith, provided the exercise of that right does not disturb law and order. No one may be compelled to belong to a religious organization or to follow a religious teaching contrary to his convictions. (*Constitution of Haiti*, 2005)

The Vodou Undercurrent

The history of Catholicism in Haiti has been well documented. The history of Vodou has not. Whereas the Catholic Church over the centuries has maintained a well-organized bureaucracy staffed by a highly educated priesthood that has chronicled the Church's activities, Vodou has not had such an organization. Instead, Haitian Voudou has consisted of clandestine practices beyond the purview of the reading public and government authorities. Also important is the fact that Vodou lore and practices were not passed from one generation to the next in written form. Instead, the content of Vodou was learned by each new generation from parents' tales, from recitals by griots (West African poets), and from the young participating in ceremonies through which slaves expressed their beliefs. Consequently, an account of the development of Vodou over the past two centuries is necessarily far less systematic and complete than is the history of the Catholic faith. Not only does Vodou lack a standard history, but there is not even a standardized spelling of its name. Several variations compete for acceptance—Vodou, Voudou, Voudoun, Voodoo, Voudun—and are assigned such varied meanings as God Creator, Great Spirit, and Great Mystery.

Although Haitian Vodou lacks a precisely documented history, the general way it evolved seems apparent. The African religions that slaves brought to the New World sustained them spiritually as they struggled to survive the trials of their forced servitude. With their family ties shattered, they found unity and solace in their faiths' invisible spirits and ancient rituals. At the same time, French priests attempted to carry out the Black Code charge of bringing Africans within the Catholic fold. This task was facilitated by the fact that African faiths and Christianity were alike in several important ways. Both placed an invisible supreme spirit at the core of the universe—*God* for Catholics and *Bondye* for Africans. In addition, Africans believed in lesser spirits—loas—that had counterparts in the Christian saints who could affect people's welfare and influence nature's forces. Both Africans and Christians offered prayers and sacrifices to win the spirits' favor. Both believed in an afterlife, in the human soul, and in demons. Both had ritual sacrifices to the spirits that included the consumption of flesh and blood (Voodoo History, 2008).

In 1970, David Nicholls wrote,

> Unlike the God of the Hebrews, the African spirits—or *loas*—were not jealous, and were quite prepared to make room for the God of the Christians. The *loas* were basically unpretentious and were content to make quite limited claims upon the devotion and the loyalty of their devotees. . . . It is sometimes said that Haiti is 90% Catholic and 100% voodoo; this statement is not, of course, entirely accurate, but nevertheless it does emphasize the fact that the duality in Haitian religious history has never been a confrontation between two separate groups of people. Almost all voodoo adherents would call themselves Catholics and most Catholics practice voodoo. . . . [The] intermittent struggle between Catholicism and voodoo has essentially been a struggle between the parish priest on the one hand, and his congregation—or certain prominent and powerful persons in the local community who would normally call themselves Catholics—on the other. (Nicholls, 1970, p. 400)

Consequently, what has evolved in Haiti over the past five centuries is a melting of African traditions that have joined with Catholicism to form a Vodou/Christian faith that can consist of a somewhat different mixture of the two foundational sources in one Haitian citizen's worldview than in any other Haitian's belief system. In effect, there are multiple versions of Vodou/ Christian faith, each version representing a particular selection of elements of African and Christian belief systems and practices. This point is illustrated in Chapters 3 through 11.

In Haiti's 1987 constitution, for the first time in the nation's history, Vodou was accorded the same official status that traditionally had been given to Christianity's Catholicism and Protestantism. However, Vodou practitioners at that time continued to fear a continuation of the persecution and vilification they had suffered over the centuries. Therefore, Vodou adherents still tended to pursue their activities covertly and, as a ruse, would "shield their beliefs with attendance at Roman Catholic or Protestant churches" (Williams, 2003). However, the fears that prevented the open practice of Vodou were largely dispelled in 2003, when the nation's president, Jean-Bertrand Aristide, declared that Vodou was an ancestral legacy, "an essential part of national identity" (Williams, 2003). Since that time, Vodou has increasingly been celebrated in the open, with its practitioners newly authorized to perform such civil ceremonies as marriages and baptisms that traditionally were the exclusive province of the Christian clergy.

Then, there is the Creole language. Across the centuries, the evolution of the Haitian religion has been paralleled by the evolution of Creole, a syncretic language derived mainly from the French language imposed by colonial authorities and from African dialects brought by the slaves. Creole has also been influenced to a far lesser extent by Arabic, Taino, Portuguese, Spanish, and English. The unlettered masses continued over the centuries to depend on an amalgam of their African tongues while the educated colonials and their mulatto progeny used French, which was the official medium of communication in schools, government, and commerce. With the passing of time, French terms for which the Africans had no equivalent, or which were ubiquitous in everyday parlance, were adopted by the populace, eventually producing a language of general use—Haitian Creole. Prior to the 1960s, French had been the only officially recognized language in Haiti. But as of 1961—and later guaranteed in the 1987 constitution—Creole became elevated to an official status equivalent to that of French.

The polyglot nature of Creole, as compared to French, can be illustrated with the following example:

> English—"Over the past five decades or more, religious beliefs and practices in Haiti have been changing at an accelerating pace."
>
> French—"Au cours de ces cinq dernières décenies, les croyances et les pratiques religieuses en Haiti ont changé à un rythme accéléré."
>
> Creole—"Nan sinkant dènye lanè yo kroyans ansam avek aspè pratik relijion te chanje anpil nan peyi Dayiti."

In summary, after the French gained control of Haiti in the 17th century, elements of Catholic doctrine and practice merged with remnants of African spiritualism to produce the present-day Vodou/Christian religion. Vodou has been adopted in some fashion by an estimated 80 percent or 90 percent of Haitians, not only within Haiti but also among many thousands of emigrants in such countries as Canada, France, and the United States.

Protestant Expansion

Missionaries and members of Christian Protestant churches first came to Haiti from North America in the early decades of the 19th century, after news spread about Haiti becoming the first black republic. In 1824, the New

York Colonization Society's effort to send free blacks to nonslavery nations received a commitment from Haitian President Jean-Pierre Boyer to pay the passage of U.S. emigrants to Haiti, to grant them land, and to pay for their support over the first four months. As a result, a shipload of free blacks from North America traveled to the island republic. Again, over the years 1861–1863, contingents of blacks freed by the U.S. Civil War also moved to Haiti, carrying with them their Protestant religion and missionaries. Most of the immigrants were Methodists, Episcopalians, and Presbyterians. However, the programs that sent North American blacks to Haiti were disappointing as a way of settling former slaves into a permanent bright future.

> Most [immigrants] were unprepared for life in a different environment. Many complained about the climate and the language barrier, and expressed contempt for Vodou and Catholicism. Haitians were often suspicious of the immigrants, whom they described as lazy and uncooperative. Most immigrants, who came from American cities, did not want to work on farms and sold the land they had received for free in order to settle in the urban centers, where they could not find work. In addition, the government's subsidy policy depleted the country's already minimal treasury by funding emigrants who often left after their four months were over. (*Colonization and Emigration*, 2008)

Estimates of the number of North American blacks who, over the decades, emigrated to Haiti range from 8,000 to 13,000, with most of the immigrants eventually returning to the United States. However, the programs had introduced Protestantism into a society that previously had been limited to Catholicism and Vodou. The potential threat of Protestant inroads on Catholicism helped convince the Vatican to negotiate the concordat of 1860 that assured the Catholic Church its solid, official status as the island's dominant religion.

The next significant stimulus to the growth of Protestantism came during the United States' occupation of Haiti over the 1915–1934 era, when Protestant missions thrived. Finally, the close of World War II set off the great surge of proselytizing in Haiti which, since 1980, has brought the proportion of Protestant adherents in the country to between 20 percent and 28 percent of the population. However, the leading denominations are no longer such traditional mainstream faiths as Episcopalians, Methodists, and Presbyterians. Instead, most Haitian Protestants are evangelicals—Baptist, Pentecostal, Assembly of God, Seventh-Day Adventist, Church of the Nazarene, and Mormon.

Through the lens of evangelicalism, missionaries and Haitians together have crafted new narratives about Haitian history and traditional culture. These narratives, while using the same scriptures as the Catholic clergy, were weighted differently in Protestantism. Whereas the [Christian] saints had lent themselves to syncretism with Vodou spirits, Protestants would stress the absolute authority of Jesus Christ and the absolute irreconcilability—even opposition—of Vodou with Christianity. For Pentecostals in particular, Vodou spirits were as real as Christ himself, and were in fact demons working as the foot soldiers of Satan. Though the [Catholics and Protestants] are all Christian, the theologies and goals of Catholics, traditional Protestants, and evangelicals in Haiti are not the same. Their stories and the stories they created about Haiti, its past, and its religion also have a different effect on their Haitian converts. (McAlister, 2012a)

Whereas Catholicism over the centuries managed to accommodate Vodou by accepting church members' African dances and celebrations, evangelical Protestant church leaders have strongly condemned any evidence of African spiritualism. Thus, a question has remained about whether Haitian Protestantism contains any vestiges of the melding of Vodou and Christian belief. Although Protestant authorities condemn all beliefs and practices associated with Vodou, I suspect that, within the religious convictions of many Haitian Protestants, remnants of African traditions still linger.

CONCLUSION

The foregoing sketch of politics and religion in Haiti over the past five centuries has been offered as a historical backdrop against which the contents of Chapters 3 through 11 can be viewed. The sketch is intended to help readers understand the details offered in those chapters regarding the central proposition to which this book is dedicated—the proposition that (a) religion in Haiti is predominantly a melding of African and Christian spiritual content and (b) such melding has resulted in a variety of belief systems whose patterns can differ from one set of believers to another—or even from one Haitian to another.

Finally, the case of present-day Haitian Vodou can be placed in a broader geographical perspective by our recognizing a similar evolutionary process in certain parts of Africa. Early in the 21st century, three major religious traditions have competed in Africa for dominance—Christianity, Islam, and indigenous African faiths. In 2010, a continentwide survey included questions about seven beliefs and four practices that were prominent parts of indigenous African religions (Pew Forum, 2010). The beliefs included "the protective power of certain spiritual people, the power of juju and other sacred objects, the evil eye, witchcraft, evil spirits, the protective power of sacrificial offerings to ancestors, and reincarnation." The practices were those of "visiting traditional healers, owning sacred objects, participating in ceremonies to honor ancestors, and participating in traditional puberty rituals."

These eleven items can be combined into a single scale to provide an overall picture of where involvement with traditional African religious is highest. This analysis shows that more than half of the respondents in three countries [Tanzania, Senegal, Mali] show high levels of traditional African religious beliefs and practice (believing or participating in six or more of the eleven items). In eight other countries [Cameroon, South Africa, Guinea Bissau, Chad, Botswana, Ghana, Democratic Republic of Congo], between one-quarter and one-half of respondents rank high on the scale. Moreover, traditional African religious beliefs and practices are common in predominantly Muslim countries, in countries with a more even mix of Christians and Muslims, and in predominantly Christian countries. For the most part, fewer respondents in the East African countries surveyed scored high on this scale compared with those in West Africa. (Pew Forum, 2010, pp. 34–35)

As noted earlier in this chapter, most of the slaves brought by the Spanish and French colonialists to Haiti had been from West Africa.

PART II

Religious Beliefs and Practices

P art II consists of Chapters 3 through 11 that are designed to facilitate readers' understanding of the origins and present-day status of Haiti's Vodou/Christian religion.

Each chapter treats an important aspect of religion. The nine chapter themes concern:

- The sources of adherents' beliefs and practices
- The organization of religion
- Religions' invisible spirits
- The creation of the universe
- Causes of events and how religious ceremonies relate to those causes
- Wise sayings and tales
- Symbols and sacred objects
- Sacred places
- Religious societies

The contents of every chapter are presented in an identical five-part sequence that traces the evolution of Haiti's present-day Vodou/Christian religion from its two principal foundational traditions—African indigenous faiths and Catholicism. The sequence consists of:

- A definition of the chapter's theme
- The theme viewed from an African traditional religions perspective

- The theme viewed from a Christian perspective, predominantly Spanish/French versions of Roman Catholicism
- The blending of African faiths and Catholicism to produce alternative versions of Vodou
- A comparison of African, Catholic, and present-day Vodou belief systems

As explained in Chapter 1, it is essential that readers recognize the particular meanings assigned throughout this book to three terms. The term *indigenous African religion* applies to the beliefs and practices of Haitians whose religion derives exclusively from the spiritual convictions of Africans (especially West Africans) before the intrusion of Christianity and Islam into Africa. The term *Catholicism* applies to the worldview of Haitians whose religion derives entirely from Roman Catholic doctrine. The label *Haitian Vodou/Christian* refers to the spiritual life of Haitians whose belief systems combine some aspects of African faiths with some elements of Christianity (especially Catholicism).

CHAPTER 3

Sources of Belief

This chapter concerns the origins of people's religious beliefs: How do religious leaders learn the beliefs and practices of their faith? How do the ordinary followers of the faith learn the beliefs and practices?

The attempt to understand African, Catholic, and Haitian Vodou/Christian belief systems begins with our inspecting (a) the origins of a religion's beliefs and (b) reasons why a religion's adherents accept those beliefs as true. The discussion opens with a scheme for interpreting the sources of religious beliefs, then continues with the reasons people adopt such beliefs, and finishes with applying the interpretive scheme to traditional African faiths, Christianity (especially Catholicism), and Haiti's present-day Vodou/Christian religion.

THE FOUNDATION OF BELIEFS

In addressing the question of how a religion's ideas and practices originate, I propose a set of concepts that, in my estimation, are assumptions on which religious convictions are founded. It should be recognized that the following interpretation of the sources of beliefs applies only to religious people, that is, to those who are convinced that spirits influence events in the world. Consequently, this proposal does not apply to people who are not religious, such as agnostics, secular humanists, materialists, realists, and atheists.

The central concept in the scheme is that religious convictions are products of a human thought process called spirit personification. The word *spirit* means an unseen power that gets things done in the world. Personification means attributing human traits to that power. Thus, when accounting for happenings, religious people explain that the world's objects and events are caused by spirits (gods, deities, angels, genies). Those spirits are personified, meaning they are invested with human or person characteristics—intelligence, motives, desires, ambitions, preferences, and such emotions as joy, anger, love, hate, jealousy, vengeance, envy, guilt, and fear. Spirits or deities also have domains of influence. A spirit whose domain is the entire universe can influence events everywhere, and thus, deserves such titles as Supreme Being or Universal God. The domains of other spirits are limited, so they can affect only certain kinds of events—protect people from illness, ensure the safety of travelers, promote success in fishing or hunting, foster the happiness of lovers, control the fate of warriors, cause crop failure, produce earthquakes, and more. In addition, spirits vary in strength. The most powerful can accomplish any feat and can vanquish any rival, so they deserve the label *omnipotent*. Strength is particularly important when spirits compete against each other, as when a virtuous spirit battles a malevolent one. Although spirits are generally invisible, under certain conditions, they can inhabit—or can assume the form of—such mundane, visible entities as humans, animals, or inanimate objects (trees, lakes, mountains, rocks, and more).

Within such a spirit-personification worldview, religious beliefs are created by the deities or spirits who then convey those beliefs to selected humans who may either keep the beliefs to themselves or share the beliefs with others.

The spirits transmit the beliefs to humans via six channels of thought or action—prayer, inspiration, dreams, visions, spirit possession, and instruction.

Prayer

Prayer consists of an individual or group intentionally communicating with a spirit—sending messages to the spirit and, if fortunate, receiving messages from the spirit. Prayers take the form of spoken words, silent thoughts, actions, sacrifices, or ceremonies directed to a spirit in order to offer thanks for blessings already received, to solicit help with problems, or to honor the spirit. The spirit's reply can be either an immediately returned message or a subsequent event—such an event as a bountiful harvest, the supplicant's recovery from an illness, the return home of a loved one, success in battle, or the like. The supplicant's belief in the spirit is strengthened when an expected response to the prayer occurs. The less frequently that prayers appear to be answered, the weaker a supplicant's trust in the spirit is likely to become.

Inspiration

Another communication channel is inspiration. For instance, at the time a person is consciously trying to find the answer to a question or trying to solve a problem, a convincing answer comes to mind. The process of pondering over the problem has produced a persuasive insight—a belief that is accepted as true. That insight can be attributed to the miraculous power of an inspiring spirit.

Dreams and Visions

Neither dreams nor visions are within a person's intentional control, but instead, they operate during altered states of consciousness. Dreams consist of images and messages people receive when they are asleep. Visions are extraordinary sights and sounds that appear to a person in a waking state, often in a trance-like condition. Religious beliefs derived from dreams and visions can be either explicit revelations of a spirit's words, sounds, and images or can be symbolic revelations. A person who receives an explicit revelation need only report precisely what the spirit said or displayed in order to divulge that belief to other people. In contrast, a symbolic revelation disguises its true meaning in a garb that must be interpreted if the message—the belief—is to be understood.

Spirit Possession

Possession has been defined by Wallace (in Walker, 1972) as "any native theory which explains any event of human behavior as being the result of the physical presence in a human body of an alien spirit which takes control of the host's executive functions, most frequently speech and control of the skeletal musculature."

Spirit possession is a source of religious wisdom, advice, and warning whenever devotees of the faith are convinced that a person's self or soul or mind can be temporarily replaced by an invisible being—a spirit—that then controls the person's speech and actions. Such beings can be either benevolent and helpful or wicked and destructive. If benevolent, they are summoned by means of welcoming rituals. If malevolent, they come uninvited and should be eliminated through exorcism rites.

Instruction

Instruction results from a spirit speaking from afar or even assuming a visible worldly form (human or animal) in order to tell people truths they should accept. Instruction is sometimes referred to as revelation. Instruction can be either direct or mediated. Direct instruction consists of information or advice passed from a supernatural being—god, minor deity, angel, deceased ancestor—to a human. Mediated instruction consists of a human—priest, pastor, shaman, seer, diviner—receiving information from a deity, and in the role of a go-between, conveying that information to other humans.

Religions are not all alike in the kinds of people considered capable of receiving messages from spirits or of interpreting messages that appear in symbolic form. Some faiths attribute interpretive power to a limited number of seers. Others extend the power to all members of the faith. Most sects identify conditions that are necessary for—or conducive to—spirit messages being transmitted to humans. Such conditions can include (a) environmental settings (holy places, ceremonies), (b) physical/mental condition (meditation, trance, deprivation, psychedelic drug state) of the individuals who receive spirit visitations, and (c) particular seasons, days, or times of day (harvest season, the summer solstice, December 25, New Year's Day, dawn, midday, sunset).

In summary, this scheme for analyzing the origins of religious beliefs proposes that personified spirits create religious wisdom that is conveyed to selected humans via conscious channels (prayer, inspiration, instruction) and subconscious channels (dreams, visions, spirit possession).

ACCEPTING BELIEFS AS TRUE

Why do people accept religious beliefs as true and use those beliefs to guide their lives?

I estimate that there are various reasons for such acceptance and that the reasons can differ from one person to another. Consider, for example, the potential influence of such factors as tradition, a line of logic, authority, social pressure, lack of alternatives, and tolerance of ambiguity.

First, when a religious faith has thrived across the centuries, such success can be accepted as evidence that the faith's beliefs and practices are authentic— that the religion's tenets are true and everlasting. A long-standing, unchanging tradition can offer people a sense of security as they attempt to cope with a turbulent, puzzling world.

Second, proponents of a religion may present a line of logic that listeners find so persuasive that they agree with the tenets and practices of the faith.

Third, people who hold positions of authority in a religion's hierarchy— kings, chieftains, ministers, bishops, priests, shamans—are expected to have intimate knowledge of the religion's beliefs and of the consequences to be expected by individuals who abide by or who violate the faith's doctrine. Therefore, followers of the faith are well advised to accept what the authorities tell them.

Fourth, when all—or at least most—people in a society share the same beliefs about life, there is reason to expect those beliefs to be true, particularly if the majority conduct their daily affairs in a reasonable manner so that they apparently are neither stupid nor mad. And even if a person feels that the majority of people have been misled and that their beliefs are no more than illusions, prudence suggests that it would be unwise to question their viewpoints and thereby attract their ire and repercussions. In other words, it would be well not to challenge the majority's convictions and then suffer the widespread disapproval resulting from the challenge.

Fifth, people are prone to accept a religion's explanations about life when those people are unaware of alternative explanations. Consequently, limiting people's access to competing doctrines helps ensure that adherents subscribe to the beliefs of a particular faith.

Sixth, individuals can differ in the extent to which they can bear uncertainty. Some people have a low degree of tolerance for ambiguity about the purpose of life, the cause of misfortune, how to cure illness, and the nature of the universe and its origins. They become distressed by such answers as "We really don't know the goal of life" or "This is one possibility, but it's just tentative" or "As yet, we can only estimate, so we need to learn more." Such individuals find security in beliefs portrayed as universal, unquestionable, everlasting truths. Religions offer such beliefs.

Now, to follow the foregoing introduction to the origins of belief and to reasons people may subscribe to a particular religion, we can consider the sources of the beliefs described throughout Part II, beginning with African worldviews, continuing with traditional Christianity (primarily Catholicism), and finishing with the Haitian Vodou/Christian version.

SOURCES OF AFRICAN RELIGIOUS BELIEFS

The convictions and practices of traditional African religions are acquired by followers of the faith through the six media already described—prayer, inspiration, dreams, visions, spirit possession, and instruction. However, significant differences exist in the form that these channels assume in different religious traditions. All indigenous African religious content has been passed orally from one generation to the next or else witnessed in ceremonies. In contrast, the core of Christian beliefs, including those of Roman Catholicism, have been in written form—the Bible—and subsequent written doctrine has been introduced over the centuries by trusted clerics. This difference in the mode of communicating religious lore helps account for the far greater number and diversity of African faiths than of Christian denominations.

Most African traditional religions have functionaries who communicate with God and the spirits on behalf of individuals and the community. This does not negate the ability of individuals to communicate with the unseen. The functionaries are trained, are initiated, and in many cases, are from a bloodline that has a special window into the unseen realm. Communication takes many forms. Chief among them are prayers that may include incantations, sacred objects, and incense.

Prayer

The main purpose of prayer and sacrifices in African religions has been to ask deities and ancestral spirits for protection and favorable conditions for the prosperity of the family and community. Women, more often than men, are the ones who offer prayers of supplication. Mothers and wives beseech the spirits to cure a family member's illness or deformity, to protect husbands and sons during the hunt or at war, to bring rain during a drought, to end their own barrenness by ensuring pregnancy, and to bless their growing children. They also thank deities for blessings received—a healthy newborn, an abundant harvest, the safe return of a lost relative. The death of a loved one can also be the occasion for a prayer of despair directed at divinities or the departed.

> My husband, you have abandoned me. My master is gone and will never return. I am lost. I have no hope. For you used to fetch water and collect firewood for me. You used to clothe and feed me with good things. . . . Where shall I go? (Mbiti, 1988)

Most indigenous African faiths include two levels of deities: (a) a Supreme Being or Ultimate God who created the universe but who is not engaged in people's daily affairs and (b) lesser deities and ancestral spirits that are the intermediaries between the earth's peoples and the sacred realm. Usually, prayers of petition or sacrificial offerings are not directed at the aloof Ultimate God, but rather, at the secondary divinities, with offerings of food and the sacrifice of animals frequently accompanying the prayers.

Although prayers have usually been attempts to seek the invisible spirits' help and favor, prayers have also served as sources of religious belief. When a prayer or sacrifice is followed by the fulfillment of the supplicant's plea, the supplicant's belief in that mode of praying is strengthened and will be used again in the future. In contrast, when the favor requested in a prayer—or in a series of prayers—is not granted, there is less likelihood that the same style of praying or the same type of sacrifice will be attempted again. In effect, the consequences that seem to follow a style of praying define, for the suppliant, how well that style works.

Inspiration

A shaman or oracle may suddenly, or by dint of extensive pondering and study, gain a persuasive religious insight or truth that is not the result of a dream or vision. The revelation is not a direct message from a deity. Rather, the insight is attributed to the inspiration of a favorite divinity or ancestral shade. Much of the religious wisdom among followers of African faiths is apparently of this inspired sort.

Dreams

Hayashida's extensive survey of African religious literature led him to conclude that:

> In traditional Africa the seen and the unseen worlds are one and hence there exists uninterrupted interpenetration and communication between the natural and supernatural worlds, or between human and superhuman realities. In dreams, this interplay from one world to the other is most completely and directly brought about without [the person] being aware of it. The "soul" exits the body temporarily, communes with spirits or divinities, and returns to the body upon awakening. If accident or witchcraft blocks its return, speedy death or illness may result. . . . The spiritual world and physical world are reconcilable companions. Perhaps we can describe African dreams this way: a clear glass rests between this world and the other world. The dreamer looks into the spiritual world, and spiritual beings can look into man's world. Only, the glass has holes in it because constant interpenetration and intermingling occur between beings from both worlds. Man cannot seclude himself safely from the encounters of the spiritual realm. (Hayashida, 1999, pp. 42–43)

Hayashida decided that African dreams can conveniently be located in five categories labeled: (a) ancestors and divinities, (b) warnings and the future, (c) witchcraft, (d) special callings, and (e) names. Dreams are not simply curiosities to wonder about. Instead, they are guides to behavior, so dreamers are expected to act in keeping with a dream's message.

A typical feature of African religions has been the belief that humans are energized by a life force that can range from very high to very low. At the highest level, a person is in excellent health—efficient, alert, active. Illness or depression involves a reduction of the force. Death is accompanied by—or caused by—a critical decline of the force. Yet the force still continues at a low level to animate the deceased who has now become an invisible spirit, lingering in the shadows to influence the fate of the living, especially the fate of descendants. That influence is often exerted through dreams that invade the sleep of the living. It is commonly believed that during sleep, a dreamer's soul can leave the body to wander about and consort with specters from the spirit world. Dreams are reports of those encounters.

Ancestors and Divinities: The spirit world of African religions is populated by a host of deities and deceased ancestors. Both of these types of spirits can appear in a person's dreams, not simply as casual visitors, but with the purpose of offering information, explanation, or advice important for the dreamer's welfare. A specter may explain the meaning of a ritual, suggest where to build a new dwelling, bless the dreamer on the verge of a journey or a new stage of the life cycle, express displeasure at the dreamer's behavior, or describe a cure for a malady the dreamer suffers from. The dreamer is then expected to take action to apply the information in daily life.

Warnings and the Future: The intent of ghostly visits is often to alert the dreamer to a future event, such as give warning about potential disaster in the days ahead—the dangers of a journey, crop failure, divorce, financial ruin, storms, illness, or death. After such visitations, a dreamer may offer sacrifices to mollify the visiting spirit, and hopefully, avoid the ill fate predicted in the dream. "Africans have sacrificed animals, mainly birds, and in many cases only their blood, to insure that their crops would prosper, that rain would come at the appropriate times, and to cause priests to go into trances and be possessed by spirits" (Nosotro, 2009).

The meaning of a dream may be either obvious or mysteriously symbolic. If symbolic, the dreamer may consult an expert in such matters—a priest who functions as a diviner willing to interpret the dream's intent. As an aid to interpretation, the diviner may toss kola nuts (from a rainforest tree), then draw the meaning from the pattern in which the nuts land. Or, as other indicators that diviners might adopt to guide their interpretations,

nine flat pieces of leather may be thrown onto a cowhide. Cowrie shells or coffee berries might be thrown in the same way. Powdered herbs, or nine twigs, might be thrown onto water in a pot, which was rocked and the arrangement then studied. The arteries in a hen's throat might be cut and the diviner counted the number of spurts till the blood stopped flowing. . . . A hen might be cut open from throat to tail and the omens judged by examining the arrangement of the fat round the entrails and the marks on them. (Welbourne, 1968)

Witchcraft: In many African aboriginal religions, some individuals are considered to be witches who can harm others through psychic means. Their witchery is thought to be an inborn power rather than a learned craft.

Frightening dreams, such as nightmares, are often believed to be the result of witchcraft. A dream in which the sleeper is chased by a wild animal can be interpreted as a witch in the guise of an elephant, leopard, jackal, monkey, snake, toad, frog, lizard, bat, or owl. During a nightmare, the dreamer may see the attacking witch and is thus forewarned of the identity of this enemy.

Special Callings: People may discover their predestined careers or callings through dreams. For example, a future priest or *nganga* may be launched on his life's work by persistent dreams about his endowment of healing and divining skills. Among the Shona of Zimbabwe, "Most men and women being called into the [priestly] profession have had relatives who themselves were *nganga*. The ancestral spirit of their dead relative encounters them in dreams to tell them of his desire to continue his craft through them" (Hayashida, 1999, p. 60).

Names: The question of what name to give to a child is a matter of great importance since the name is not merely a convenient label but is thought to influence the bearer's personality and fate. A parent may depend on a dream to guide the selection of a child's name, particularly when a respected ancestor appears in the dream, thereby suggesting a bond between the ancestor and the infant that warrants assigning the child the ancestor's name.

Conclusion: In Hayashida's analysis of 90 dreams from a variety of African cultures, three-fourths of the dreams offered either guidance or warning of danger. He concluded that dreams in African religions were not just "a minor appendage to one's life and welfare," but rather, were "a sacred implement to help forge one's decisions in the marketplace of life, and sometimes even one's destiny" (Hayashida, 1999, p. 73).

Visions during Trances

As noted earlier, visions are supernatural images and messages that a person experiences while awake. The dominant and most dramatic visions in African religions have appeared when a person has entered a state of trance. In the shift from the waking state to a trance condition, "the ego and rational mind are bypassed, strong emotions and feelings are invoked, and powerful altered states of consciousness are accessed" (The Secret Life of Trance, 2003). Dianne Stewart (in Glazier, 2001, p. 21) has identified trance as one of the main features distinguishing African religions from traditional Christianity.

Spirit Possession

Trance can exist without being explained as possession, but in African traditional religions, some degree of trance usually does exist, barring faking, when the term possession is used. Most altered states of consciousness are explained as possession.

Entering a trance state is an intentional act, with the changed psychic condition induced by drum-accompanied chanting and dancing or by the participant inhaling medicinal vapors or drinking an intoxicant. During the trance, the possessed person receives images and messages from the spirit world—instruction, explanation, guidance, prediction, or information important to the visionary's family or community. Shamans often attribute their knowledge of medicine to messages conveyed by deities during a trance session. In some African cultures, the entranced individuals' souls are said to travel out of their bodies into the spirit world. Sometimes, the essence of a deity or ancestor is thought to pass from the ethereal universe into the body of a possessed dancer, so that the spirit

> can be physically incarnated and present in this world. In these music-religious traditions, the rhythm of the drums also plays a central role. Gods or deities (called *loa* among the Fon or *orisha* among the Yoruba) have their own distinctive rhythm and chant that is played by a small drum ensemble. The priests and priestesses dance for long periods of time, entering into trance states, until one or more of them is possessed by a deity, usually signaled by shaking that comes over the possessed dancer. The personality of the dancer disappears and is replaced by that of the deity. The dancer's face, body language, movements, and behavior change dramatically. (The Secret Life of Trance, 2003)

> If the drums don't play, the gods don't come; . . . art participates in the ritual process not only by honoring the deities but also by calling them into presence and action. . . . The arts—costume, dance, poetry, music—create the appropriate atmosphere for worship. (Stam, 1997, p. 212)

According to Walker (1972), in Nigeria and the Dahomey kingdom (now Benin) of the past, individuals who became possessed had to wear special beads without which their deity would not arrive. The apparition would come only on his own worship day, arriving in front of his cult house when his special drum rhythm was sounded and after *vèvès* (special designs) and the proper sacrifices had been made. The phenomenon of becoming possessed was not a spontaneous fusion of the visiting deity's personality and that of the devotee. Instead, it was a learned role acquired only after long practice.

Instruction

As explained earlier in this chapter, the term instruction means a process of informing adherents about the content of their religion (descriptions of deities, rules of behavior, rituals, and the like) and about happenings in their lives (physical ailments to be cured, decisions faced, problems to be solved, predictions of future events). Not only may instruction arrive in dreams and trances, but it is often conveyed to a believer through a diviner—an individual endowed with the psychic power to reveal mysteries from the spirit world. "The main function of diviners, mediums, oracles, and seers is to find out hidden secrets of knowledge and pass them on to other people" (Mbiti, 1991, p. 157). Such divination has always played a key role in indigenous African faiths.

Summary

Adherents of traditional African religions believe that the tenets and practices of their faith originate in the invisible world of spirits and are conveyed to humans through prayer, inspiration, dreams, visions, spirit possession, and instruction. Three of the most important channels to the spirit world are dreams, visions acquired during trance states, and divination by a seer who has special skills of communicating with deities and with the souls of deceased ancestors.

SOURCES OF CHRISTIAN BELIEFS

Christian beliefs are those found in the Bible, along with subsequent embellishments and interpretations by theologians, pundits, priests, ministers, and evangelists. Christian denominations can vary in their conceptions of who is qualified to receive and explain the religion's beliefs and practices. The Roman Catholic Church is perhaps the clearest example of a hierarchy of belief analysts, with the analysts on the upper rungs of the ecclesiastical ladder regarded as closer to God and thus capable of rendering more authentic versions of doctrine than do clerics on lower rungs. The pope is at the pinnacle of the hierarchy and the most trusted authority on God's intentions. Then, the authenticity of belief interpretations descends by degrees through cardinals, archbishops, bishops, priests, nuns, and lay persons. In contrast, Protestant tradition teaches that each member of the faith is capable of communicating directly with God through prayer, inspiration, dreams, or visions. However, some Protestants—mainly ministers, pastors, and evangelists—are credited with deeper knowledge of the Bible and more accurate skills of analysis. Hence, through sermons, prayer meetings, and revival sessions, such experts guide parishioners in understanding their faith's doctrine and applying the doctrine in everyday living.

Consider, now, examples of beliefs in the Bible that Roman Catholics assume were received from God through prayer, inspiration, dreams, visions, spirit possession, and instruction.

Prayer

Praying in Catholic culture assumes many forms. Individuals can engage in silent moments of meditation, in spoken pleas for help or expressions of thanks at mealtime and bedtime, and in such acts as fingering prayer beads, lighting candles, or gesturing (making the sign of the cross). A group, during a church service or special prayer session, may recite in unison a prayer from the Bible, sing a prayerful hymn or anthem, or listen to an individual—a priest, pastor, or evangelist—voice a supplication, with the audience at the close of the prayer endorsing the appeal by uttering "Amen."

Inspiration

The thought process of inspiration can be credited for many of the detailed beliefs in Catholic culture. The contents of the Bible that are not attributed to direct revelations from God are generally considered the result of divine inspiration. Such is also the case of many writings about Christianity over the past two millennia—Saint Augustine's *Immortality of the Soul,* Dante's *Inferno* and *Purgatorio,* Saint Thomas Aquinas's *Summa Theologiæ,* Saint Gregory the Great's *Dialogues,* Saint Ignatius Loyola's *Letters,* and hundreds more. Likewise, parishioners often regard the content of weekly sermons in churches as inspired truths. Thus, inspiration as a source of belief is apparently responsible for a large portion of most Catholics' worldview.

Dreams

Not only has dreaming been reported in the Bible, but Christians over the centuries have experienced dreams of a religious nature. The five functions of dreams in Christian culture have been those of providing information, giving advice, prophesying future events, promoting God-and-person dialogue, and frightening people.

As a prime New Testament example of dreams' informational function, prior to Jesus' birth, God sent an angel to inform Joseph in a dream that Joseph could properly wed the pregnant Mary because the infant Jesus whom Mary carried in her womb was not the result of an illicit sexual affair. Instead, the pregnancy was divine, conceived in Mary by the Holy Ghost (Matthew 1: 20).

Three biblical examples of advice are (a) God commanding Abemelech in a dream to return Sarah to her husband (Genesis 20: 3–7), (b) God ordering Jacob in a dream to return to his own homeland (Genesis 31: 10–13), and (c) God sending an angel in a dream to advise Joseph to take his wife Mary and infant Jesus to Egypt so as to prevent King Herod from slaying the child (Matthew 2: 13).

The prophecy role of dreams is illustrated in God's telling Moses, Aaron, and Miriam, "If there be a prophet among you, I the Lord will make myself known unto him . . . and will speak to him in a dream" (Numbers 12: 6). Thereafter, prophets' predictions would often come to them in dreams.

The manner in which God promotes dialogue with humans is shown by the following Bible passage: "In Gideon the Lord appeared to Solomon in a dream by night, and the Lord said, 'Ask what I shall give thee.'" And Solomon replied, "'Give [me] an understanding heart to judge thy people, that I may discern between good and bad'" (I Kings, 3: 5, 9).

The frightening function of dreams was referred to by Job when he complained to the Lord, "Thou scarest me with dreams" (Job 7: 14).

The content of dreams in Judeo-Christian tradition can be either explicit or symbolic. As noted earlier, dreams are explicit whenever their images tell exactly what they mean. Dreams are symbolic whenever their meaning is cloaked in imagery or in events that must be interpreted to reveal their intent.

In the Bible, when God spoke to Laban in a dream, the meaning was explicit: "Take heed that thou speak not to Jacob either good or bad" (Genesis 31: 24). In contrast, the images in a dream of the prophet Daniel were symbolic—four great beasts coming from the sea. They included a lion, a bear, a leopard, and a fantastic 10-horned critter with iron teeth, brass claws, and human eyes. In Daniel's interpretation, the beasts symbolized a sequence of four kingdoms that would rule in the Middle East, with the fourth kingdom destroying the other three (Daniel, 7: 1–28).

Sometimes, a dreamer is able to explain the meaning of symbolic images, as did Daniel. But in many cases, individuals with special insight are needed to interpret the codes and signs. Such was the case when the Jewish slave

Joseph in the book of Genesis revealed what the Egyptian Pharaoh's dreams foretold. The Pharaoh had dreamt of seven well-fed cows followed by seven starving cows, and then of seven healthy ears of corn on a stalk along with seven dried-out, shrunken ears. The Pharaoh was distressed about what his dream might portend until Joseph solved the puzzle by explaining that seven years of good harvests would be followed by seven years of drought, so the Egyptians would be wise to store up foodstuffs during the seven years of plenty for use during the seven years of famine (Genesis 41: 1–31).

Visions

Visions—as extraordinary sights and sounds that appear to people in their waking state—can achieve for Christians the same range of functions as do dreams. Visions are able to inform, advice, prophesy, foster God-and-humans dialogue, and frighten.

Perhaps the best known biblical vision involved a Jewish tentmaker named Saul, born in the city of Tarsus, whose life was transformed in his early adulthood by a blinding, miraculous appearance of Jesus while Saul traveled on the road to Damascus. Jesus' words to Saul converted the tentmaker to Christianity, in that Saul changed his name to Paul, and thereafter served as the missionary who was mainly responsible for bringing non-Jews into the Christian fold during the first century CE. The vision not only informed and advised Saul, but also astonished and frightened him (The Acts 9: 1–22; 13; 9).

An instance of a prophecy was Daniel's vision in the Old Testament that enabled him to predict the succession of kingdoms that would rule (Daniel 12: 1–45).

Across the centuries and up to the present day, dreams and visions have conveyed religious meanings to many Christians, both to leaders—popes, priests, ministers, evangelists—and to ordinary parishioners who accept the messages as guides to their beliefs and behavior.

Spirit Possession

The expression *speaking in tongues* appears often in the Bible's New Testament, particularly in the letters that the apostle Paul sent to Christian groups in various Mediterranean communities, as illustrated in the following passages.

> Though I speak with the tongues of men and of angels, and have not charity, I become as sounding brass, or a tinkling symbol. (1 Corinthians 13:1)

> I would that ye all spake with tongues. (1 Corinthians 14:5)
>
> I thank my God, I speak with tongues more than ye all. (1 Corinthians 14:18)

Over the centuries, various interpretations have been offered for such passages. One version holds that Paul was referring to the Holy Spirit expressing God's words through the medium of a possessed human.

In modern times, there are Christians who maintain that they themselves are conveyors of God's word via the process of spirit possession. Consider, for example, the following assertions by two Christian women.

> For me, it is almost as if I am able to tap into God's heart and what he wants. I don't really know what I am saying, but I know it is what God wants me to say and speak. It is more of an enlightenment. You can feel him all around you, and you can feel him speaking through the words that you are saying. (Mabrey & Sherwood, 2007)

> The Charismatic Renewal of the Catholic Church began in 1967. One of the charisms of its many members is the ability to pray in tongues, to have a prayer language in which to praise God. The gift of tongues is a gift that the Holy Spirit gives us. Very often the words with which I might pray fall short. I really do not know what is best for me in a particular situation. By opening to the Holy Spirit, I allow Him to pray through me and for me. For me, the gift is generally expressed in song. I may be walking and I will begin singing praises to God in a language I do not know. It is also a marvelous tool for discernment as it allows me to pray, again, in accordance with God's will. It is not I who prays but God himself who prays through me. . . . God may choose to speak or more often sing through me in the middle of a prayer group. I do not have the gift of interpretation, but somebody in the group will translate what I just said or sang into words that can be understood. (DebChris, 2007)

Instruction

Instruction can be divided into two major types—direct and mediated. It is direct when it involves God revealing a truth or issuing a command to a selected person or group. Instruction is mediated when the person to whom God has spoken then serves as an intermediary who conveys God's message to others. For example, in the biblical book of Exodus (20: 2–17), God dictated to Moses ("mouth to mouth . . . and not in dark speeches" [Numbers 12: 8]) 10 commandments embossed on stone; then, Moses became the mediator who passed the commandments on to the people of Israel.

Throughout the Bible's Old Testament, God is also reported to have spoken directly to a variety of other Jewish leaders—Abraham, Joshua, David, Solomon, and more—who then informed their followers of the content of such messages.

A further example of a mediator is Saint Paul, whose letters to members of churches in Rome, Corinth, and Ephesus appear in the Bible's New Testament. In his epistle to the Ephesians, he contended that what he was telling them were truths he had received directly from God "by revelation" (Ephesians, 3: 3).

The four gospels in the Bible's New Testament (Matthew, Mark, Luke, John) tell of Jesus—in his earthly semblance as the Son of God—issuing truths and advice to his disciples and to audiences who attended his sermons. Hence, his lectures might be viewed as a combination of direct and indirect instruction since he is depicted in the gospels as both divine (the originator of truths) and human (the teller of truths to ordinary earthlings).

Mediated instruction can become a two-stage process. In the first stage, a person who receives a communication directly from God can transmit its content to others (as through the Bible); those others then convey the message to additional people. Such is the case with the preaching of today's priests and ministers and the lessons taught by missionaries and Sunday school teachers. In delivering homilies, pastors typically use the Bible in two ways. The first way involves the pastor quoting a passage of biblical scripture, then interpreting the passage (offering an exegesis) to show what the passage means in relation to historical events and people's daily lives. Below are three examples of verses that provide themes for such sermons.

> *Functions of mercy, truth, and fear.* By mercy and truth iniquity is purged, and by fear of the Lord men depart from evil. (Proverbs 16: 6).

> *Steadfast faith in Jesus.* Blessed are ye, when men shall hate you, and when they shall separate you from their company, and shall reproach you, and cast out your name as evil, for the Son of man's [Jesus'] sake. Rejoice ye in that day, and leap for joy, for, behold, your reward is great in heaven. (St. Luke, 6: 22)

> *The end of the world.* But the day of the Lord will come as a thief in the night, in which the heavens shall pass away with a great noise, and the elements shall melt with fervent heat, the earth also and the works therein shall be burned up. (II Peter, 3: 10)

A second way of using the Bible consists of a priest selecting a topic as the focus of discourse, then drawing on relevant passages of scripture to illustrate the Bible's pertinence for that topic. Over the centuries, typical themes of such instruction have been:

What It Means to Obey the Lord
The Wages of Sin
The Nature of Charity
That Old Deluder Satan
Men's and Women's Roles
Sacrifice as a Virtue
The Rewards of Chastity

Summary

In the foregoing discussion, God was identified as the originator of Christian beliefs, with the beliefs then communicated to humans through prayer, inspiration, dreams, visions, spirit possession, and instruction. Catholics can differ among themselves in how much faith they invest in each of those sources. Some people accept all six sources as persuasive bases of conviction. Others would trust prayer and inspiration, but not dreams and visions. Still others would place their confidence in the interpretations of particular mediators, such as specific priests or evangelists.

AFRICAN AND CATHOLIC SOURCES COMPARED

Followers of traditional African faiths and Catholicism acquire their beliefs and practices through the same six communication media—prayer, inspiration, dreams, visions, spirit possession, and instruction. However, there are significant differences between the two religious traditions in the nature of the media.

For example, instruction in Roman Catholic practice has depended heavily on written documents, principally the Bible, whereas traditional African lore has been passed on orally and by means of ceremonies. As a result, African religions have been far more numerous and diverse in their beliefs and practices than Catholicism.

African and Catholic traditions have also varied in other important ways. Dianne Stewart has proposed that African religions exhibit six major features that have distinguished them from Western Christianity:

(1) a notion of the divine as a community (communotheism), (2) ancestral veneration, (3) divination and herbalism, (4) ritual food offerings

and animal sacrifice, (5) persuasion trance as essential in worship, and (6) a belief in neutral mystical power which can be accessed by humans. These characteristics can be observed in systematic and unsystematic configurations within African-Caribbean and African-American cultural and religious life. (Stewart in Glazier, 2001)

Four of those features concern how people acquire their religious beliefs and practices. Traditional Africans, but not Catholic clerics, are convinced that:

- The invisible souls of dead ancestors linger about and have the power to affect the descendants' destiny.
- Diviners are valuable for interpreting the meaning of puzzling events and for passing on messages from deities and ancestral shades to the religion's living adherents. The techniques diviners use to ply their trade differ significantly from the methods Catholic clerics employ for communicating with the spirit world.
- The offerings of food and sacrificed animals that accompany prayers are thought to be effective in soliciting the goodwill of deities and ancestors that inhabit the invisible spirit world.
- Trance is a powerful device for obtaining knowledge from the spirit world.

Most Christian dream revelations have been attributed directly to the supreme being—God—or to a close emissary, such as an archangel. In contrast, most of the images and messages in Africans' dreams have originated from ancestral spirits or from divinities of less stature than a supreme being.

In summary, while both Africans and Catholics have depended on the same general media for acquiring their beliefs and activities, the specific means used in each tradition for utilizing those media have often been quite different. Therefore, people living in a society—as in Haiti—with strong African and Christian traditions are obliged to adhere solely to one of the religions or else to meld aspects of both, thereby forging a mixed Vodou/Christian faith.

SOURCES OF HAITIAN VODOU/CHRISTIAN BELIEF AND PRACTICE

So far in this chapter, my purpose has been to identify the sources from which adherents of African religions and of Christianity (especially Catholicism) have derived their beliefs and practices. By discovering and comparing those sources, I hoped to understand both (a) the sources of Haiti's Vodou/

Christian faith and (b) how Vodou/Christian devotees can, without apparent contradiction or confusion, subscribe to a melding of two separate traditions.

As my analysis of African and Catholic belief sources has suggested, I conclude that, in both traditions, adherents acquire knowledge of their chosen faith by means of the same six modes of persuasion—prayer, inspiration, dreams, visions, spirit possession, and instruction. So, in their channels of belief acquisition, the two religions are compatible. It then should come as no surprise that those media are also the sources of belief in a combined Vodou/Christian faith. However, there can be distinctions in the role of each medium in that combined faith. Consider, for example, Professor Roberto Strongman's response when interviewed by Dr. Claudine Michel.

MICHEL: Do Vodou leaders pray?

STRONGMAN: The mechanism for the communication with the gods is not supplication. It's collaboration. Because you're doing something for them—for the *lwa*—, they do something for you. Whereas in Christianity, it's more like, "Please do this for me. I do everything you ask. I can't do anything more."

MICHEL: Vodouisants do use the term *praying*, but it's mostly referring to Catholic practices. You are probably right that I've never heard anyone say, "Let's go pray to the gods—to the lwa." They don't say *worship* either.

STRONGMAN: Even bilingual Haitians would never say in English, "Let's go worship or pray." Instead, it would be "Let's go to *service*. We're going to serve" [na pral sevi lwa yo]. The term is, "to serve" rather than "to worship."

MICHEL: What is the purpose of prayer-like activity in Vodou/ Christian faith?

STRONGMAN: Primarily it's to commune, to spend time with someone, and also to please, appease, and be protected—to have a life of harmony. (Strongman, 2011)

So, the African and Catholic components of Vodou/Christianity are alike in the six forms of communication I have identified, but the two underlying traditions can differ in certain details. How, then, can such differences be rationalized so that adherents might logically subscribe to a version of Vodou/Christianity? The answer, I suggest, can be found in the principles-of-accommodation that were introduced in Chapter 1. Consider, for example, the four African practices mentioned earlier regarding the roles of deceased ancestors, diviners, food offerings, and trance in transmitting beliefs and practices. I estimate that by applying principles-of-accommodation, the ostensible conflict between those roles and the Catholic tradition can be explained away in the following fashion.

- *The in-name-only principle:* When elements of two religions have the same meanings but bear different names, those elements can compatibly coexist within a combined belief system.

Example: Deceased Ancestors. In African tradition, the ghosts of dead ancestors hover about to guide their living relatives through warnings and advice. In Catholic tradition, devotees who had lived miraculous lives can become saints following their earthly death to serve thereafter as invisible patrons for people living various life roles—the roles of travelers, residents of particular cities, specialists in various occupations, and more. Therefore, people's guardian saints are, symbolically, their relatives, promoting the welfare of their adopted charges with warnings and advice, not unlike the relationship between the Africans' shades of ancestors and their earthly progeny. Thus, the ostensible conflict between a belief in African deceased ancestors and a belief in Catholic patron saints can be rationalized as an instance of *in-name-only*.

- *The add-on principle:* If a belief from Religion A does not contradict or violate a belief of Religion B, then Religion A's belief can be accepted by devotees of Religion B.
- *The tolerance principle:* Religions can differ in the extent to which they accept add-on beliefs and practices. A more tolerant tradition will permit greater importation of add-ons than will a less tolerant tradition.

Example: Diviners. As noted earlier in this chapter, African diviners have typically used objects such as cowrie shells, berries, or twigs in their effort to predict future events or locate lost items or missing people. Catholic tradition, which does value prophecy as a means of obtaining esoteric information, does not recommend the use of such objects in the process. In fact, official Catholic writings draw a distinction between divination (which is condemned) and prophecy (which is respected).

Divination is the seeking after knowledge of future or hidden things by inadequate means. The means being inadequate they must, therefore, be supplemented by some power which is represented all through history as coming from gods or evil spirits. Hence the word *divination* has a sinister signification. As prophecy is the lawful knowledge of the future divination, its superstitious counterpart is the unlawful. (Divination, 2008)

Prophecy, in its strict sense, means the foreknowledge of future events, though it may sometimes apply to past events of which there is no memory, and to present hidden things which cannot be known by the natural light of reason. St. Paul, speaking of prophecy in 1 Corinthians 14, does not confine its meaning to predictions of future events, but includes under it divine inspirations concerning what is secret, whether future or not. (Prophecy, 2008)

However, the Christian Bible does not specifically prohibit the use of such objects as cowrie seeds or pebbles in prophesying, so a tolerant interpretation of prophecy could permit their use as acceptable add-ons to help a seer envision unseen events. In addition, during the centuries of slavery in Haiti, the Spanish and French Catholic authorities did tolerate certain of their African chattels' rites, apparently considering such antics of no religious import. Ergo, by dint of such tolerance, Vodou/Christian faith could rationally include practices of prophecy that employed traditional African techniques.

- *The variations-on-a-theme principle:* Religions that share the same basic belief (same theme), but manifest that theme in different practices, can exist compatibly together.
- *The separate-compartments principle:* People can compartmentalize their lives in a way that insolates one set of beliefs or activities from another set, thereby allowing inconsistencies and conflicts between different compartments' contents to go unrecognized.

Example: Food offerings. Associating food and drink with religious rites designed to honor deities and to solicit their favor is a feature of both African and Christian faiths. The food-and-drink theme is shared by both belief systems, but is simply manifest differently in each one. Thus, a Vodou/Christian faith can tolerate both (a) food offerings to deceased ancestors at a private altar in a devotee's home and (b) wine and wafers during the public observance of mass in a Catholic cathedral, especially when, in the devotee's mind, each practice is relegated to a separate mental compartment.

- The *in-name-only principle* (as defined above).

Example: Trance. Catholic doctrine, as described in the *Catholic Encyclopedia*, rejects trance as an element of the unacceptable practice of spiritism (Spiritism, 2008). Furthermore, trance, as observed in African religious rites, has been considered a pagan activity by Catholic clerics who have seen—or have heard of—African devotees being transported into an altered state of consciousness (mystic absorption so intense as to cause a temporary loss of awareness of their surroundings) that resulted from chanting, dancing to drum rhythms, and perhaps, ingesting psychedelic drugs.

At the same time, Catholic doctrine accepts and exalts supernatural ecstasy, which is defined as:

> a state which, while it lasts, includes two elements: (a) the one, interior and invisible, when the mind rivets its attention on a religious subject, and (b) the other, corporeal and visible, when the activity of the senses is suspended, so that not only are external sensations incapable of influencing the soul, but considerable difficulty is experienced in awakening such sensation. (Ecstasy, 1912, 1992)

For adherents of a Vodou/Christian worldview, African trance and Catholic supernatural ecstasy can easily be rationalized as the same phenomenon by different names.

CONCLUSION

In this chapter, I reviewed the sources of beliefs and practices for adherents of both African indigenous religions and Christianity (especially Catholicism) and have concluded that those sources in both traditions are basically the same—prayer, inspiration, dreams, visions, spirit possession, and instruction. It then seems reasonable to recognize why those six would also be the foundations of belief and practice in a combined Vodou/Christian belief system. I have suggested as well that ostensible conflicts between African and Christian beliefs, which might make the two traditions appear incompatible, could be explained by the principles-of-accommodation introduced in Chapter 1 that can make Vodou/Christianity a rational faith.

CHAPTER 4

The Organization of Religion

This chapter concerns religious groups' structure, ways of transmitting the faith from one generation to the next, and the nature of a religion's membership. My intent is to estimate the contribution that African and Roman Catholic traditions have made to the structure, development, and membership of the present-day Vodou/Christian belief system.

African faiths must have the longest history of any of the world's religions because the first humans—*homo sapiens*—have been traced to Africa as far back as perhaps 200,000 years. And down through the millennia thereafter,

> each ethnic group located in a particular territory developed its own religion, usually associated with places of origin, with particular myths, with different ways of understanding God's role in its localized societies, and with the role of the spiritual world in its communal and social life. In that sense the indigenous religious traditions date back to ancient societies and ancient land associations. Over the centuries, groups moved to other areas looking for natural resources needed for their subsistence. . . . All those groups had varieties of accounts concerning their origin, as well as ritual specialists who knew how to communicate with the world of the divine, and with the spirits, and who also had access to places associated with their religion. The world of the spirits, be they ancestral or nature spirits, exercised a constant intervention in the world of humans, especially in the life of their descendants, and therefore needed to be controlled and predicted. (Shaw, 2009)

THE STRUCTURE OF RELIGION

As a result of the way religious practices evolved in Africa, in modern times, there has not been a monolithic indigenous spiritual organization on the African continent. Instead, many hundreds of forms of belief and practice have evolved, with each form governed by a particular village's authorities— or at most, by regional rulers. It is true that all of the continent's faiths have shared certain features in common, such as belief in the influence of invisible spirits on people's lives and the need to appeal to those spirits for aid or favors. However, those features are simply defining traits of religions everywhere, not just in Africa. Therefore, in terms of both organizational structure and spiritual practices, it is proper to speak of traditional African religions in the plural rather than to speak of a singular indigenous African religion.

TRANSMITTING THE FAITH ACROSS GENERATIONS

Until well into the 19th century, most devotees' knowledge of African religious beliefs and practices was spread entirely by word of mouth rather than in written or pictorial form. Even today, by far, the dominant manner of informing adherents of their faith's belief system is oral or in the form of observable rituals. Thus, across the millennia, the accuracy of religious lore that passed from one generation to the next necessarily depended on the memory and creativity of the speaker or performer; and that person could be a religious leader, parent, minstrel, tribal historian, raconteur, or the like. A narrator's vagueness of memory could distort the account that the audience received, and new material could be added to the narrative as an inspired storyteller introduced truths that ostensibly were from the spirit world. Hence, with the passing of time, the elaborate variety of beliefs and practices found in recent centuries would spread by voice and ritual throughout the continent.

MEMBERS OF THE FAITH

The people who associate themselves with a religion are commonly referred to as believers, members, adherents, devotees, or followers. Adherents of traditional African faiths can be divided into two basic types, those of leader and follower—or of provider and consumer. The position of leader (provider) in African religions is similar to that of the rabbi in Judaism, priest/minister in Christianity, and imam in Islam. Followers (consumers) are advocates of the faith who lack expertise in holy matters and seek the wisdom, guidance, and help of the leaders. In Judaic, Christian, and Islamic settings, the followers comprise what is often called the congregation or the religious laity.

The Religions' Leaders

There is no general African language word for a religious leader. Instead, ethnic groups and tribes have their own labels for spiritual authorities, such labels as *Babalawo, Babaaláwo,* or *Awo* among the Yoruba and *Dibia* among the Igbo. In English language descriptions of African religions, such leaders have usually been referred to as priests.

Leaders' Roles

As spiritual authorities, African religious leaders usually perform multiple functions that can include those of: interpreter of sacred lore, mediator, prophet, counselor, healer, diviner, shamanic journeyer, spirit possessor, ritual expert, and weather controller. Usually, a leader will not attempt to provide all such services but will specialize in a few. For instance, one individual may be a good diviner but not well versed in conducting sacrificial ceremonies. Another may be a skilled herbalist or a talented drummer or singer. Thus, a leader's main clientele will consist of persons seeking aid in the leader's area of expertise; seekers then turn to other spiritual authorities for help with problems beyond a particular leader's specialization.

Consider, then, the nature of the several specializations. First, a leader in the role of interpreter of sacred lore instructs devotees in the religion's beliefs about: (a) the names and roles of invisible spirits (theology), (b) proper behavior toward deities and fellow humans (morality), (c) the origin of the universe and of human life and death (creationism), (d) human nature (people's motives, strengths/weaknesses, body/soul relationships), and (e) the reasons behind good and bad fortune (causality). Competent leaders can recite prayers and songs relating to the principal deities of their faith and can prepare shrines needed by devotees. They can also administer sacrifices and perform dances honoring the spirits (Traditional African Elders, 2008).

Next, a leader in the role of mediator serves as a messenger and a negotiator between the religion's followers and the invisible gods. Lay members of a faith are usually considered unfit to contact the spirits directly, other than to honor them with offerings and ceremonies. Consequently, discovering the gods' intentions and judgments is generally the responsibility of trained spiritual authorities.

Religious leaders can also be credited with a gift of prophecy that enables them to reach beyond the normal boundaries of time and space. They can accurately envision events from the past and the future. They can also visualize distant events occurring at the present moment—a skill that may include the ability to contact the shades of dead ancestors.

As counselors, religious adepts help their followers make decisions about choosing whom to wed, what occupation to adopt, when and where to hunt, when to take a trip, and the like.

Healers specialize in diagnosing and treating people's physical and mental/emotional ailments by means of herbs and potions or by conducting ceremonies intended to exorcise evil spirits and foil witches or sorcerers who are thought to have caused the ailments.

Divination is the art of using sacred rituals to discover answers to baffling questions. In one typical form, a divination session begins with a client asking a question, such as "Why did my child die?" or "Will my crops fail this season?" In response, the diviner casts a selection of small objects (such as cowry seashells, pieces of metal, bits of colored glass) onto a table, then offers an interpretation of the objects' arrangement—an interpretation that is intended to dispel the client's puzzlement.

The term *shaman* can be defined as "A member of certain tribal societies who acts as a medium between the visible world and an invisible spirit world and who practices magic or sorcery for purposes of healing, divination, and control over natural events." The expression *shamanic journeyer* identifies a shaman's sensation of having his or her mind becoming detached from the body during a trancelike state and traveling to witness events in distant sites (Grisso, 2011). Such a psychic journey may be used by a religious authority to discover answers to questions brought by a troubled follower, such questions as "My son disappeared—where is he?" and "What happened to our beloved ancestor's sacred altar?"

As noted in Chapter 3, the expression spirit possession refers to the belief that an individual's psyche can be replaced—usually only temporarily—by a supernatural being. The way a person thinks, speaks, and acts when possessed is believed to be the action of an intrusive shade, so the individual who owns the body is not responsible for that behavior.

In addition, religious authorities function as ritual experts whenever called upon to organize sacred ceremonies. Rituals often mark stations in the cycle of the year, as in the case of herding and hunting rituals or of rites marking the rhythm of agriculture and of human life. There are also craft ceremonies—such as ones bearing on weaving, smithing, and fishing—as well as rituals for building a home or introducing a new tribal chief.

Finally, some religious leaders specialize in efforts to control the weather, particularly by summoning rain during times of drought through prayer and the use of sacred objects, such as burning special types of wood. Or, as among the Madi of Uganda, rainmakers conduct ceremonies that require sacred stones for winning the support of deities that determine weather conditions (Lacy, 2009).

In addition to the foregoing kinds of leaders, a special type of functionary in African religions is the *griot* (masculine) or *griotte* (feminine). Griots are masters of words and music, combining the skills of the minstrel, storyteller, genealogist, tribal historian, advisor to tribal chiefs, entertainer, messenger, and praise singer. "Though [the griot] has to know many traditional songs without error, he must also have the ability to extemporize on current events, chance incidents, and the passing scene. His wit can be devastating and his knowledge of local history formidable" (Oliver, 1970). Different tribes have their own terms for griots, such as *jeli* in northern Mande, *jali* in southern Mande, *guewel* among the Wolof, and *gawlo* among the Fula in Pulaar (Hale, 1998).

Leaders' Training

Traditional religious leaders, past and present, typically have learned their profession through an apprenticeship system, which could begin either in adolescence or adulthood. It is a process that can take years, depending on the complexity of the knowledge and skills that apprentices must memorize and practice under the guidance of an established authority. Neophytes must "participate in spiritual work led by an elder, then conduct spiritual work supervised by an elder, then be tested on their ability to do that spiritual work alone" before they qualify to provide service on their own (Traditional African Elders, 2008).

> Among the Yoruba, . . . training and years of dedication are still the hallmark of the most learned and spiritually gifted Awos. This is why on average, most Ifa initiates train for as long as a decade before they are recognized as "complete" Babalawos. (Addo, 2011)

Frequently, the profession of religious leader passes within a family from one generation to the next. For instance, the training of a griot begins within the family unit, with boys and girls learning from their griot parents, then moving to a formal griot school, and finally to an apprenticeship with a master griot (Lot, 2002). As a result, "Griots are very different from the rest of society—almost a different ethnic group" (Hale, 1998).

The Religion's Followers

Prior to the spread of Islam throughout North Africa and before the European colonization of regions south of the Sahara, virtually all native peoples could be considered adherents of indigenous religions. In more recent times, and particularly since the 19th century, increasing numbers of Africans have adopted Islam or Christianity, or else, they have subscribed to practices representing a combination of African traditions and either Islam or Christianity, with the Christian segment often that of Roman Catholicism.

As can be expected in any religion, the followers of African traditions have varied in their dedication to the faith. Some followers have believed more deeply in religious doctrine and engaged more consistently with African spiritual practices than have others. The most faithful devotees have diligently attended worship sessions conducted by leaders at regular intervals and on special occasions throughout the year. In addition, members have engaged in

> continuous indirect worship on a daily basis through the divinities and ancestors at all times during the day by each family and individual. The ritual altars in the African villages are the indigenous peoples' way of reaching out and praising the Great Creator. To the Africans they are the boundary between heaven and earth, between life and death, between the ordinary and the world of the spirit. The constant pouring of drink, food, and sacrificial animal blood makes them sacred and no one would dare abuse them. Some altars are simple; especially the ones in homes, but some communities and villages have communal altars for the entire village as vehicles for channeling the positive forces from the Great One and the ancestors to the whole community. (Addo, 2011)

CATHOLICISM'S STRUCTURE AND MEMBERSHIP

Roman Catholicism is a far newer faith than are the traditional African belief systems. To arrive at its present-day version, Catholicism originated barely 2,000 years ago, when Peter, one of Jesus' immediate disciples, was credited with establishing the Christian church headquarters in Rome. Peter served as the first pope—the organization's top administrator and spiritual leader. However, Christianity was not an entirely new invention. Instead, it was an effort to reform the current practice of Judaism. Therefore, Roman Catholicism's roots extend back at least 2,000 additional years to the formal beginnings of Judaism (Timeline for the History of Judaism, 2011). The Old Testament, which comprises three-quarters of the Catholic Bible, consists of Judaism's sacred scriptures.

Over the past 2,000 years, extensions of Catholic doctrine have been added to the Bible's contents by periodic councils and revered pundits in the form of interpretations and clarifications. Notable among the councils have been the Council of Trent (1545–1563) and The First Vatican Council (1869–1870). Important pundits were such sanctified clerics as Augustine (354–430), Dominic de Guzmán (1170–1221), and Thomas Aquinas (1225–1274).

Many of the roles assumed by members of the Catholic faith are much like those filled by members of indigenous African faiths. However, African and Catholic structures and modes of transmitting doctrine from one generation to the next have been remarkably different. Because the Roman Catholic Church's organizational form and the positions occupied by its members are so intimately entwined, the following section addresses both matters together—structure and membership.

Organizational Structure

The Roman Catholic Church is the largest religious denomination on earth, with more than one billion adherents—19 percent of the world's population (Markham, 1996, pp. 356–357). The Church's organizational structure is too complex to describe completely in this chapter. As a substitute, I offer a simplified version—one that can be compared readily with the patterning of traditional African religions.

The Roman Catholic Church assumes the form of a hierarchy in which authority and spiritual authenticity (extent of intimacy with God) are greatest in the single person at the top of the organization (the pope). Authority and authenticity then descend through levels in which officials represent diminishing degrees of power and responsibility, finally reaching ordinary believers—the faith's ultimate consumers—at the base of the edifice. Peter Drucker, commenting about the long-lasting effectiveness of the structure, noted that in the 13th century,

> Pope Gregory IX published the first comprehensive collection of papal rulings on ecclesiastical law. In doing so, he established the first code of canon law, which is the first "management text". No other organization to this day equals the Catholic Church in the elegance and simplicity of its structure. There are only four layers of management: pope, archbishop, bishop, and parish priest. (Drucker, 1998)

In the following much-simplified version, the structure can be visualized as an outline of functionaries, their training, and their duties (Boudinhon, 1912; Roman Catholic Church Hierarchy, 2007; Rudd, 2011).

1. Priests
   1.1 Parish priests
   1.2 Bishops
   1.3 Archbishops
   1.4 Cardinals
   1.5 Pope
2. Deacons
3. Monks, Friars, Sisters, and Nuns
4. The Laity

Priests

The designation priest identifies a man who, following years of study in a Roman Catholic seminary, is ordained, meaning that he is officially appointed to the religion's priesthood. He is then qualified to: (a) conduct worship services (principally the mass), (b) teach the Bible, (c) hear parishioners' confessions of sin and to absolve them of those sins, (d) baptize people, (e) officiate at marriages, (f) comfort the ill, (g) offer the last rites to persons who are on the brink of death, (h) counsel people at decision points in their lives, (i) serve on church committees, and (j) aid in community projects.

Parish priests: Roman Catholic churches are organized under districts called dioceses or sees. The region served by each church within a diocese is called a parish. A recently ordained priest's typical assignment will be to take charge of a parish church, and most priests will spend their entire working lives in that role. However, some parish priests, after years of impressive service, are judged to be particularly skilled leaders, so they are elevated to the status of bishop. Those bishops who are considered particularly talented may be advanced to the position of archbishop. Furthermore, some bishops may be raised to an even more select status—that of cardinal. Finally, one priest whose service over the years has been judged exemplary will be chosen to become the pope, the supreme leader of the international Roman Catholic Church.

Bishops: A bishop is in charge of a diocese, responsible for the conduct of parish priests within his jurisdiction. In addition, bishops have special privileges and duties. For example, only bishops are allowed to administer the Sacrament of Holy Orders and are empowered to absolve any parishioner who is liable to be excommunicated for abortion. Followers of Roman Catholicism have been officially reminded that "In matters of faith and morals, the bishops speak in the name of Christ, and the faithful are to accept their teaching and adhere to it with a religious assent" (Pope, 2011).

Archbishops: Some districts in the Roman Catholic organizational scheme are especially large or have unusual historical significance and are thereby designated as archdioceses, each one headed by an archbishop who wields authority over the bishops and dioceses within his domain.

Cardinals: A cardinal typically is an ordained bishop who bears two chief responsibilities: (a) be available to the pope as a consultant and (b) join the other cardinals in electing a new pope when that office becomes vacant. Cardinals, like archbishops, are usually answerable only to the pope for their behavior.

Pope: As the peak official in the Roman Catholic Church, the pope is considered to be the successor to Peter, who, 2,000 years ago, was the apostle of Jesus assigned to establish the church in Rome and to serve as the first pope. The pope currently in office bears a variety of titles reflecting his supreme position in the Church—such titles as His Holiness, Holy Father, Vicar of Jesus Christ, and Bishop of Rome. According to Catholic doctrine, the pope's judgments in matters of faith and morals are to be accepted as infallible—that is, unquestionably, the word of God (Roman Catholic Church hierarchy, 2007).

Deacons

The position of deacon in the Catholic hierarchy is that of an assistant to a priest. Deacons are qualified to preach sermons and to perform baptismal and marriage services and also to assist priests in conducting holy communion and the mass. There are two types of deacons—transitional and permanent. A transitional deacon is usually a priest-in-training who, during the final six months or so before being ordained as a priest, is appointed to the deaconate. A permanent deacon is a man at least 35 years old who has undergone an extensive preparatory program before assuming the role of deacon as a lifelong vocation. Deacons, unlike priests, can be married men.

Monks, Friars, Sisters, and Nuns

Men who enter a monastery and dedicate their lives to praying and contemplating the mysteries of their religion are known as monks or friars. They may also spend part of each day at an occupation, such as making wine or aiding members of the community who are needy, sick, poor, or uneducated. Women who, in a similar manner, enter a convent, are known as sisters or nuns.

Laity

The ordinary members of the Catholic faith—the recipients of the services provided by priests, deacons, monks, and sisters—are referred to as the laity. There are well over one billion people in the world who identify themselves as Catholics. However, such members vary significantly in the degree to which they actively practice their faith by attending church services, praying, confessing their sins to a priest, and contributing funds to the Church.

TRANSMITTING THE FAITH ACROSS GENERATIONS

Until very recent times, African religions were passed solely in spoken form from one generation to the next. Even today, word of mouth is the chief mode of spreading indigenous faiths. In contrast, Catholicism—along with other forms of Christianity—has been propagated in both written and spoken form over the centuries. The primary written version has been the Bible—a combination of the Old Testament (Judaic lore, prior to the arrival of Jesus) and the New Testament (the teaching of Jesus and his followers during the first century CE). Over the past two millennia, the Bible has been supplemented with additional written interpretations by councils and individual clerics. At the same time, oral versions of the religion have also played an important role as priests have interpreted the faith for parishioners by means of sermons. In addition, Sunday school teachers, along with parents, have instructed children in God's commandments with tales from the Bible and catechisms (questions and answers about the religion). By Catholics having the fundamental version of their religion in written form, the stability of the doctrine would continue basically intact 2,000 years later.

AFRICAN RELIGIONS AND CATHOLICISM COMPARED

In terms of organization and membership, African faiths and Catholicism have a variety of characteristics in common. Members of both traditions have included leaders and followers, that is, purveyors and recipients. Likewise, in both traditions, leaders perform a variety of functions. However, African faiths and Catholicism have differed dramatically in their administrative structures. African religions have been local, with decisions about doctrine and the duties of leaders and followers made at the village or regional level. Furthermore, the number of adherents of a particular African faith has been limited to the thousands.

Until very recent times, African religions were passed solely in spoken form from one generation to the next. Even today, word of mouth is the chief mode of spreading indigenous faiths. In contrast, Catholicism—along with other forms of Christianity—has been propagated in both written and spoken form over the centuries. The primary written version has been the Bible—a combination of Old Testament (Judaic lore, prior to the arrival of Jesus) and the New Testament (the teaching of Jesus and his followers during the first century CE). Over the past two millennia, the Bible has been supplemented with additional written interpretations by councils and individual clerics. At the same time, oral versions of the religion have also played an important role as priests have interpreted the faith for parishioners by means of sermons. In addition, Sunday-school teachers, along with parents, have instructed children in God's commandments with tales from the Bible and catechisms (questions and answers about the religion). By Catholics having the fundamental version of their religion in written form, the stability of the doctrine would continue basically intact two thousand years later.

THE VODOU/CHRISTIAN FAITH

Over the past five centuries, the structural evolution of the two primary sources of the Vodou/Christian faith (African religions and Catholicism) has differed dramatically. Whereas Catholicism has remained basically the same across the centuries, African religions as fashioned into Haitian Vodou have not. Thus, the following account of the development of Vodou is lengthier and more complex than the account of Catholicism within a Vodou/Christian worldview.

Vodou Structure and Membership

Across the decades, as the successive waves of slaves were carried to Haiti from African villages, the slaves brought with them the concept of proper religious structure that they had experienced in their homeland. For them, the organization of religion was local, specific to their own village or region. Decisions about which deities to worship and which rituals to practice were made by local religious leaders. Thus, as the enslaved Africans settled into their new life in the Caribbean, they continued their familiar religious practices, although without the established priesthood of their African experience.

Vodou Structure

When the slaves from a particular locality were placed together in their Haitian setting, they established a measure of consistency in their religious practices.

Consequently, different African traditions would evolve in different areas of the island. However, the form of their faith was not identical to that of their homeland because of the influence of slaves from other African regions who worked together with them in the same sugar plantation or silver mine. In effect, new versions of old religions resulted in multiple variants of Vodou. Those variants shared certain characteristics in common, such as a belief in a distant, revered supreme being as well as in lesser deities and deceased ancestors to whom adherents prayed. But, in other ways, the variants differed—as they continue to differ today.

> Haitian Vodun is a ritual syncretism that incorporates the rites of several African ethnic groups into one kaleidoscopic religious drama. The beliefs and practices vary significantly, depending on the ethnic composition of the various sects. Arada, Nago, Congo, and Petro Vodun each represent slightly different practices. Arada is predominantly Dahomey; Nago, Yoruba; Congo, the ethnic practices of slaves from the Congo regions; Petro, predominantly Creole. These divisions, though obvious to scholars, are not conscious sectarian divisions among the devotees; they are merely liturgical. (Vodun, 1988)

Vodou Membership

The members of both Vodou and Catholicism fit into a hierarchy of power and prestige. But while Catholicism has a monolithic, worldwide structure, the Vodou hierarchy is local, limited in form and complexity to each local variant or chapter of the faith.

At the pinnacle of hierarchy is the top leader—the houngan or hongan (male priest) or *mambo* (female priest). The number of mambos is greater than the number of houngans as the priestly lineage is most often passed along matrilineally. Only fully trained and installed houngans and mambos can officiate at ceremonies, including during initiations. The Vodou priestly class consists of men and women who have gained respect for their leadership, knowledge of African lore, and supernatural insight. They are expected to be skilled healers and herbalists, able to explain ways of interacting with the spirits and to serve as therapists, counselors, and medical doctors for their community. They provide space for temples (*hounforts*) and often pay for the education and healthcare of their initiates. Within the nonreligious community, they also may be asked to mediate disputes and decide matters of justice. Because houngans and mambos do not have salaries paid by organized religions to ministers, they usually ask fees for their services.

An entire subset of ceremonial activity has developed around proving the authenticity of houngans and mambos, with secret passwords, handshakes, salutations, and *langaj* (code words) that enable houngans and mambos to recognize one another (Racine, 2012).

The words houngan and mambo reflect the syncretic nature of Vodou as derived from multiple African sources.

> The title *hungan* is probably of Haitian peasant origin. *Hu* in the Fon language is the word for divinity, while *nganga* is derived from a Congo word meaning "he who deals with occult forces." *Hungan* may be translated as "the one who is possessed with divinity." (Vodun, 1988)

> The word for a voodoo priestess, *mambo* or *manbo*, is a combination of the Fon word for *mother* or *magical charm* and the Congo word for *healer*. (Dakwar & Wissink, 2004/2009)

There are two ranks of houngans, *houngan asogwe* (high priest) and *houngan sur pwen* (junior priest). A houngan asogwe is the highest member of clergy in voodoo and the only one with authority to ordain other priests. In descending order beneath the houngan and mambo are several levels of aides or initiates (*hounsis*) who bear ritual and community responsibilities commensurate with their defined status. But most Vodou followers (Vodouisants) are noninitiates (*bosal*) who incur no responsibilities beyond serving the deities (loa or lwa) in their own private lives (British Broadcasting Corporation, 2011).

> In Dahomean Vodou, anyone can become an initiate, an adherent of the religion, and even a ritual assistant; however, the priesthood is generally reserved for the descendants of the royal priesthood. The office can only be conferred through the maternal bloodline, apart from the very rare occasions when spirit sends someone outside that bloodline to the priesthood. (British Broadcasting Corporation, 2011)

A 1934 survey of a Haitian rural population of 30,000 listed 200 houngans, another 1,500–2,000 assistants to houngans, and 18,000–23,000 members of the rank and file. Thus, an estimated three-quarters of Haitians in rural settings were adherents of Vodou in the mid-20th century (Walker, 1972, pp. 7–8).

Controversial Types of Members

Two sorts of individuals often associated Vodou—but frequently denied by followers of the religion—are zombies and bokors.

Zombies: Writers who accept zombies as authentic elements of Vodou religion typically identify a zombie as:

a person who has been almost-killed, and then later raised from the almost-dead by a voodoo priest, to be used as slave labor for the rest of their miserable life. Zombies can move, eat, hear, and speak, but they have no memory and no insight into their condition. Dr. Wade Davis, an ethnobiologist from Harvard, went to Haiti to discover how to make a zombie. First, make them "dead", then make them "mad" so that their minds are malleable. Often, a local "witch doctor" secretly gives them the drugs . . . a mixture of toad skin and puffer fish. You can put it in their food, or rub it on their skin. The victims soon appear dead, with an incredibly slow breath, and an incredibly slow and faint heartbeat. (Kruszelnicki, 2004)

The term zombie is apparently a derivative of the African Kongo word *nzambi*, meaning "soul" or of the word *nzumbe* in the Bantu language of Angola's North Mbundu culture.

Bokors: A bokor is a sorcerer or magician who casts spells upon request. Bokors are not necessarily priests, but rather, are practitioners of sinister arts, usually not accepted by mambos and houngans. The term bokor or caplata may be applied to either a Vodou priest or a conjurer who deals in both the light and dark arts of magic. Bokors are often said to be the creators of zombies. The stereotypical voodoo curse is the product of such malfacteurs, who are viewed as dangerous by neighbors and much disapproved by serious Vodouisants.

Zombies and bokors are found only on the fringes of the Vodou reli-gion, belonging to the realm of secret societies, not the everyday praising of the gods (*lwa*). Do Haitians believe that the dead rise and become, at best helpers and at worst slaves? To some [Haitians], zom-bies are just folktales, to others they are as possible as a car crash, and to still others they are somewhere in between. Most Haitians see zombies as a metaphor for hard life without reward, a loss of control, or worse— a loss of faith. (Davis, 2012)

The Catholic Component of the Vodou/Christian Faith

Whereas the multiple African religions changed substantially during their transformation into a rather unified form of Haitian Vodou, Catholicism remained largely unaltered within the merged Vodou/Christian worldview. The one notable way in which Catholicism did adjust was in its tolerating the slaves' African-based beliefs and rituals when the blacks joined the Catholic Church. This ostensible tolerance was apparently not a willing—and certainly not an enthusiastic—acceptance of what Catholics considered pagan practices. Rather, the Catholic clerics' appearance of leniency likely resulted from a combination of: (a) Haiti's blacks confining their Vodou rites to clandestine gatherings so that colonial authorities were unaware of such activities, (b) the Spanish and French colonialists not recognizing that slaves' festivities (dancing and chanting to drumbeats) were religious rituals, and (c) colonial authorities wishing to avoid unnecessarily antagonizing the thousands of workers on whom the success of plantations and mines depended.

RATIONALIZING THE VODOU/
CHRISTIAN STRUCTURE

Finally, consider the organization of the Vodou/Christian faith in terms of the central question posed in Chapter 1: By what form of logic could rational humans subscribe simultaneously to such contrasting worldviews as those of Vodou and Catholicism?

To account for why a combined Vodou/Christian structure can be defended as reasonable, I propose a principle-of-accommodation from Chapter 1.

- *The in-name-only principle:* When elements of two religions have the same meanings but bear different names, those elements can compatibly coexist within a combined belief system.

The organizational systems of Vodou and Catholicism have much in common. Both are in the form of hierarchies, with the degree of religious knowledge, authority, power, and responsibility descending by successive levels from the people at the top of the hierarchy to those at the bottom. In Vodou, mambos and houngans are at the pinnacle, with initiates beneath them on decreasing levels, and ordinary Vodouisants (*bosal*) at the bottom. In Catholicism, the pope is at the pinnacle, priests (cardinals, archbishops, bishops, parish priests) beneath the pontiff, lesser clerics (brothers, sister, deacons) beneath the priests, and the ordinary laity at the bottom.

Vodou and Catholicism also have in common two major media for transmitting beliefs and practices from the religious authorities to the believers. Those media are speech and ritual performances. Lecturing and storytelling have been dominant means of spreading the gospel in both traditions, while such rites as African dance sessions and the Catholic mass have conveyed much of the emotional spirit of the religions.

Although the African faiths from which Vodou has evolved were not traditionally transmitted in written form—as has been true of Catholicism with its Bible and explanatory texts—recent decades have witnessed a growing body of Vodou writings from which Vodouisants and prospective converts to Vodou can learn about the faith.

Thus, in their organizational structure and methods of transmitting religious lore, Vodou and Catholicism have been quite compatible.

CONCLUSION

The purpose of this chapter has been to compare the organizational structure of indigenous African religions and Catholicism and to identify the effect of those traditions on the present-day Vodou/Christian faith that is practiced by a majority of Haitians. The comparison has led me to propose that the marked structural similarities between the African and Catholic belief systems go a long way toward explaining why Haitians can reasonably subscribe to a combined Vodou/Christian belief system.

CHAPTER 5

Spirits

The word spirits, as intended throughout this book, refers to invisible beings that are described in religious lore. The spirits' role in the universe is usually that of hovering about and influencing events, including influencing what happens to each of the world's inhabitants. Spirits do not always remain invisible. On occasion, some adopt a perceptible form, such as that of an animal (a praying mantis among the Khoisan peoples of South Africa or a serpent in Dahomey, West Africa), a human (Christianity's Jesus), or an inanimate object (the sun, lightning, rain).

Spirits differ from each other in the amount of power they wield and in the aspects of life they affect. In West African Yoruba tradition, the supreme power controlling the entire universe is Olorun or Olodumare, just as God is the ultimate, all-encompassing power for Christians. More limited in influence are spirits whose domain is a particular location or facet of life. Catholics recognize Saint Christopher's spirit as the guardian of travelers and Saint Andrew's spirit as the protector of fishermen. The Igbo of Nigeria identify Ani as the guardian of the earth and Igwe as the guardian of the sky. Among West African Ewe, Kabye, Mina, and Fon societies, the minor deity Sakpata is the controller of diseases.

Spirits are also credited with personality traits. In African traditions, the Yoruba divinity Ogun is the god of war and the hunt—fearsome and terrible in revenge—while the demigod Eshu is mischievous. The biblical book of Deuteronomy portrays the Judeo-Christian God as merciful, compassionate, angry, vengeful, and jealous.

The following discussion focuses first on the gods and apparitions of African indigenous faiths, then turns to Catholicism's spirits and specters, and finishes with spirits recognized in Haitian Vodou.

AFRICAN SPIRITS

The invisible beings that populate traditional African religions form a hierarchy of power and responsibilities. However, specialists in African religions can differ in their views of how many levels compose this hierarchy. One interpretation holds that there are three tiers: (a) the supreme divine power at the pinnacle, (b) lesser deities in the middle, and (c) the spirits of deceased ancestors at the base. Another proposal places: (a) the supreme power at the top, followed by (b) lesser divinities, (c) ordinary spirits that inhabit particular places, and (d) the souls of dead ancestors (Turaki, 2000).

The Supreme Being

Belief in a high god is widespread throughout Africa, with the name of this ultimate supernatural power varying from one culture to another. Rather than believing in a single god (monotheism), some adherents of African religions subscribe to a version of henotheism, meaning the worship of a principal god while also accepting the existence of other deities.

The supreme power in African faiths is known by different names within different ethnic groups. Thus, the high god is referred to by the

Yoruba of Benin as Olorun (King of the Sky) or Olodumare (the Almighty)

Igbo of Nigeria as Chukwu (Great in Size)

Dogon of Mali as Amma (the Creator)

Asante of Ghana as Nyame (the Creator)

Zulu of South Africa as Unkulunkulu (the Great One)

Massai of Kenya as Ngai

Wimbum of Cameroon as Nyai

The supreme being is typically assumed to be male. However, for the Ewe of Ghana and Benin, the principal god is a female-male partnership in which the female component, Mawu, is gentle and forgiving and the male partner, Lisa, serves as a judge who punishes the guilty. The pair is sometimes referred to as a single androgynous deity, Mawu-Lisa.

Usually, the high god is credited with creating the universe and with wielding the ultimate control over life on earth, but this divinity is not directly available to humans. People who seek the deity's attention and aid must do so through the mediation of lesser spirits—demigods.

Lesser Divinities

African religions are replete with an expansive panoply of minor spirits that affect all aspects of human experience. Consider, for example, minor deities in three of the ethnic groups that were important sources of slaves shipped to the Americas—the Igbo and Yoruba of Nigeria, and the Ewe/Fon of Dahomey (now the nation of Benin).

For the Igbo (Ibo), invisible spirits or *alusi* populate the sky and earth. Sky spirits manifest themselves through such phenomena as thunder, lightning, sun, moon, and rain. Earth spirits inhabit rocks, hills, caves, trees, lakes, rivers, forests, and plots of land. The guardian of the earth is the earth mother, Ani/Ala. Spirits attached to each day of the Igbo four-day week bear the names Eke, Orie, Afor, and Nkwo. Every major occupation has a patron alusi that protects and strengthens hunters, farmers, fishermen, medicine men, and members of other vocations. Human spirits, called *chi*, determine people's destinies. Igbo diviners are said to conjure up spirits that furnish potions designed to protect friends or harm enemies (Igbo Religion, 2008).

The several hundred minor divinities in Yoruba religion are called *orishas*. The orisha Esu is a trickster who rewards devotees and also punishes them when they go astray. Orunmila is the orisha of wisdom and divination while Ogun is the orisha of iron and war. The female deity Oshun is the goddess of water and is revered as a great mother. Her devotees hold festivals that have become important cultural events in the Nigerian town of Oshogbo. Other orishas are divinized historical figures—kings, cultural heroes, founders of cities—whose spirits can be invoked along with personifications of such natural forces as the earth, wind, trees, rivers, lagoons, seas, rocks, hills, and mountains (Religion—Africa, 2009).

The faiths of the Yoruba peoples of Western Nigeria vary significantly from one part of the region to another; the same deity may be male in one village and female in the next, or the characteristics of two gods may be embodied in a single deity in a neighboring region; in the city of Ile Ife alone, the trickster god is worshipped under three different names. These variations inevitably arose as the myths were passed by word of mouth. (Horton, 1989)

The traditional Ewe/Fon (Dahomey) religion was called Vodun, an espe-cially influential source of Haitian Vodou. Lesser divinities for Ewe/Fon adherents have included:

Agé—patron god of hunters, and the wilderness (plus the animals within it)

Avrikiti—god of fishermen

Ayaba and Loko—sister goddesses

Gleti—moon goddess

Gu—son of Mawu and Lisa. Gu is the god of war and patron deity of smiths and craftsmen. He was sent to earth to make it a nice place for people to live, and he has not yet finished this task.

Okanu—god of dreams

Sakpata—god of smallpox

Zinsu and Zinsi—semi-divine twin magicians

Fa or Ifa—god of wisdom and knowledge

Nana—goddess of fertility and creativity

Egberun—deities of prosperity and protection, also for seers and clair-voyance. (Dahomey Mythology, 2009)

In summary, the African religious traditions that were carried by slaves to the New World included a great host of invisible demigods that were believed to affect all aspects of life. As a consequence, they deserved respect and obe-dience because they were feared and revered.

Regional Differences

Ellis's (1890/1970) 19th-century studies of religion across the Gold Coast (Ghana) and the Slave Coast (Togo, Benin, Nigeria) convinced him that the extent of ethnic groups' contacts with other peoples influenced the sorts of spirits they worshipped. In the most westerly portion of this region (the Tshi-speaking people of Ghana), villages tended to be isolated from each other—particularly those in the interior. Their people had little or no contact with tribes—or even villages—other than their own. Village gods were many, each deity associated with a specific place or object and each with a distinct name. Hence, most Tshi gods were strictly local, limited to a particular village. Rarely did any god bear a name worshipped throughout a tribe. However, Ellis found that as he traveled east, peoples' conceptions of spirits differed.

Although there were still spirits identified with particular places and objects, there were also ones whose powers were far more encompassing, not limited to a single object in a specific village. In the east, the name and characteristics of a particular deity were recognized throughout a tribe and even beyond. Thus, among the Ewe-speaking peoples of Togo and Benin,

> Instead of a thousand different [Tshi] villages possessing each a god, each of whom resembles all the others in general attributes and functions, but is believed to be essentially separate and individual, we find [among the easterly Ewe] the same gods, worshipped under the same name, in every town and in every considerable village, represented by images modeled on a common plan, and possessing in every case identical attributes and functions. (Ellis, 1890/1970, p. 13)

In effect, tribes in the east conceived of overarching gods whose domains encompassed many villages and tribes. Ellis considered this a higher level of abstract thought and theological maturity than that in belief systems that recognized only local deities attached to specific objects. The highest level of the ability to think more abstractly and broadly would be found in religions that envisaged a supreme being whose realm was the entire universe—visible and invisible. For example, the Yoruba of Nigeria worshipped the supreme god Olodumare, as well as dozens of orishas who were personified aspects of nature.

Ellis proposed two conditions that he thought contributed to the differences between tribes in their level of theological sophistication as represented by their beliefs about spirits. One condition was the opportunity of people to learn a variety of religious concepts from different cultures. The eastern tribes appeared to have more vision-expanding opportunities as a result of greater contact with varied cultures. Thus, tribes farther east—the Ewe and Yoruba—enjoyed more opportunities than did the westerly Tshi when it came to communication with people other than their fellow villagers. The second influential condition was the existence in a society of an organized priesthood, which the Slave Coast possessed, but was "as yet unknown on the Gold Coast" (Ellis, 1890/1970, p. 14).

Deceased Ancestors

Throughout sub-Saharan Africa, certain dead ancestors are believed to linger about as invisible spirits with mystical powers, equipped to help or harm their living kinsmen. These shades of departed relatives can be "both punitive and benevolent and sometimes even capricious" (Kopytoff, 2009).

Consequently, living relatives are cautioned to appease the spirits of dead forbearers with such offerings as favorite foods and sacrifices, especially at times of crisis or during such critical life transitions as childbirth, the adolescent rite of passage into adulthood, and marriage. On those occasions, the eldest members of the clan will serve as the proper mediators between the living and the dead.

For example, among the Suku (in Angola and the Democratic Republic of the Congo), an appeal for the aid of an ancestral spirit is made either at the deceased relative's grave or at a crossing of paths.

> The old men "feed" the dead certain foods considered to be their favorites: particular kinds of forest mushroom and wild roots, palm wine, and sometimes even manioc, which is the Suku staple. A small hole is dug in the ground and the food is put into it. Communication with the dead takes the form of a conversational monologue, patterned but not stereotyped, and devoid of repetitive formulae. One speaks the way one speaks to living people: "You, [such and such], your junior is ill. We do not know why; we do not know who is responsible. If it is you, if you are angry, we ask for forgiveness. If we have done wrong, pardon us. Do not let him die. Other lineages are prospering while our people are dying. Why are you doing this? Why do you not look after us properly?" The words typically combine complaints, scolding, sometimes even anger, and at the same time appeals for forgiveness. (Kopytoff, 2009)

In Mbiti's (1991) experience, spirits of relatives who died more than five generations earlier are viewed with suspicion and apprehension, unless they are ghosts of highly respected famous personages. However, ancestors who died more recently are considered still part of their families and are more to be trusted. They stay close to where they dwelt while alive and show concern for the welfare of their living kin. The most recently dead are believed to be frequently present in the houses of their children, overseeing daily activities since they are the spirits most directly concerned about the welfare of their offsprings.

The living relatives propitiate the departed by pouring them drinks and leaving them bits of food. Ancestral spirits may often visit surviving relatives in dreams or visions to warn of danger, give advice, or make their wishes known. In some parts of Africa, villagers' attempts to expand the ancestral plot of farmland or to build houses in a nontraditional shape would be opposed by ancestral spirits because the new would depart from established custom.

Summary

Invisible spirits in many traditional African religions form a hierarchy of three main tiers—an all-powerful supreme being at the apex, a multiplicity of demigods and lesser deities in the middle, and the souls of departed ancestors at the base. The supreme being created the universe and, in most versions of the faith, continues to affect the fate of the world and its inhabitants. The demigods, subservient to the supreme god, are attached to, and influence, specific aspects of life—places, plants, animals, weather conditions, people's activities, and more. Ancestral souls can affect the lives of their living descendants. Thus, family members are advised to honor the departed so as to earn the spirits' support in times of trouble and to avoid the spirits' wrath that can be invited either by misbehaving or by neglecting forbearers.

SPIRITS IN CATHOLICISM

The collection of Catholic spirits can be depicted as a three-tier hierarchy that involves different levels of power and responsibility—God, angels, and saints.

The Supreme Being

God, also known as The Lord, is male and occupies the top tier. He is said to be all-powerful (omnipotent), all-knowing (omniscient), and existing everywhere at once (omnipresent, ubiquitous). The biblical Old Testament's pre-Christian Judaic doctrine describes God as a single being. But according to Jesus in the New Testament's gospels, God takes the form of a trinity—a tripartite entity consisting of God the Father, Jesus the Son, and the Holy Ghost or Holy Spirit. God created the universe and all of its contents. Since that early time, he has continued to monitor events and influence them.

Angels

The second level of the hierarchy is populated by angels, all created by God. Angels are invisible, occupy no space, and are indeterminate in number. On extremely rare occasions, an angel may assume a temporary human form in order deliver messages to selected persons on earth. Three important archangels are Gabriel, Michael, and Raphael. Most angels are beneficent, serving as God's aides, messengers, and heralds of God's glory. But one especially powerful archangel is a devious, malevolent enemy of God, of righteousness, and of humankind. He is identified in biblical texts by various names—Satan, the Devil, Lucifer, Belial, Beelzebub, the Serpent, the Evil One, and Prince of Demons. Satan was one of God's creations who—when overcome with pride and ambition—disobeyed the Lord and was no longer worthy of God's blessing and support. Ever since Satan's fall from grace, his mission has been to lure humans into evil deeds. Satan's own angels help him pursue that goal.

Saints

The third tier is inhabited by the spirits of Christian saints. Those spirits are the souls of humans who, when alive on earth, led such blessed, miraculous lives that, upon their death, they deserved special recognition and assignments in their afterlife. Whereas all Christian denominations recognize as saintly such early luminaries as Jesus' disciples and Paul of Tarsus, it has been the Roman Catholic Church that has assumed the task of systematically conferring postmortem sainthood on individuals during more recent centuries. The process of verifying that a deceased human deserves to be a saint is called canonization, a procedure introduced in the 10th century CE. Prior to that time, saints were chosen by public acclaim.

> The process begins after the death of a Catholic whom people regard as holy. Often, the process starts many years after death in order give perspective on the candidate. The local bishop investigates the candidate's life and writings for heroic virtue (or martyrdom) and orthodoxy of doctrine. Then a panel of theologians at the Vatican evaluates the candidate. After approval by the panel and cardinals of the Congregation for the Causes of Saints, the pope proclaims the candidate "venerable."
>
> The next step, beatification, requires evidence of one miracle (except in the case of martyrs [who died for the Christian cause]). Since miracles are considered proof that the person is in heaven and can intercede for us, the miracle must take place after the candidate's death and as a result of a beatified or "blessed"; the person can be venerated by a particular region or group of people with whom the person holds special importance. Only after one or more miracles will the pope canonize the saint (this includes martyrs as well). The title of saint tells us that the person lived a holy life, is in heaven, and is to be honored by the universal Church. Canonization does not "make" a person a saint; it recognizes what God has already done. (All about Saints, 2006)

Some canonized souls are designated patron saints since they are thought to protect and promote particular groups or places. Saint John-Baptist de la Salle is the patron of teachers, Saint Joan of Arc is the patron of rape victims, Saint Hubert is the patron of dogs and hunters, and Saint Genevieve the patron of the city of Paris. Dozens of other guardian saints are assigned their own groups and places. Patron saints are responsible for protecting those designated groups and places on the basis of the saints' imagined character traits and talents.

The total number of saints and beatified, as listed in historical sources and Catholic archives, exceeds 10,000.

It is useful to recognize that according to Christian doctrine, an invisible ethereal essence of each human continues to exist following the person's death. That essence is the soul, which, upon departing from the inert body at the time of death, will dwell eternally in heaven, hell, or limbo. However, souls of the nonsaintly are not considered spirits (as the concept spirits is intended in this chapter) because Christian culture does not portray those souls as influencing events in the world as God, angels, and saints do.

An important feature of Christian spirits is each one's set of personality traits. For example, as noted earlier, the Bible's Old Testament describes God as powerful, wise, merciful, jealous, fearsome, vengeful, angry, and loving.

Behold, God is mighty . . . in strength and wisdom. (Job 36: 5)

For the Lord thy God is a merciful God. He will not forsake thee. (Deuteronomy 4: 31)

For thou shalt worship no other god; for the Lord . . . is a jealous God. (Exodus 34: 14)

God is greatly to be feared in the assembly of the saints, and to be had in reverence of all those that are about him. (Psalms, 89: 7)

Vengeance belongeth unto me, I will recompense, saith the Lord. (Hebrews 10: 30)

God judgeth the righteous, and God is angry with the wicked every day. (Psalms 7: 11)

For the Lord your God . . . loveth the stranger, in giving him food and raiment. (Deuteronomy 10: 18)

Summary

Christian theology assumes the presence of a variety of invisible spirits that can affect events of the world. The spirits are located on three tiers, representing three major levels of power that range from God's omnipotence at the top, through the assigned acts of angels in the middle, to the saints' limited roles at the bottom. Humans can seek help from the spirits through prayer and the ceremonies described in Chapter 7.

AFRICAN AND CATHOLIC SPIRITS COMPARED

African religions and Catholicism share a variety of beliefs about invisible spirits. Both traditions place great faith in the existence of invisible beings that created the universe and continue to affect all events in the world. In both traditions, the spirits are organized under a structure of strength of power and breadth of influence. Beings on the upper levels of a hierarchy have greater power and broader influence than those on the lower levels. Most African faiths have a single god at the peak. Catholicism also places a single supreme being (or a trinity that functions as a unified being) at the pinnacle of the structure. Traditional Africans and Catholics use honorific ceremonies, prayer, gifts, and sacrifices to solicit the aid of spirits and to avoid the spirits' ire.

However, African faiths and Catholicism also differ in several important ways. Catholic doctrine does not invest objects of the world—other than humans—with souls or spiritual qualities, whereas African belief systems attribute personality characteristics and mystical powers to all sorts of things—animals, plants, landforms, waterways, objects in the sky, and more. Nor does Catholicism propose that shades of deceased ancestors affect the fate of living relatives, as does the typical African worldview. Although in both traditions, the top level of their three-tier spirit hierarchies is the same (a single omnipotent god), the second and third tiers differ. The second tier in African religions is crowded with an enormous host of deities that are associated with particular objects, places, and activities in the world. In contrast, Catholic lore's second tier is occupied by angels who serve as emissaries of the supreme being. The third level in African faiths contains the spirits of dead ancestors who have attained their status simply by dying. However, the saintly souls on the third level in the Christian scheme are the shades of unusually holy people who had worked miracles when alive and whose saintly character has been formally verified by church authorities.

SPIRITS IN HAITIAN VODOU/CHRISTIAN RELIGION

The Haitian Creole word for spirit is lwa or loa, a term whose origin apparently derives from the French term *loi*, meaning law (Singh, 2008). The total number of spirits in a combined Vodou/Christian belief system extends into the thousands. Haitians do not venerate—or even know about—this entire panoply of spirits. Instead, each adherent adopts (is mounted by) only one or a few selected spirits that are instinctively identified as truly one's own. These are the only lwa to whom Vodouisants appeal through prayer and whom devotees honor with rituals, gifts, and sacrifices.

One doesn't serve just any *lwa* but only the ones they possess, which is a matter of one's individual nature and destiny, and sometimes a matter of which spirits one has met and who take a liking to oneself. Since the spirits are individuals, they respond best to those whom they know or have been personally introduced to. Which spirits a person has may be revealed at a ceremony, in a reading, or in dreams. However anyone may and should serve their own blood ancestors. (Rock, 2002)

Two noteworthy features of the Vodou/Christian faith's voluminous congregation of invisible beings are (a) the African origins of Vodou spirits and (b) the Vodou versions of Catholic saints.

Vodou Spirits' African Origins

When the slaves brought to the New World the lwa from their various tribal areas, the separate sets of beliefs gradually resolved into a complex, interwoven web of spirits. Important African ethnic groups that contributed to this emerging Vodou worldview were the Fon, Yoruba, Angolan, Nago, Ibo, Dahomeans, Congos, Senegalese, Haussars, Caplaous, Mondungues, Mandinge, and Angolese (Voodoo, African Spiritual Religious Systems, 2011). Thus, a particular lwa often bore more than one name, with each name from a different tribal tradition. In addition, the Catholic influence sometimes affected the title of a spirit. For instance, the supreme god in Haitian Vodou is called Bondye, a derivative of the French expression *bon Dieu*, meaning good God. Vodouisants consider Bondye the creator of everything and aloof from everyday affairs, so that devotees never attempt to contact him for help.

The slaves carried the three-level African religious hierarchy to the Americas as well, with Bondye at the pinnacle, scores of lesser demigods (lwa, loa) on a second tier under the supreme master, and the spirits of deceased ancestors beneath, on a third tier. Ancestral spirits are referred to as loa Ghede.

The lwa have been organized into a variety of pantheons or nations. The most obvious grouping is between Rada, composed of generous and benevolent spirits, and Petro, occupied by malevolent shades that practice

black magic Voodoo and the Voodoo of angry, mean loa. Dangerous things happen in Petro, including death curses, the making of zombi and wild sexual orgies. By virtually all scholarly estimates one can find, Rada accounts for about 95 percent of Voodoo, if not more. Thus, the spectacular tales of black magic, while very real, are extremely limited. Petro is not the typical Voodoo, but it does exist. (Corbett, 1988)

Every lwa is envisioned as a complex being with multiple characteristics, with each lwa associated with a color, a number, a day of the week, and preferred fruits or vegetables. For example, consider the nature of five important lwa—Legba, Erzulie, Agwe, Papa Ghede, and Dumballah (Introduction to Voodoo, 2004; Corbett, 1990; Dumballah Wedo, 2012; Erzulie, 2012; Morgan, 1997).

Legba is the elderly keeper of the gate at the crossroads between the earthly world and the world of invisible spirits. He is the originator and regenerator of life, as symbolized by both the sun and a phallus. Legba came to the Vodou pantheon from West Africa's Yoruba culture. He is a great orator, serving as the chief communicator between Bondye and the earthly Vodouisants. In Vodou ceremonies, he is the first to be invoked. No other lwa is allowed to enter into the ceremony without Legba's permission. Legba is also a trickster, so it is wise to be wary when he is present.

Erzulie is the earth mother, goddess of love—the muse of beauty and of jewelry, dancing, luxury, flowers, and finery. Her symbol is a heart. Her colors are pink, blue, white, and gold. She is skilled at using dreams to predict the future. She wears three wedding rings, one for each of her husbands—Dumballah, Agwe, and Ogoun. Erzulie is a much-loved lwa, often identified in Catholic iconography with the Virgin Mary, Mater Doloroso (Our Lady of Sorrows), or Saint Barbara Africana.

Agwe is the sovereign of the seas, especially honored by people who live near the ocean. He wields influence not only over the flora and fauna of the sea but overall the ships as well. His symbols are tiny boats, brightly painted oars, and seashells. When Vodouisants' conduct rituals to honor Agwe:

> The service is quite different from others since it is on the sea itself. A barque is prepared with all sort of Agwe's favorite foods, including champagne. This barque is then floated over where it is believed the sacred underwater world exists. If the barque sinks, then Agwe has accepted the sacrifice and will protect the water interests of those who have prepared the sacrifice. Were the barque to float back into shore, then the service has been refused and a different manner of placating Agwe would have to be devised. (Corbett, 1990)

Papa Ghede (also known as Baron Samedi) is an old man dressed in black who serves as the lwa of death and resurrection. He is stationed at the crossroads where life meets the afterlife, and thus, is people's primary contact with the dead. His symbol is a cross on a tomb. His colors are black, purple, and white. He is also a clown with a rude sense of humor, a coarse fellow known as the lord of eroticism with a ravenous appetite for food and drink. Papa Ghede loves children and seeks to protect them so they will enjoy long lives.

Dumballah is a beloved, innocent father figure in the guise of a benevolent snake that serves as a source of peace and tranquility. He is the lwa of purity, of platinum and silver, and the granter of riches. His purpose in life is to bring wealth, happiness, optimism, and purity of thought to the Vodouisants that adopt him as their lwa. He is known as the original servant to the creator, Bondye. In that capacity, Dumballah formed the stars and shaped the earth's hills and valleys. He used lightning bolts to forge metals and create sacred rocks and stones. "When the sun showed through mist settling on the plants and trees, a rainbow was born. Her name was Ayida Wedo. Dumballah loved her and made her his wife. They are still together today, the serpent and the rainbow" (Dumballah, 2012).

Like these five spirits, each of the additional lwa in Haitian Vodou's vast pantheon displays multiple attributes that devotees can consider when they are choosing which lwa to adopt as their own.

Vodou Versions of Catholic Saints

As explained by Jules Anantua, head of the Haitian Ministry of Cults (Religions), the historical reason for African religions melding with Catholicism to form a Vodou/Christian faith is that:

> Vodou has always been practiced clandestinely, first by the slaves brought here from Africa, but even after independence, because Catholicism became the official religion in Haiti in 1860. In order for Vodou to survive, it had to borrow symbols from the officially recognized religion. Most Vodou spirits have their counterparts in Christian saints. Attending services of the Catholic Church and praying to St. Patrick for luck or the Virgin Mary for love were means of addressing the relevant Vodou loa. Individual spirits govern separate realms, from fertility to war to ocean travel, each with its own symbol, favorite colors, and preferred offerings. Attending services of the Catholic Church and praying to St. Patrick for luck or the Virgin Mary for love were means of addressing the relevant Vodou loa. Individual spirits govern separate realms, from fertility to war to ocean travel, each with its own symbol, favorite colors, and preferred offerings. (Williams, 2003)

Consequently, most Catholic saints have been envisioned by Vodouisants as African deities. Thus, Legba is also the Catholic Saint Peter, the one who holds the key to the door of communication between God and humans. As noted earlier, Legba's symbol is a cross, which represents Vodou's crossroads, and in Catholicism, symbolizes the cross of Jesus. Dumballah-Wedo (Danbala), the serpent deity of Africa's Dahomey, is associated with Saint Patrick, who, according to myth, freed Ireland of snakes. Shango, the Vodou god of lightning and thunder, is Saint John the Baptist, who is said to control the storm clouds. Ogun is the Vodou god of iron and thus the god of war; he is closely associated with Saint James the Elder, portrayed by the Catholic Church as a knight in steel-plated armor (Vodun, 1988). In an alternative Yoruba version of the deity/saint equivalents, the demigod Shango is depicted as the Catholic Saint Barbara, the Yoruba Obatala as Catholicism's Our Lady of Mercy, and the goddess Oshun as the Virgin Mary. Ogun, the Yoruba god of iron who carried ritual swords, became associated with Saint Peter and his iron key of heaven. Agwe Tawoyo, who rules the sea, is Saint Ulrich's counterpart (Rock, 2002).

> Ezili Danto, one of several variations of the Vodou goddess of love, melds into the persona of the Catholic Church's Black Madonna as well as Our Lady of Lourdes and a saintly character known as Mother of Salvation as well as Our Lady of Prompt Succor. (LaBorde, 2009)

Important lwa are celebrated on saints' days, such as Ogun on Saint James's Day, July 25; Ezili Danto on the feast of Our Lady of Mount Carmel, July 16; Danbala on Saint Patrick's Day, March 17; and the spirits of the ancestors on All Saints' Day and All Souls' Day, November 1 and November 2 (McAlister, 2012b).

Although traditional African demigods have been equated with Catholic saints in Haiti's Vodou/Christian belief system, there is one significant distinction between lwa and saints.

> The Catholic saints are dead white people who, when on earth, did some good deeds. . . . In contrast, the lwa are disembodied energetic forces that course through the universe, so they never had a body, although they can have a body when they descend to talk to a person when they go into a trans-possession. At that point they are given somebody else's body. (Vodun, 1988)

RATIONALIZING THE VODOU/CHRISTIAN SPIRITS

The spiritual components of Vodou and Catholicism have so much in common that it does not seem difficult—by applying some slight adjustments—

to defend the conception of spirits in a combined Vodou/Christian faith as a convincing, internally consistent worldview. I propose that those adjustments can be effected by applying three principles-of-accommodation from Chapter 1.

First, there is the structure of the two religions' spirit systems. The invisible shades in both Vodou and Catholicism are arranged on a three-level hierarchy that has: (a) a supreme god at the top, (b) demigods (created by the supreme being) in the middle, and (c) deceased humans at the bottom. Thus, in their basic designs, the two structures appear to qualify for the *variations-on-a-theme* principle from Chapter 1.

However, there are some differences between the occupants at each level of the hierarchy. For example, Vodouisants do not pray directly to the supreme being, Bondye, whereas Catholics communicate directly with the Christian God. The middle tier of the Vodou system is occupied by lwa with whom devotees communicate, whereas Catholicism places angels in the middle tier; Catholics are not expected to communicate with angels, except when angels are sent by God to carry messages to Christians. Although the lowest tier in both Vodou and Catholicism is populated by dead humans, in Vodou, the beings are ancestors who drift about to influence the fate of living relatives, while in Catholic tradition, the influential deceased humans are saints—individuals who led exceptionally blessed lives and performed miracles. I believe that these apparent differences between the two religions can be accommodated within a combined Vodou/Christian faith by the application of two additional principles-of-accommodation—*nonconflicting add-ons* and *tolerance*.

An example of a nonconflicting add-on is the Vodou belief that a religion's devotees appeal to demigods (lwa) for aid, rather than appealing to the supreme god at the apex of the hierarchy. Catholic biblical lore does not proscribe devotees' actively seeking the aid of an angel, so such behavior can be tolerated in a Vodou/Christian faith. Indeed, such a belief is implied in a Catholic motorist keeping an image of Saint Christopher, patron saint of travelers, on the car's dashboard.

Both the add-on and the tolerance principles can be invoked in a Vodou/Christian faith to allow dead relatives of Catholics to influence the lives of living descendants. Indeed, it is not unusual for Christians to imply that their lives are affected by the lingering spirit of a departed family member: "I feel so guilty, because my father would have been terribly upset at my being jailed for drunk driving" or "Grandmother would be so proud of me for earning a bachelor's degree."

CONCLUSION

My dual intent in Chapter 5 has been to (a) trace the concept of invisible spirits in Haiti's combined Vodou/Christian worldview back to its origin in traditional African religions and Catholicism and (b) propose why the resulting portrayal of spirits qualifies as a reasonable, integrated belief system.

CHAPTER 6

The Creation of the Universe

$\mathbf{A}$frican, Catholic, and Vodou/Christian religions offer explanations of how the universe was formed, with descriptions in all three traditions including a creator, a creation process, and creation products. This chapter addresses not only the origin of the universe in general, but also of human nature in particular. The following account opens with African views, continues with traditional and present-day Catholic doctrine, and concludes with Haitian Vodou/Christian beliefs.

AFRICAN VERSIONS OF CREATION

It is apparent that African traditional religions offer a myriad of creation explanations, with each story representing the view of a particular ethnic group or tribe. Among scholars who write about Africa, there is no agreement on the number of ethnic groups throughout the continent. Estimates are often cast vaguely as "hundreds" or "several thousand" groups that have their "own distinct language, traditions, arts and crafts, history, way of life, and religion" (Oracle Think Quest, 1998).

There are roughly 120 ethnic communities in [Tanzania] representing several of Africa's main sociolinguistic groups. (U.S. Department of State, 2011)

There are over 70 distinct ethnic groups in Kenya, ranging in size from about seven million Kikuyu to about 500 El Molo. Kenya's ethnic groups can be divided into three broad linguistic groups—Bantu, Nilotic, and Cushite. (African Studies Center, 2011)

Thus, within each of Africa's more than 50 countries, there are multiple interpretations of the beginning of the universe and its inhabitants. Across the centuries, those interpretations were passed from one generation to the next as oral tales, rather than in a permanent written form. Consequently, any creation myth was subject to variations that each new raconteur chose to introduce. This meant that within a given ethnic group, there were often alternative versions of creation. With so many different ethnic groups and with the possibility of varied versions within a particular group, the number of African creation stories became very great. In this brief chapter, I can describe only a few of those accounts, so I have limited the description to six that feature West African regions from which most of the slaves were taken to the Americas during the centuries of Spanish and French colonial control of Haiti.

Each of the six examples is identified by the name of the ethnic group and the names of the countries in which most members of that group have resided. Each description is divided into two sections. Section 1 lists the participants in the tale. Section 2 traces the sequence of the story's events. The first two examples are alternative versions of Yoruba creation beliefs, illustrating variations that can arise within a single oral culture. The last four examples are Fulani, Fang, Efik, and Mandinka tales.

Yoruba—Version 1

People of Yoruba heritage live mainly in Nigeria, Benin, and Togo.

Participants: The characters in the story include Olorun, chief god who ruled the sky; Olokun, goddess who ruled the earth; Obatala, a lesser god; Orunmila, god of prophecy; Eshu, a messenger god; and humans (Yoruba Creation Myth, 1997).

Event Sequence: In the beginning, the world consisted only of the sky and the earth's water and marshland below. One day, Obatala received Olorun's permission to descend to the earth and create dry land that could be inhabited by all kinds of creatures. When Obatala sought advice from the god of prophecy about how to carry out this mission, he was told he would need: (a) a gold chain long enough to reach the earth, (b) a snail's shell filled with sand, (c) a white hen, (d) a black cat, and (d) a palm nut, all carried in a bag. Other gods contributed the gold that was fashioned into a chain, which Obatala hung from a corner of the sky and began to climb down to earth.

But the chain was not long enough, so his advisor, Orunmila, told him to pour the sand from the snail's shell and release the hen. The hen immediately started scratching. Wherever the sand flew, it formed dry land, hills, and valleys. And Obatala jumped to a hill which he named Ife.

When Obatala planted the palm nut, it suddenly produced a full-grown tree that spread more nuts that grew into trees until the land was covered with palms. Obatala built a hut and settled down to a pleasant earthly life with the cat as his companion; but he soon became bored and decided to create beings like himself to keep him company. As he molded clay into human figures, he paused periodically to drink palm wine, so that each new figure became more distorted. While still intoxicated, he summoned the chief god, Olurun, to breathe life into these creatures. The next day, now recovered from his drunken condition, Obatala was dismayed at the disfigured humans he had fashioned. He vowed never to drink again and would become the official Protector of the Deformed.

The newly created people built huts, tilled the land, and prospered, so that Ife was soon a thriving city. All of the gods, except Olokun, praised Obatala for his project. Olokun was furious because she was the goddess in charge of the entire region under the sky and she had not been consulted about Obatala's plan to develop and populate the earth. So when Obatala returned to the sky for a visit, Olokun generated enormous waves from her vast oceans, flooding the earth and drowning inhabitants. People who had fled to the mountaintops begged the god Eshu, who was visiting the earth, to return to the sky and report the tragedy. Eshu agreed to carry the news only if the people would sacrifice animals to him and Obatala. After the people sacrificed a few goats, Eshu returned to the sky. Orunmila, the prophesy god, was appalled at Eshu's tale of destruction and climbed down the golden chain to cast magic spells that caused the flood waters to recede and the land to dry out, thereby saving the remaining people from the great flood.

Yoruba—Version 2

Participants: The characters in the tale include Olorun, the principal deity; orishas, other heavenly beings, including Obatala; Orumila, an orisha who could predict the future; Sankofa, a bird that carried the spirits of all orishas; Chameleon, a messenger orisha; and humans (Anderson/Sankofa, D.A., 1991).

Event Sequence: Before there were any humans in the universe, the all-powerful supreme being, Olorun, lived with orishas around a baobab tree in the sky, where they were supplied with everything they could wish for, including fine clothes and gold jewelry. All of the orishas, except Obatala, were content to live by the baobab tree. However, Obatala was restless. When he gazed down through the mists, he saw an enormous empty ocean in which he thought he could create solid land and populate with beings.

After Olorun gave permission to attempt the venture, Obatala asked Orunmila what he needed for such a project. Orunmila produced a sacred tray on which he sprinkled baobab root powder, followed by 16 palm nuts, and then studied the patterns the kernels made in the powder. After eight repetitions of this act, Orumila advised Obatala to prepare: (a) a golden chain, (b) sand, (c) palm nuts, (d) maize, and (e) the sacred egg that carried the special spirit of each orisha. The orishas furnished all their gold, which a goldsmith melted to create a chain. Obatala collected all of the sand in the sky and put it in a snail shell along with the baobab powder and the palm nuts, maize, and other seeds from around the baobab tree. He wrapped the egg in his shirt to keep it warm during his journey to earth.

For seven days, Obatala climbed down the golden chain, but did not know what to do when he reached the end, as he was suspended over the ocean. Orunmila shouted, "Pour the sand from the shell into the water below." Obatala released the sand, which spread to form a massive land mass. As Obatala dangled at the end of the golden chain, his heart beat so loudly that the egg cracked, releasing Sankofa, the bird that carried the spirits of all the orishas. The spirits blew the sand to form hills, valleys, and lowlands.

When Obatala dropped from the chain, he landed on a spot he dubbed Ife, "the place that divides the waters." As he explored the region, he scattered seeds from his pack. The seeds suddenly sprouted and the land turned green. When he came to a pond and bent to take a drink, he saw his visage reflected in the water. He was so pleased with this sight that he grabbed black clay from the edge of the pond and started to mold it into the sight he had seen. He liked the first attempt, so he tried another, and then even more. Now very thirsty, he took fermented juice from a palm tree and drank so much that he became intoxicated. And the images that he next molded were flawed—some without eyes and others with distorted limbs. When he later recovered from his intoxication, he was distressed at what he had done and vowed to eschew wine in the future.

In the sky, the supreme god, Olorun, sent the orisha Chameleon down the golden chain to investigate Obatala's project. When Chameleon reported that Obatala's figures were both unfinished and lifeless, Olorun lit gasses which exploded into a fireball that dried the lands around Ife and baked Obatala's clay figures. Olorun next blew his breath across Ife, turning the figures into Ife's first people. And the fireball started the spinning of the earth, as it continues today.

Fulani (Fula, Fulbe)

The Fulani people are distributed throughout most countries of West Africa.

Participant: Doondari/Gueno, supreme master of the universe

Event Sequence: The Fulani creation tale assumes a poetic form that begins with a nurturing product of the cattle-tending Fulani culture—milk—and then advances: (a) to the creation of humans, (b) through the destruction of a sequence of human traits because of undue pride, and (c) finally ends with envisioned human redemption when the compassionate master of the universe defeats the specter Death.

At the beginning there was a huge drop of milk. Then Doondari came and created the stone. The stone created iron, and iron created fire. Fire created water, and water created air. Then Doondari descended a second time. He took the five elements and shaped them into man. But man was proud, so Doondari created blindness, and blindness defeated man. But when blindness became too proud, Doondari created sleep, and sleep defeated blindness. When sleep became too proud, Doondari created worry, and worry defeated sleep. When worry became too proud, Doondari created death, and death defeated worry. Then when death became too proud, Doondari descended for the third time. He came as Gueno, the Eternal One. And Gueno defeated death. (Sky Flowers, 2011)

Fang (Fan, Fans)

Members of the Fang ethnic group dwell mainly in Gabon, Cameroon, and Equatorial Guinea.

Participants: A tripartite deity consisting of Nzame (strength), Mebere (leadership), and Nkwa (beauty); three initial chiefs of the earth—elephant, leopard, and monkey; Original Fam—chief of the earth who exemplified power and turned evil; Second Fam/Sekume—virtuous chief of the earth; Mbongwe—Sekume's wife; humans—descendants of Sekume and Mbongwe

Event Sequence: When the universe began, there was only a three-part deity consisting of Nzame, Mebere, and Nkwa. After Nzame created the universe, Mebere and Nkwa advised him to make a chief to rule the earth. At first, Nzame devised an elephant, leopard, and monkey as joint chiefs, but was unhappy with the result, so the three deities decided to fashion a creature that looked more like themselves. They produced Fam (power) and put him in charge of earthly matters, promising him life ever after. The elephant, leopard, and monkey willingly obeyed Fam's orders, and all went well until Fam grew vain and overbearing. He abused the animals and stopped worshipping Nzame, boasting in song that "I rule here." The angry Nzame responded with thunder and lightning that destroyed everything in the world except Fam, who had been promised life ever after. Nzame banished Fam to the underworld. And even though he disappeared from sight, he continued to linger about, causing trouble. What would the deities do now? They decided to spread new soil over the burned earth and to plant a tree. The tree grew and dropped seeds that produced more trees. The leaves that fell on the sea turned into fish, and leaves that fell on the land became animals, producing the world we see today.

To rule the earth, Nzame created a new Fam, one who would not be guaranteed everlasting life, but who would eventually die. This new Fam was Sekume, the ancestor of all subsequent humans. Sekume himself created the first woman, Mbongwe, from a tree. Each offspring they produced was complete with a body and a soul. The soul appeared as the tiny spot in the middle of the eye. The soul enlivened the body and was the body's shadow. When the body died, the soul lived on. Today, Fang parents still warn their children to be cautious about what they say because the original Fam is likely listening and apt to cause trouble (Leeming, 2010, pp. 107–108).

Efik

The Efik population is distributed mainly across Nigeria and Cameroon.

Participants: Abassi, the deity who created the universe; wife of Abassi; humans—a man, a woman, and their children.

Event sequence: After creating the earth, Abassi produced a man and a woman to dwell there. But then, he feared the two would become so ambitious and self-serving that they would damage the earth by growing crops, hunting animals, and producing destructive offspring. As Abassi then planned to destroy the pair, he was deterred by his wife, Atai, who pled to let them live. Abassi finally agreed, but he now insisted that the two humans take their meals with him, thereby eliminating their need to farm and hunt. He also forbade them to procreate. By requiring the pair to be with him at all mealtimes, he could keep them continually under surveillance.

As the weeks advanced, Abassi's fears proved well-founded. The man and woman planted crops and enjoyed consuming their own food, so they started ignoring the bell that announced Abassi's mealtimes. This infuriated the deity. He blamed his wife for this predicament, shouting, "See what you've done! Those two are feeding themselves, producing children, and forgetting all about me." In response, Atai sought to compensate for her poor judgment through using her magic powers to control humans by making them vulnerable to social discord and death (Efik Creation Myth, 2011; Leeming, 2010, pp. 101–102).

Igbo (Ibo)

The Igbo people live predominantly in southeastern Nigeria.

Participants: Chukwu (Chiukwu, Chineke), the supreme being; Eri, first human male; Nnamaku, first human female, Eri's wife; Nri, Eri's and Nnamaku's first son; a blacksmith; slaves; Ala, the earth goddess.

Event Sequence: After the supreme deity, Chukwu, created a universe of sky and a water-soaked earth below, he fashioned the original ancestor of all humans, Eri, and sent Eri down to earth, accompanied by Nnamaku, the world's first woman. She would be Eri's wife. When Eri complained about the dampness of the marshy earth, Chukwu sent a blacksmith to use his fiery bellows and charcoal to dry the land.

Throughout Eri's lifetime, Chukwu sent food to nourish the growing family. But upon Eri's death, the food stopped, and Eri's first son, Nri, complained bitterly to Chukwu about the loss. In response, Chukwu ordered Nri to sacrifice his first son and daughter, then bury the pair in separate graves. Nri obeyed, and soon yams grew from the son's grave and cocoyams (taro) from the daughter's burial site. Nri's family feasted on yams and cocoyams, and for the first time, could sleep peacefully. Later, Nri killed and buried two slaves—a man and a woman. An oil palm sprung from the male slave's grave and a breadfruit tree from the female's grave. With this new food supply, Nri and his people prospered. Chukwu next directed Nri to share his food items with people other than his own relatives, but Nri refused, protesting that he had earned the foods by sacrificing his children and his slaves. Instead, he demanded seven fowls, chalk, goats, and a pot in which to cook those ingredients, along with yams to produce *ifejioku*, a spirit drink. He offered the potion to everyone who asked, and they took it home to use in ceremonies.

Within the hierarchy of deities that developed under Chukwa's rule, one that rose to great prominence was Ala, the earth goddess, whose important role is reflected in the shrines to the goddess found in virtually all traditional Igbo villages (Onwu, 2002).

Human Nature

In African religious traditions, human beings are composed of both a physical, viewable body and an incorporeal, invisible self or soul.

> Most indigenous African religions have a dualistic concept of the person. In the Igbo language, a person is said to be composed of a body and a soul. In the Yoruba language, however, there seems to be a tripartite concept: in addition to body and soul, there is said to exist a "spirit" or an *ori*, an independent entity that mediates or otherwise interacts between the body and the soul. (Rooke, 1980)

The Yoruba of Nigeria teach that the essence of each person is a deceased ancestor's *okan* or heart-soul that is transmuted into a newborn as the invisible sense-of-self that the person will carry throughout the lifespan. Among the Nupe of Nigeria, the *kuci* or personal soul of a neonate is the soul of an ancestor that has returned to *Soko* (the supreme god) for a period of time before it animates a newborn descendant. The Nupe "illustrate the inevitability of the process of rebirth [of the soul] by comparing the journey of an ancestor's *kuci* after death to the path of a stone thrown in the air: sooner or later it has to land somewhere" (Rooke, 1980).

In African religions, a person's soul is often thought to extend beyond the individual person to merge with the souls of others who share the same culture. This notion seems similar to the collective unconscious proposed by the Swiss psychiatrist, Carl Jung.

CATHOLIC PERSPECTIVES ON CREATION

Present-day Christians' conceptions of how the universe and its occupants originated appear in two main varieties: (a) the literal account in the Bible and (b) a modern science account that considers the biblical description to be ancient observers' naïve estimate of how the world and its occupants came into being.

Creation According to Genesis

The traditional explanation among Jews, Christians, and Muslims of how the universe began is the description that appears in the first two chapters of the book of Genesis in the Jewish Torah and the Christian Bible. The following summary of that creation story is from the Bible authorized by King James I of England in 1611.

In the beginning God created the heaven and the earth. And the earth was without form and void; and the darkness was upon the face of the deep. And the Spirit of God moved upon the face of the waters. And God said, "Let there be light," and there was light. . . . And God called the light Day, and the darkness he called Night. And the evening and the morning were the first day. (Genesis, 1: 1–4, 1611)

On the second day God formed a region—a dome-like firmament—that he called heaven. On the third day, he created dry land below heaven which he called earth; and he produced waters that he called seas, along with grass and fruit trees. On the fourth day he created the sun to light the day and the moon and stars to light the night, and he attached stars to the heavenly firmament. On the fifth day he created all sorts of fish for the seas and fowl for the skies. On the sixth day he declared, "Let the earth bring forth every living creature after his kind—cattle, and creeping thing, and beast of the earth after his kind: and it was so."

And God said, "Let us make man in our image, after our likeness: and let them have dominion over the fish of the sea, and over the fowl of the air, and over the cattle, and over all the earth, and over every creeping thing that creepeth upon the earth. So God created man in His *own* image . . . male and female created He them. And God blessed them and . . . said unto them, "Be fruitful, and multiply, and replenish the earth, and subdue it: and have dominion over . . . every living thing that moveth upon the earth." (Genesis 1: 1–28, 1611)

In a more detailed passage, the second chapter of Genesis explains that:

The Lord God formed man of the dust of the ground, and breathed into his nostrils the breath of life; and man [named Adam] became a living soul. . . . And the Lord God caused a deep sleep to fall upon Adam . . . and took one of his ribs . . . [from which he] made a woman [Eve]. (Genesis, 2:7, 21–22, 1611)

In summary, the creator was God, the creation process was a six-day series of acts, and the creation product was the earth and its life forms—plants, animals, and humans in essentially the same condition as they exist today. The final product in Christian lore includes invisible elements of the cosmos—God, a Holy Spirit, angels, souls of the dead—in addition to the earth's viewable contents.

Today, there are several versions of the biblical creation story's details. One is young earth creationism, which proposes that (a) God produced the universe and everything within it during six days and (b) the Earth is only a few thousand years old—perhaps 4,000, maybe 6,000, or possibly 10,000. Another version accepts the notion that the Earth is millions of years old, but holds that God originally created humans complete in their present form, distinctly different from all other manner of life. A third version rejects the notion of macro-evolution (all species tracing their origins back to a common simple-celled organism) but accepts micro-evolution (changes within a given species as the result of selective breeding or adjustments to changed environments, as with humans in intense-sunlight tropical regions developing more protective dark skin pigment than humans in temperate zones).

Creation According to Modern Science

Although across the centuries, the biblical account was accepted in Jewish, Christian, and Muslim societies as the true story of human beginnings, a few people doubted that the Genesis version was literally true because the story contained logical inconsistencies. For instance, how could God differentiate day from night on the first day of creation when he did not create the sun and moon until the fourth day of creation? However, most Jews, Christians, and Muslims accepted the Genesis account as the god-given truth.

Then, in the mid-19th century, Europeans and Americans alike were stunned by a proposal that men and women had not been created suddenly in their mature form by a supreme heavenly power. Instead, in the opinion of a group of scientists, humans had evolved gradually over eons of time from simpler forms of animal life through a process of mutation and natural selection by which varieties of animals that were well suited to survival as their environments changed would prosper, and those not well suited would die off. Therefore, humans were not unique beings, entirely separate from other animals. They were part of a complex pattern of linked life forms. The detailed version of that proposal appeared in the book *The Origin of Species* (1859) by Charles Darwin, an English naturalist; and the scheme became known as the theory of evolution.

Darwin's theory was not greeted with joy in his day, nor is it universally accepted by Christians today. In the late 19th century, the theory was condemned from most pulpits; and the general public did not welcome the unattractive likelihood that their close biological relatives might have been apes and monkeys and that more distant ancestors could have been chickens, toads, and garden slugs. However, a massive accumulation of empirical evidence over the decades gradually convinced scientists of the theory's worth, so that today, most of biological science is founded on an updated version of the theory of evolution called neo-Darwinism.

Whereas Darwin's proposal explained how humans represented one link in a chain of connected forms of life, it did not explain how the universe itself began. Such an explanation came later. During the 20th century, the most popular secular science account of cosmic origin was labeled the big bang theory. According to the theory, about 13.7 billion years ago, the cosmos was born from the explosion of an extremely hot, dense core of matter and energy. Since that time, the galaxies, stars, and planets produced in the explosion have been traveling through space in all directions, producing an ever-expanding cosmos. However, scientists continue to puzzle over what might have been the original source of the scorching, dense matter that produced the big bang. Present-day Christians who accept the Darwinian and big bang explanations in preference to the Genesis account usually contend that God was the source of that energy and of the processes by which the universe continues to enlarge and life forms evolve.

Therefore, in this revised Christian account of the origin of the cosmos and its life forms, God is still the creator, but the creation process consists of the universe's contents gradually evolving from simpler to more complex forms with the passing of time. Hence, the product of creation—the cosmos and its elements—is not fixed or static but is ever-changing.

In the 21st century, Christian denominations known as conservative, fundamentalist, or evangelical have clung to the Genesis story, whereas church groups labeled moderate or liberal have accepted the Darwinian and big bang explanations, with God identified as the original force behind those phenomena. Fundamentalist groups have included Southern Baptists, Jehovah Witnesses, Mormons, Pentecostals, and Conservative Lutherans. Moderates have included Presbyterians, Episcopalians, Liberal Lutherans, Methodists, Christian Scientists, and Unitarians.

From the time of the earliest colonization of Haiti until the end of the 20th century, the official Catholic explanation of the universe's creation was the account in the Genesis. For example, the early-20th-century *Catholic Encyclopedia* endorsed the doctrine that: (a) "the material of the universe was created by God out of no pre-existing subject", (b) "the various species of living beings were immediately and directly created or produced by God, and are not therefore the product of an evolutionary process", and (c) "the individual human soul is the immediate effect of God's creative act" (Creationism, 1912, 1992).

When recent popes of the Roman Catholic Church continued to advocate a biblical view of creation, many Catholic high schools and colleges in Europe and in the Americas were teaching Darwinism and the big bang theory in their science classes; and the Vatican's chief astronomer endorsed the secular science theories (Thomas, 2007). But early in the 21st century, the Vatican's position on Biblical creationism changed. Pope Benedict XVI updated the tradition by accepting the reality of evolution and the big bang while, at the same time, contending that God had produced those phenomena.

Hence, the six-day description of creation in Genesis was tacitly abandoned. In 2007, Pope Benedict XVI objected to the notion that a Christian version of creationism and science's evolution were

> presented as alternatives that exclude each other. This clash is an absurdity because on one hand there is much scientific proof in favor of evolution, which appears as a reality that we must see and which enriches our understanding of life and being as such. . . . [On the other hand,] science does not answer the great philosophical question, "Where does everything come from?" (The Vatican, 2007)

In 2011, Pope Benedict XVI implicitly accepted a version of the big bang theory while, at the same time, contending that God was the cause of the event.

> The universe is not the result of chance, as some would want to make us believe. Contemplating [the universe], we are invited to read something profound into it: the wisdom of the creator, the inexhaustible creativity of God. (Pope Benedict, 2007)

FUNDAMENTALIST-PROTESTANT VIEWS OF CREATION

As noted in Chapter 2, the rapid increase of Protestantism in Haiti over recent decades has been chiefly among such fundamentalist denominations as Southern Baptist, Pentecostal, Assemblies of God, Seventh-Day Adventist, Church of the Nazarene, and Mormon. Those evangelical groups have traditionally accepted the account of creation in Genesis as the literal truth, so it seems likely that many of their followers in Haiti continue to advocate such beliefs. However, in recent times, a growing number of fundamentalists have embraced the evolution and big bang explanations of the universe, while crediting God as the creator. For example, in 2009, the official manual of the Church of the Nazarene declared that:

> We oppose any godless interpretation of the origin of the universe and of humankind. However, the church accepts as valid all scientifically

verifiable discoveries in geology and other natural phenomena, for we firmly believe that God is the Creator. (Creation, 2009, p. 371) (See also: Ham, 2010; Tenneson & Badger, 2010; Yong & Elbert, 2003.)

Human Nature

The dominant Catholic view of human nature is a version dating back to Aristotle (384–322 BCE)—a conception later reformulated by Saint Thomas Aquinas (1225–1287 CE). In this revised version, each person consists of both a visible physical being—a body—and an invisible soul. The soul includes the person's sense of self or sense of me. The soul, which some people call the mind, contains a variety of faculties or powers that bear such labels as intellect, memory, reasoning, willpower, reverence, humor, feelings, and more, with the total number of faculties and their labels sometimes differing from one version to another. Faculties operate during a person's purposeful, conscious awareness while awake as well as at an unintentional, unconscious level, with hints of the unconscious thought processes revealed in dreams (Faculties of the Soul, 1912, 1992).

Throughout the centuries, debate has continued over how individuals' souls originate. The traducian position in the debate contends that God created the first souls in Adam and Eve, and since that time, each new person's soul is one transferred through the parents' souls into their offspring. From a traducian perspective, an important faculty of the human soul is an inherited tendency to commit sin passed down through successive generations since the time of Adam and Eve, who committed the original sin of disobeying God. In contrast to a traducian interpretation is creationism, a belief that God imbeds a newly created soul into each human fetus sometime before birth. Catholic doctrine favors the traducian interpretation over creationism (Traducianism, 1912, 1992).

In Catholic belief, each person's soul is a separate entity, not connected to anyone else's soul. Whereas people's bodies disintegrate following physical death, their souls continue into an afterlife, existing in an invisible condition throughout eternity.

AFRICAN AND CATHOLIC VIEWS COMPARED

Both the African and Catholic conceptions of the beginning of the universe share the belief that a supreme being spontaneously initiated the creation process out of nothingness. Whereas in the Christian biblical version, God was the sole creator, in the typical African tale, the supreme being—Olorun

(Yoruba), Doondari (Fulani), or Abassi (Efik)—was assisted in the task by a variety of demigods that the supreme being fashioned. However, the exact steps in the creation process differ not only between African and Catholic versions but also among the African explanations themselves.

The African and Catholic traditions are also alike in their conception of human nature as consisting of both (a) a physical body that expires and gradually disintegrates on the occasion of death and (b) an invisible soul, which is the essence of a human being's personality that continues into the future as an incorporeal umbra.

CREATION IN HAITIAN VODOU/CHRISTIAN BELIEF

The Internet and a typical university library (journal articles, books) contain a great many African religions' accounts of creation. But the same is not true of Haitian Vodou creation stories. An intensive search of Internet websites and a library, guided by such descriptors as Haitian creation or Haiti's Vodou creation tales, yields virtually nothing. How, then, can we account for such an apparent lack of Vodou visions of how the universe began?

I assume that when slaves were taken to the Americas in the 16th and 17th centuries, they bought with them the tales of creation from their African religions, and those accounts were passed on by word of mouth to each new generation. However, that was long ago, so memories of the tales could be expected to dwindle over the past three centuries as a result of competition from the Christian version of creation that Catholic priests taught in their efforts to Christianize the Haitian population. The Catholic account, unlike the ephemeral African oral tales, was printed in a permanent form— the revered Bible—where the story enjoyed the prominence of appearing at the very beginning of the tome.

According to Professor Patrick Bellegarde-Smith, in his dual role as a Vodou scholar and practitioner,

> Haitians have no single version of creation, because every ethnic group in Africa has its own story of creation, and Haiti is a compendium of hundreds of African ethnic groups, with a French overlay. So Haitians often adopt the Christian story of creation, which has become the accepted truth in most Haitians' hearts. (Bellegarde-Smith, 2011)

Bellegarde-Smith's personal view of creation includes the conviction that there is no conflict between Vodou and scientific evidence, so "We are talking about the creation of the universe fourteen billion years ago." As a Vodou devotee and university professor, he subscribes to such scientific theories as Darwinism, the big bang, and anthropologists' proposals about the origin of homo sapiens.

> We have scientific evidence in terms of Mitochondrial DNA that gives us direct access to the remains of an early female called Lucy by anthropologists [discovered in Ethiopia in 1974 and estimated to have lived 3.2 million years ago], showing that all of us on the planet have descended from common ancestors, and this is where the so-called nature religions like Vodou never clash with a scientific understanding of the world. (Bellegarde-Smith, 2011)

Another explanation for the paucity of Vodou creation stories has been suggested by Professor Roberto Strongman (2011), who speculates that many Haitians do not concern themselves with how the universe was created because they tacitly assume that the universe and its contents have existed forever, with no beginning and no end. "Having no creation myth makes the lwa more eternal."

> Vodou is about the here and now. European philosophy [as represented in Catholicism] speaks about "This is the way things started and this is the way things are going to end." It's very much about linearity, progress, and chronologies that are sequential and grand—but grand in a very naïve way. Vodou is not really making such plans. Vodou concerns what is important now. It's *presentism*. (Strongman, 2011)

So I conclude that the most frequent version of creation offered by devotees of Haiti's Vodou/Christian religion will likely be the account in the opening chapters of the Bible's book of Genesis.

As for human nature, Vodou/Christian lore agrees with traditional African and Catholic beliefs that people are composed of both a physical self and an eternal, invisible soul. In some writers' opinions, the soul may be segmented, consisting of various parts that serve particular functions (Bellegarde-Smith, 2011).

One explanation of the zombie phenomenon attributes the condition to a damaged soul.

> The soul consists (in basic terms) of that which is shared between all sentient beings and is constantly recycled; that which allows the body to stay alive, and that which is the seat of personality and spirit. In Vodou,

a zombie has had this latter part of the soul removed by a malfacteur. It is theorized that malfacteurs skilled in the use of herbs and poisons may use dried parts of the blowfish to induce temporary paralysis followed by brain damage that would deprive persons of their ability to think for themselves. However, regardless of the rumors, there are very few documented cases of zombification. (Rock, 2004)

RATIONALIZING THE VODOU/CHRISTIAN ACCOUNT OF THE CREATION OF THE UNIVERSE

I propose that (a) the dominant version of creation in Haitian Vodou/Christian religion is the biblical explanation at the beginning of the book of Genesis and (b) such dominance can be accounted for by the *availability* principle introduced in Chapter 1.

- *The availability principle:* When there are alternative versions of re-ligious belief or practice, adherents are apt to adopt the version that is most available, that is, most frequently encountered.

Therefore, I find it likely that most Haitians, because of Catholic or Prot-estant training, are better acquainted with the dominant Christian version in the Bible than they are with traditional African stories about the world's beginnings.

CONCLUSION

As described in this chapter, the dominant version of the creation of the uni-verse in present-day Vodou/Christian religion has been the Catholic biblical account.

CHAPTER 7

Causes and Ceremonies

The word *causes*, as intended throughout this book, refers to explanations of why an event occurred the way it did. I am proposing in this chapter that a religion's ceremonies are designed to explain—and frequently to influence—the how and why behind important happenings in people's lives. Throughout this book, the term *ceremony* is defined as a formal act or set of acts performed as prescribed by ritual or custom.

The chapter opens with a discussion of two types of causation, then continues with descriptions of African, Catholic, and Haitian Vodou/Christian ceremonies.

DIRECT AND MEDIATED CAUSES

The expression *direct cause* refers to explanations which propose that an event—such as a thunderstorm or the loss of a car key—was the result of an earlier observed condition or event. Thus, an observed configuration of clouds, humidity, and temperature change is said to have caused the thunderstorm. The motorist's carelessness is said to have caused him to misplace his ignition key somewhere around the house. Secular scientific explanations of cause are of this direct variety. In effect, the scientist's task consists of: (a) observing conditions that preceded an event, (b) identifying which of those conditions have consistently been correlated with the event, and (c) adducing a persuasive line of logic showing that the selected conditions inevitably lead to such an outcome, and therefore, can be considered the cause of the event. So, from this perspective, there is a direct connection between a previous condition and a subsequent event.

In contrast to direct explanations of events, mediated explanations assume that a supernatural being or power has served as an intermediary between an initial condition or event and a subsequent one. Hence, the thunderstorm occurred because (a) as an initial event, a group of people performed a dance as an appeal to a supernatural power to end a drought and (b) the mediating supernatural spirit responded favorably to the appeal by (c) producing a rainstorm. In another application of a mediation viewpoint, unwanted events can be blamed on people's having angered a mystical spirit or power. For instance, (a) a motorist used a supernatural spirit's name as a curse word, thereby (b) offending the spirit, who responded by (c) distracting the attention of the motorist so the motorist lost his car key. Or, perhaps the key was lost only inadvertently (accidentally) and not because an invisible spirit was displeased. However, the motorist can still trust mediated cause in order to recover the key. He can: (a) appeal for the spirit's help in finding the key on the assumption that (b) the all-wise spirit knows where the lost key fell, and (c) will reveal that location to the motorist or perhaps to a confidant of the motorist.

People who subscribe to a religion are apt to employ both direct and mediated causal reasoning. When the connection between an initial event and a subsequent event seems obvious, nearly everyone will attribute the outcome to the direct influence of the initial event. Thus, throwing sand on

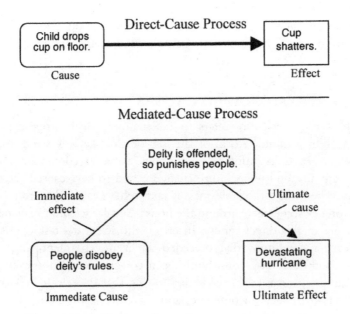

Figure 7.1 Direct and Mediated Cause Processes.

the fire is judged to be the cause of the fire going out. Slapping the mosquito is said to be the reason the mosquito died. Failing to water the corn patch is blamed for the corn stalks withering. But religious people are prone to apply a mediated interpretation when an event's origins and causal process are not readily apparent. Thus, assuming the influence of a spirit-mediator seems necessary for solving such questions as: Why did the child contract the fatal illness? Why did an earthquake destroy so many buildings and so many lives in Haiti in 2010? Why did the enemy win the war? Why did the economy fail? Why did the ship sink in the storm? Why did the swarm of locusts arrive to devour the crop? Why did I win the lottery?

Indigenous African religions, Catholic doctrine, and Vodou/Christian faith all depend heavily on mediated explanations of events whose causes seem puzzling. Thus, differences among religions are not about whether supernatural beings cause events, but instead, the differences are about the way the mediation process operates, and especially, about how people can make the process operate in their favor. In other words, how can people most effectively appeal to the spirits in order to achieve their aims? The answer—for traditional Africans, traditional Catholics, and Vodou/Christian devotees—is through ceremonies.

For convenience of discussion, I address two forms of ceremony—prayers and rites—with prayers often included within rites.

The words *prayer* and *praying* identify remarks, silent thoughts, or observable actions that people address to one or more invisible spirits. As noted in Chapter 3, prayers can be designed to serve various purposes, including those of: (a) appealing for a deity's aid, (b) thanking deities for blessings received, (c) paying tribute to a deity, (d) expressing contrition for misbehavior, (e) begging forgiveness for one's misdeeds, and (f) declaring faith in a spirit's wisdom and power. Prayers can be cast in various forms. The most common forms are oral remarks and silent thoughts. However, prayers can also consist of other types of actions—performing an Igbo dance, drawing symbols on Fulani pottery, fingering Catholic rosary beads, singing a Catholic anthem, or worshipping at a Vodou altar. To add strength and conviction to a prayer, supplicants may end their plea with good words—a benediction. A typical Catholic benediction reads, "In the name of the Father, the Son, and the Holy Ghost," in reference to the trinity of God, Jesus, and the Holy Spirit. Or "Amen" may be intoned by listeners at the end of a Christian prayer to signify the adherents' endorsement of the prayer's content. In Yoruba culture, the word *Ashe*—meaning "so be it"—serves the same purpose.

Rites or rituals are activities—cast in an established pattern and infused with spiritual significance—that are performed on special occasions for their symbolic value as prescribed by a group's religious tradition. Whereas most rites are intended to serve one or more of the aims of prayers, some are designed for additional purposes—to initiate newcomers into the religion, to honor a worthy member of the faith, to commemorate a significant event in the life cycle (puberty, marriage, death), or to punish a person who has violated sacred rules.

The following discussion focuses on traditional African ceremonies, followed by Catholic ceremonies, and the function of ceremonies in present-day Haitian Vodou/Christianity.

INDIGENOUS AFRICAN CEREMONIES

Traditional African religions have included an extensive panoply of rituals that differ from one region to another—even from one community to another. The fact that religious lore was orally passed from one generation to the next helps account for this great variety of sacred rites since each new practitioner might introduce novel activities and interpretations unencumbered by written accounts from the past. Because it is not possible in this brief chapter to describe all versions of prayers and rites, the following account represents only a sample of the types of prayers and rituals.

Traditional African Prayers

African prayers, as appeals to invisible spirits, have assumed a variety of forms—words spoken aloud, silent thoughts, sacrifices, songs, dances, graphic designs, sculptures, and edifices. In the religions of West Africa, devotees have used prayer to express their respect for the supreme being at the top of the deities' hierarchy, such gods as the Yorubas' Olodumare and the Igbos' Chukwu. However, supplicants usually have directed their pleas for help and their expressions of thanks to spirits of lower rank and to the shades of deceased ancestors, who are often described as the supreme god's messengers. Only the deceased who lived honest lives, did not die from mysterious diseases, and had full burial rites can become ancestral spirits. In contrast, the shades of evil persons are destined to wander about as *akalogolu,* which appear on lonely roads to frighten the living (Iwuama, 2000).

Purposes of Prayer

African devotees have adopted prayer as a means of fulfilling a variety of needs (African Religions, 2009; Ibo Religion, 2008; Igbo Religion, 2008):

Offer thanks for one's good fortune and for blessings received—"We raise our voices in thanks to Ani for protecting us during the flood."

Exalt and pay tribute to a deity—"The mighty Osun be praised."

Appeal for protection—"Ifa, deliver me from evil people. Deliver me from talebearers. Prevent me from unending weeping."

Appeal for favors—"Morning has risen. Great Jengi, take away from us every pain, every ill, every mishap; Jengi, let us come safely home."

Appease an angered spirit—"Almighty Father, prayer is our sacrifice. You are the one we have offered the sacrifice for. Do accept our sacrifice."

Issue advice, suggestions, or orders to a deity to perform particular tasks— "May the year bring blessings of money and children."

Types of Indigenous Prayers

Varieties of prayer range from daily personal devotions to periodic group litanies.

Daily Prayer: At the opening of the day among the Igbo, the father prays to the spirits, asking them to bless the family throughout the day. In like manner, at the end of the day, the Bambuti Pygmies will pray, "Oh, God, Thou hast given me a good day; give me a good night" (Mbiti, 1969/1999).

Occasional Prayer: Particular events in people's lives call for expressions of gratitude or appeals for protection and help. As a prayer of thanksgiving among the Pygmies, when a baby is born, the mother and father lift the infant toward the sky and pray,

To Thee, the Creator, to Thee, the Powerful, I offer this fresh bud, new fruit of the ancient tree. Thou art the Master, we Thy children. To Thee, the Creator, to Thee, the Powerful Khmvoum, I offer this new plant. (Mbiti, 1988)

Appeals for protection are common when men go to war, as illustrated in this wife's prayer from the Banyarwanda culture in Uganda:

Let him be saved with those who went with him! Let him stand firm with them. Let him return from the battle with them. (Mbiti, 1988)

Established Group Prayer: Supplications in time of need often take the form of traditional appeals that the faith's followers have memorized, such as a song of the East African Galla at the time of drought: "Come to us with a continued rain, Oh, God, let it fall." And when Galla hunters fail to find game, they chant "Oh, Mutalabala, Eternal One . . . We pray Thee to let us kill today before sunset" (Mbiti, 1969/1999).

Prayer Accompanied by Offerings: Frequently, adherents of indigenous African faiths have offered gifts or sacrifices when praising invisible divinities or when seeking the spirits' help. For example, elderly men among the Igbo extend fresh water to the spirits during morning prayers.

Personal Prayer: At a time of need, a supplicant spontaneously creates a plea, such as this appeal by a childless Burundi woman, "Oh, Imana of Urundi, if only you would help me! . . . Oh, Imana, if only you would give me a homestead and children! I prostrate myself before you, Imana of Urundi. I cry to you: Give me off-spring, give me as you give to others. Oh, Imana of mercy, help just this once!" (Mbiti, 1988)

Responsive Prayer: The expression responsive prayer refers to a pattern of appeal to sacred spirits that involves each of a leader's comments being followed by assent and by embellishing remarks from an audience. Here is such a litany from the Aro tribe in Sierra Leone in which the mother of a sick child is the leader, with her women friends forming a responding chorus (Mbiti, 1991).

> *Mother*—"Oh spirits of the past, this little one I hold is my child; she is your child also; therefore, be gracious unto her."
> *Chorus*—"She has come into a world of trouble: sickness is in the world, and cold and pain; the pain you knew, the sickness with which you were familiar."
> *Mother*—"Let her sleep in peace, for there is healing in sleep. Let none among you be angry with me or with my child."
> *Chorus*—"Let her grow. Let her become strong. Let her become full-grown. Then will she offer such a sacrifice to you that will delight your heart."

Traditional African Rites

John Samuel Mbiti, a Kenyan-born Anglican cleric and authority on indigenous African religions, explains that:

> [T]here are no sacred books in African religion. Instead, it is a living religion which is written in the lives of the people. Africans celebrate their religion, they dance it, they sing it, they act it in rituals and festivals. These embody what people believe, what they value, and what they wish to apply in daily life. . . . Ultimately all rituals are for the welfare of the individual and society, aimed at preserving and prolonging human life. (Mbiti, 1991)

In subscribing to a mediated interpretation of causality, adherents of traditional African religions direct their rituals at invisible spirits that can serve as either helpful forces or doers of evil. Thus, religious rituals can be intended to gain the favor of helpful forces or to defeat evil ones. It is also the case that potentially helpful deities or spirits can turn destructive if they are displeased by people's behavior, so adherents' rites can be designed to mollify such spirits.

Rites can be routine, customary, or critical. Routine rituals are ones carried out as daily or weekly habits intended to honor deities and seek their aid or to ward off evil spirits. An example would be the morning prayers that elders offer to demigods. Customary rituals are rites of passage from one stage to another in the lifespan (birth, naming, puberty, marriage, status as an elder, death), or are designed to celebrate seasonal occasions (planting time, harvest time). Critical rituals are performed at times of crisis to win the spirits' support in producing a favorable solution to such emergencies as personal illness, an epidemic, war, crop failure, lack of game to hunt, drought, flood, and destructive fire.

Mbiti (1991) has divided rituals into four categories—personal, health, homestead, and professional.

Personal rites are performed at stages of the lifespan, beginning with the mother's pregnancy and continuing with the individual's birth, naming, teething, puberty, circumcision or clitidectomy, engagement, marriage, childbearing, eldership, old age, death, and after death as an invisible spirit.

Health rituals are designed to reveal the mystical cause of a disease, who has been responsible for the disorder or sent it to the victim, how to cure the malady, and how to neutralize the cause of the illness so it will not recur.

Homestead rituals are intended to promote the welfare of the family by blessing the construction of a new home or barn, showing hospitality to visitors, protecting the departure and return of family members, implementing major changes in the family (births, marriages, deaths), strengthening social ties, and defining the duties and rights of family members.

Professional rituals are designed to improve people's skills, such as skills for hunting, fishing, making spears, building canoes, trapping animals, curing illnesses, divining the future, predicting rain, blacksmithing, conducting religious rites or witchery, or performing the functions of a ruler—that of a tribal chief, king, queen. Professional rituals are intended to ensure that high occupational standards are maintained.

Rituals can vary markedly in their complexity, ranging from the simple to the extremely elaborate, as illustrated by the following examples.

Libation

A libation consists of pouring a liquid into a cup or bowl to honor an ancestor. The pouring may simply precede a person taking a drink or it may be
performed to solicit good fortune with such an enterprise as going on a trip,
searching for a lost object, or entering a new occupation.

Libation in traditional African cultures is a magico-religious ritual and
is part of worship and prayers, which expresses the indispensable spiritual
unity between the living and the dead. It represents one way that the African concepts of communion among family, lineage, and clan members are
reinforced. Belief in the reliance of human beings on the supreme being, the
ancestors, and the deities is also reflected in African libation practice (Peek &
Yankah in Walker, 2010).

Welcoming Ritual

Among the Igbo of Nigeria, the act of greeting a visitor to one's home typically begins with a kola nut rite. Kola nuts are products of the kola tree, an
evergreen indigenous to West Africa. Cutting open a kola nut reveals seeds
which, when chewed, release caffeine that serves as a stimulant for the user.

At the time that a respected visitor is greeted at an Igbo home, one or
more kola nuts are presented on a dish or wooden platter. The householder
accepts the platter from an attendant or one of his wives, then touches a nut
to his lips to signify that the nut is offered in good faith, attesting that the
host is free from malice. The nut is then passed from one person to another
of those present, thereby ensuring that the welcome of the visitor is indeed
sincere. Next, an elder holds the kola nut up and says a prayer to the ancestors. Among the Igbo, "The kola is a symbol of life, and for this reason,
many profound and mysterious interpretations and formalities are accorded
it" (Ukaegbu, 2003).

Morning Worship

Among the Yoruba, the daily morning prayer is usually a private ceremony
involving a single person equipped with water and kola nuts. He stands at an
altar and calls the name of the deity he is summoning, inviting the spirit to
attend to the plea of "this child". The worshipper may shake a rattle to help
attract the spirit's attention and then will pour the libation on the ground or
shrine. Next, the supplicant tells the reason that he is calling on the spirit. He
splits the kola nut and awaits a sign that the spirit has accepted the entreaty
(Adelowo, 1990).

Rite of Passage—Leaving Childhood

The most frequently described rite of passage in nearly every society is the ritual around the age of puberty that signals a youth's advance from childhood into the beginning of adult life. In African societies, this coming-of-age rite has involved the boy or girl being separated from the community, prepared for adulthood, then received back into the community. The separation can be for a few days, weeks, or years at a location away from the village or at a special enclosure in the community. During the separation, initiates learn the skills necessary to participate in the society as adults.

Among the Krobo of eastern Ghana, girls are secluded for three weeks, during which they are trained in appropriate female behavior, personal grooming, domestic skills, dance, and the art of seduction. The Senufo in the Ivory Coast initiate girls into the secret women's society of Poro through a process that lasts for a period of seven or eight years. Ritual songs, dances, and masks or other artwork feature prominently in many initiation rites. Senufo girls achieve womanhood through a ceremonial dance called the Ngoron, the steps of which can take up to six months to master, marking the culmination of the girls' ritual training. Among the Nkanu people of Angola and the Democratic Republic of the Congo, specialized sculptors create masks, figures, and carved panels that are used to educate initiates about symbolic meaning, appropriate and inappropriate behavior, and other adult knowledge. . . . Male circumcision is common throughout Africa while female "circumcision," or female genital cutting (FGC), varies in prevalence. The Krobo of eastern Ghana do not practice FGC; instead, they mark the back of an initiate's hand with a tattoo of fine blue marks to symbolize her maturity and the completion of her ritual training. (Hipple, 2008)

Rite of Passage—Elder Status

Far less common than the ritual that marks the transition from childhood into early adult status is a rite celebrating a mature adult's crossing the threshold from middle age into advanced age. The Igbo have such a rite called "setting an altar" for the supreme god, Chukwu.

The ritual prepares initiates to establish an altar at which they can offer daily prayers. The objects used in the rite are two white chickens, a castrated goat, seed yams, a tall pole, an eagle feather, and a white cloth. The feather is stuck into a yam that, together with one chicken, is tied to the top of the pole, which is then planted between two standing ironwood planks, forming an offering to Chukwu. The goat is also dedicated to Chukwu, along with the second chicken. The animals are later slaughtered and shared in a communal meal. The ceremony ends when the initiate is brought to sit in the place where, until then, the elderly director of the rite had been sitting. The initiate then prays, using water in chalk and a kola nut, as every elder does each morning (Ikenga-Metuh, 1984, pp. 22–23). The ritual illustrates the frequent use of animal sacrifices in African rites and the key role that such items as kola nuts and yams are assigned.

Seasonal Rituals

Another Igbo ceremony illustrates the nature of rites observed to attract the spirits' blessings on newly planted crops or to thank the spirits for a successful harvest. To honor their Deity of Yam and Wealth (*ife-ji-oku*), the Igbo annually conduct a festival just before the harvest of new yams. The yams to be sacrificed to the deity would be planted one month before the others. The farmer then kills a chicken and sprinkles its blood on a few choice yam plants, which are then dug up and carried to a barn, where a shrine to the yam god is located. At the altar, each item among the offerings is introduced to the spirit by a worshipper.

> The kola nut is broken and bits placed on the shrine: "Eat this kola and keep the yams in the small farm so if the rain be too much, they will not drown; and if the sun is too strong, it may not cause them to wither."
> The chicken's throat is slit and the blood sprinkled on the shrine: "*Ifejioku,* see the fowl I have brought you." The carcass is given to the children who take it home to prepare for communion meals.
> The yams are presented: "If I plant yams as small as this, when I dig them up, may they be as long as this." He indicates with his hands the size he desires.
> The worshipper next prays that fever will not attack his people and that all his ventures will prosper. The ritual ends with a great feast. (Ikenga-Metuh, 1984, p. 23)

Exorcism

Frequently, devotees of African faiths identify ostensibly malevolent individuals as witches who command power that can exceed that of ancestors and divinities. For example, the Gelede ritual-masquerades of the Yoruba are lavish spectacles designed to represent and honor witches who can either bring wealth and fertility or cause disaster in the form of disease, famine, and barrenness. To combat misfortune brought on by witches, diviners are sought to provide protective medicines and amulets and to counteract the work of witches through exorcism rites (African Religions, 2011).

Among the followers of the Vodun religion of Benin, the adolescent coming-of-age ceremony involves a youth seeking to receive and adore the Fá, who is the supreme being's messenger. The youth makes overtures to the Fá and awaits a response. A negative answer to the plea requires an exorcism rite in which the initiate offers sacrifices "to cast off *Kù* (death), *Azon* (illness), *Hwê* (guilt and legal summons), and *Hên* (poverty, wretchedness)." As the final step in the exorcism process, the youth takes a ritual bath in flowing water, and his "hair, nails, a piece of his loin-cloth and everything that in him that symbolizes impurity are buried in the sacred wood" (Zinzincohoue, 1993).

The Arts in Rituals

Chanting, drumming, dancing, masks, and costumes are conventional components of most African communal ceremonies.

Group rites are lively affairs, typically held outdoors, either in the village center or in the forest nearby, with the audience gathered around a wide circle within which the participants perform. The intent of such rites is to contact deities or spirits of ancestors in order to honor and thank them or to solicit their blessing and aid. Certain songs can be identified with particular spirits, so music can summon a specific spirit to join the ritual.

> In many healing or possession rituals, the success of the ritual revolves around the music and how well it is played, thus affecting whether or not an individual will go into trance and become possessed. . . . [The] dance seems inspired by music and not vice versa. It is in many ways an extension of the music through movement, and works alongside it to create the necessary conditions for possession and communication with the spirit world. Dance in itself does not seem to have the same power as music to call directly on the spirit world. Cyclic rhythms have huge power in sending a person into an "other" level of consciousness. Even an onlooker can become wrapped up in the hypnotic nature of repeated rhythms. (Jobarteh, 2008)

> In Western Africa . . . trance, induced naturally or chemically with certain drugs, is related to possession by spirits and deities, and thus is an instrument of ritualistic and religious importance because it provides the basis for experiencing the "sacred" or the "supernatural." In other words, through listening to music and dancing, a qualitative change occurs in the minds of individuals that facilitates what they perceive as a religious or transcendental experience. (Papadimitropoulos, 2009)

Although various musical instruments—drums, flutes, rattles, whistles—can accompany African chanting and dancing, by far, the most prominent instruments are drums of many sorts. They are usually carved from solid logs or consist of narrow wooden panels bound together by metal hoops, with stretched animal skin forming the heads. Sometimes, drums are made from large gourds and calabashes.

The relationship between the performers and the audience can differ from one religious sect to another. In some communities, interaction between the actors and observers is encouraged, with members of the audience clapping in rhythm and joining in the chant, whereas in other communities, such behavior is forbidden. In a Yoruba *egungun* festival honoring deities and ancestors, a performer can run through the gathering of spectators,

> fondling the men and women of his choice and sometimes scaring the audience by sneaking up behind them. . . . The fact that the dancer leaves the space of the stage and enters the spectators' space shows that in Yorubaland, there is no distinction between the audience and the performer. This works well with the notion of improvisation and spontaneity as the possibilities of interaction between the two realms (stage and audience) is endless. (Bastian, 2008)

Almost all ancestral dances are "masked affairs because they articulate the roles of ancestors that are not seen by humans. . . . The colors and styles of masks as well as the songs, music, and dancing are forms of storytelling . . . of the community's origin, practices, and teachings of the ancestors, the myths and legends, and the character, virtues, and morals of the spirit that the masks symbolize" (Monteiro-Ferreira, 2009).

Funerals

Traditional funerals in West Africa can differ from one ethnic group to another and from one type of person to another—the elderly, the young, the highly respected, the physically flawed, the wicked.

However, several features of funerals are common to nearly all of the region's religions. For example, families spend great amounts of money to ensure that the deceased will receive a proper reception in the spirit world. Some funds pay the cost of the funeral itself—the coffin, the burial plot, and personal goods that the deceased may need in the life hereafter, such as eating utensils, walking sticks, and blankets, which are placed in the grave. Other funds are for the elaborate celebrations that follow the burial—for drummers, flute players, decorations, fancy apparel, and food and drink for the many guests.

Funeral rites may last a week or more. Among the Yoruba, the first day is labeled the *Ojo Isinku*, the most important of the seven days of ritual, when family and friends mourn the loss of the loved one, with women often wailing in great anguish. The third day, *Itaoku*, is dedicated to feasting and celebration. The fourth day, *Irenoku*, is for play. The seventh, *Ijeku*, closes the ritual celebration. Thus ends the week of sacrifice to ensure the deceased's acceptance by the ancestral spirits (Drewel, 1992, p. 41).

A Yoruba man in recent times explained that the post-burial celebrants

> think dancing and enjoying after the death will depict the deceased's achievements on earth, how he or she was able to behave to the community. . . . It is not that they are extravagant. They do it for a meaning. If they don't do it, then the deceased who is joining the ancestors will be concerned and unhappy—and be wandering—because he has not been remembered. The deceased will have to answer queries [from the ancestors]: "Why are you not properly initiated, why sent to us? Perhaps you have not performed well. Have you not achieved well? If you have performed well, why is posterity forgetting you?" The only way for us on earth to judge the deceased is to know how much honor was given to him who died by his descendants. (Drewel, 1992, p. 42)

Without a proper funeral, the newly departed

> may become a wandering ghost, unable to "live" properly after death and therefore a danger to those who remain alive. It might be argued that "proper" death rites are more a guarantee of protection for the living than to secure a safe passage for the dying. There is ambivalence about attitudes to the recent dead, which fluctuate between love and respect on the one hand and dread and despair on the other, particularly because it is believed that the dead have power over the living. (Anderson, 2001)

Summary

Indigenous African religions are founded on a belief in mediated causality, which means that difficult-to-explain happenings in life are assumed to be caused by mediators—by invisible spirits that control what happens to people. Religious ceremonies are intended to win the favor and support of benevolent spirits and to negate the destructive efforts of evil spirits. Over the centuries, a great variety of prayers and rituals has been created in myriad African communities to influence deities and the spirits of ancestors. Communal rites have typically featured chants, drumming, dances, masks, and costumes.

CATHOLIC CEREMONIES

As in African religions, Catholic ceremonies include prayers and rituals designed to solicit the approval and aid of divinities and to ward off evil forces.

Catholic Prayers

Roman Catholics offer a variety of types of pleas to achieve diverse outcomes.

Purposes of Catholic Prayers

Praying serves such purposes as:

- Giving thanks for one's good fortune and for blessings received— "We gratefully thank Thee, Lord, for this bountiful meal Thou hast provided."
- Exalting and paying tribute to a deity—"Almighty, true and incomparable God, you are present in all things, yet in no way limited by them. You remain unaffected by place, untouched by time, unperturbed by years, and undeceived by words."
- Appealing for a deity's help—"Lord, lead us not into temptation, and deliver us from evil."
- Drawing a deity's attention to a problem that should be remedied—"Dear God, please comfort the Johnson children who are so distraught at the death of their mother."
- Issuing advice, suggestions, or orders to a deity to perform particular tasks—"Bless our missionaries who labor in foreign lands."
- Begging forgiveness for having done wrong—"Please, God, show mercy on me, for I didn't realize that my failing to tell the truth would cause so much grief."
- Expressing faith in, and respect for, a deity's wisdom and power—"We know that Almighty God will not forsake us in our hour of need."
- Promising to do penance for having misbehaved—"To compensate for my wrongdoing, I will give baskets of food to the needy this holiday season."

Appealing to have a loved one transported to a place of eternal bliss—
"Lord, we deliver the soul of this precious departed child to thy keeping in heaven."

Bargaining with a deity—"If you fix it so our team wins, I'll faithfully attend all the weekly religious services the rest of this year."

Types of Catholic Prayers

Catholic prayers can be divided into five types—scriptural, doctrinal, available, occasional, and personal.

Scriptural prayers are ones taken directly from the Holy Bible. The most popular is the Lord's Prayer from the book of Matthew (6:10–13).

Our Father in heaven, hallowed be your name, your kingdom come, your will be done, on earth as it is in heaven. Give us today our daily bread. And forgive us our trespasses, as we also have forgiven those who trespass against us. And lead us not into temptation, but deliver us from evil.

A second often-used scriptural prayer is from the biblical book of Psalms, expressing faith in God's support. The 23rd psalm begins in the following manner.

The Lord is my shepherd; I shall not want. He makes me lie down in green pastures, he leads me beside quiet waters, he refreshes my soul. He guides me along the right paths for his name's sake. . . .

Doctrinal prayers are ones created by revered Catholic clerics in the past, ones that since have been adopted as official prayers of the Church. Each doctrinal prayer is cast in a set form to be uttered verbatim. An example is the Hail-Mary verse, built from several passages in the biblical book of Luke.

Hail Mary, full of grace, our Lord is with thee. Blessed art thou among women, and blessed is the fruit of thy womb, Jesus.

Another doctrinal prayer is known as *The Golden Arrow*. It came in a vision from heaven reported by a Carmelite nun in Tours, France, in the 1840s. She announced that she had received it as a revelation of how sinners can make amends for blasphemy (Sister Mary of Saint Peter, 1843).

May the most holy, most sacred, most adorable, most mysterious, and unutterable name of God be always praised, blessed, loved, adored, and glorified, in heaven, on earth and under the earth, by all the creatures of God, and by the Sacred Heart of Our Lord Jesus Christ in the most holy Sacrament of the altar.

The Catholic prayer custom known as the rosary is composed of a required series of scriptural and doctrinal prayers. The expression *rosary* literally means a garland of roses, in reference to the string of prayer beads that are used to count the cycle of prayers in the rosary routine. In using the rosary, a devotee fingers each bead representing the sequence, starting with the Lord's Prayer and continuing with 10 repetitions of the Hail Mary, followed by a single praying of Glory Be to the Father, and occasionally, by the Fatima Prayer. The series may be repeated numbers of times, with the devotee each time meditating about the 15 Mysteries of the Rosary that reflect the stages in the life of Jesus.

Some doctrinal prayers are in the form of a litany in which the priest or leader opens with a traditional formal statement to which the audience replies with a formal response that is followed by a further statement and another audience response. An example is the Litany of the Saints practiced today much in the same form as in the time of Pope Gregory the Great (540–604CE). The following brief segment illustrates the pattern it assumes (Litany of the Saints, 2011).

Leader—"O God, the Father of heaven."

Audience—"Have mercy upon us."

Leader—"O God the Son, Redeemer of the world."

Audience—"Have mercy upon us.

Leader—"Holy Virgin of virgins."

Audience—"Pray for us."

Leader—"Saint Michael."

Audience—"Pray for us."

Leader—"Saint Gabriel."

Audience—"Pray for us."

Leader—"All ye holy Angels and Archangels."

Audience—"Pray for us."

Available prayers are published entreaties composed by Catholic clerics or by the laity and made available to followers of the faith. There are thousands of such prayers, including many on the Internet (A treasure of 3,360 prayers, 2011). Here are two examples—the first with a celebratory Christmas theme and the second expressing contrition (Prayers, 2011).

> Hail, and blessed be the hour and moment at which the Son of God was born of a most pure virgin at a stable at midnight in Bethlehem in the piercing cold at that hour. Vouchsafe, I beseech Thee, to hear my prayers and grant my desires. Through Jesus Christ and His most Blessed Mother.
>
> My God, I am sorry for my sins with all my heart. In choosing to do wrong and failing to do good, I have sinned against you whom I should love above all things. I firmly intend, with your help, to do penance, to sin no more, and to avoid whatever leads me to sin. Our Savior Jesus Christ suffered and died for us. In his name, my God, have mercy.

Perhaps the most famous prayer of the available sort is a quatrain children are taught to recite at bedtime. As these samples illustrate, the last two lines may assume different variations.

> Now I lay me down to sleep,   Now I lay me down to sleep,
> I pray the Lord my soul to keep; I pray the Lord my soul to keep;
> If I should die before I wake,   When in the morning light I wake
> I pray the Lord my soul to take. Teach me the path of love to take.

Occasional prayers are ones composed for a particular event, such as by a priest for a sermon, by a mother for a child's birthday, by a father for his daughter's wedding, by a grandparent as a blessing before a family dinner, or by a college president to open a convocation.

Personal prayers are spontaneous oral or silent communications directed to God by an individual who creates the prayer on the spur of the moment, often at a time of crisis (a threat of danger, a loved one's death or injury) or at a time of good fortune (winning a game, finding money).

Prayers are frequently in the form of poems and songs, either selections from the Bible or hymns created by Christian composers over the past two millennia. Perhaps the most revered set consists of the 150 verses attributed to King David in the Bible's book of Psalms.

Catholic Rites

As explained earlier, I am using the term rites or rituals to identify activities—cast in an established pattern and infused with spiritual significance—performed on occasions specified by a group's religious tradition. There are far more Catholic rituals than can be described within this short chapter.

Therefore, I selected five to represent different types of ceremonies in Roman Catholicism—the mass, confirmation, Epiphany, anointing the sick, and Lent.

The Mass

The most basic Catholic rite is the mass—a communal form of worship directed by a priest to honor the sacrifice made by Jesus when he died on the cross and thereby took on himself the sins of faithful followers from that day forward. The rite consists of conventional utterances by the priest, conventional responses from the audience, the priest's reading a passage from the Bible and offering a sermon (homily) related to the passage, and the devotees partaking of the ritual of the Eucharist (drinking wine and eating bread symbolic of Jesus' blood and flesh). Catholics are urged to attend mass each Sunday and on special days, including such holy days of obligation as January 1 (Mary, Mother of God), January 6 (the Epiphany—the three kings' appearance), the Friday before Easter (Good Friday), and November 1 (All Saints Day).

As these examples illustrate, rarely does an important Christian ritual depend for its form and timing on seasons of the year or on the celebrants' locations or lifestyles. Instead, form and timing are dictated by events in Jesus' life (his birth, his ministry, his death, his reappearance on earth, his ascension to heaven) or in the lives of those associated with him (his mother, his disciples). Exceptions to this pattern are ceremonies honoring saints, with the time of such events usually determined by the date of a saint's birth, death, or most prominent miracle.

Confirmation

The rite of passage signifying a Roman Catholic youth's becoming a mature member of the church is the rite of confirmation. "It is the occasion when young people, who had been baptized as infants, now put their 'personal signature' on their parents' decision" (Luebering, 2011). The rite is usually performed in early adolescence, at the putative age of discretion or age of reason, when the recipients of the ritual are told:

> Recall then that you have received the spiritual seal, the spirit of wisdom
> and understanding, the spirit of right judgment and courage, the spirit
> of knowledge and reverence, the spirit of holy fear in God's presence.
> Guard what you have received. God the Father has marked you with his

sign; Christ the Lord has confirmed you and has placed his pledge, the Spirit, in your hearts. (Catechism of the Catholic Church, 1993, ¶ 1303)

Youths who intend to be confirmed are typically required to go through a training period, extending from a few months to a couple of years, during which they study the Bible and Catholic lore, faithfully attend weekly mass, and engage in Christian service activities with fellow initiates. The exact nature of the preparation, the age at which initiates are confirmed, and the contents of the ritual are determined by each local parish. The timing, but not the form, of Christian ceremonies that signify religious milestones in an ordinary person's life (baptism, confirmation, marriage, funeral) depends on that person's birthday and the availability of the service. The ceremony always includes the mass, which may be accompanied by such additional activities as group prayers, individual prayers, meditation, choral music, instrumental music, pageants, processions, dramas, the lighting of candles, and feasting.

Epiphany

The general term *epiphany* means a sudden insight into the meaning of something. In Christian lore, epiphany refers to a specific case of revelation—the discovery made by the three wise men (Magi, Persian priests) of Biblical fame when they chanced upon the birth of Jesus. In present-day Roman Catholic practice, that occasion is celebrated as a feast day on January 6, the 12th day after Christmas. The celebration can consist of two major activities: (a) a special mass at the church and (b) feasting and revelry at homes and sites of pleasure.

The following is a typical form that the church service may assume:

If any Mass in the whole year should be celebrated with all possible magnificence, with music and incense, it is [the Epiphany High Mass] as a great offertory procession, led by the three Magi. . . . Three representatives of the parish bring gold, frankincense, and myrrh, together with the bread and wine for the Offertory, while the choir chants special antiphons from the Epiphany liturgy. At the altar, the gifts are presented to the officiating priest, who may then read over them the special blessing the Church gives for gold, incense, and myrrh on this feast day. Such a procession can help all the people enter more fully into an understanding of the Epiphany mystery, and its theme of offering adoration and praise to God. (Epiphany Mass, 2011)

The feasting part of the day varies from one nation to another. In France and Belgium, celebrants eat the *gâteau des Rois*, a highly enriched pastry, or *galette des Rois*, a puff pastry with almond cream. In Spain and some Latin American and Caribbean cultures, sweet wine, fruit, and milk are left for the Magi and their camels while the celebrants dine on a special epiphany bread called *Roscón* (Barbezat, 2014).

Anointing the Sick

In Roman Catholicism, the term *sacraments* refers to seven rites introduced by Jesus and described in the biblical New Testament. Each of the seven is considered to be a sign of the sacred—an indicator of God's grace and a special occasion "for experiencing God's saving presence." The word *grace* means unmerited mercy that God has given to believers by sending Jesus to die on a cross and thereby rescue the faithful from eternal damnation. The seven sacraments are: (a) baptism, (b) the Eucharist, (c) penance and reconciliation (confession of sins and promise to reform), (d) confirmation, (e) marriage, (f) holy orders (priests being ordained), and (g) anointing the sick. The ultimate rite—anointing the sick—is also known as the last rights, unction, or extreme unction.

The intended purpose of anointing the sick is officially described in the following fashion:

> The special grace of the sacrament of the Anointing of the Sick has as its effects: the uniting of the sick person to the passion of Christ, for his own good and that of the whole Church; the strengthening, peace, and courage to endure in a Christian manner the sufferings of illness or old age; the forgiveness of sins, if the sick person was not able to obtain it through the sacrament of penance; the restoration of health, if it is conducive to the salvation of his soul; the preparation for passing over to eternal life. The anointing of the sick is not a sacrament for those only who are at the point of death. Hence, as soon as anyone of the faithful begins to be in danger of death from sickness or old age, the fitting time for him to receive this sacrament has certainly already arrived. (Catechism of the Catholic Church, 1993, ¶1514, ¶1532)

The rite is conducted by a priest who anoints the ill person's forehead with olive oil that has been blessed and says, "Through this holy anointing, may the Lord in his love and mercy help you with the grace of the Holy Spirit." The priest then anoints the recipient's hands and prays, "May the Lord who frees you from sin save you and raise you up." The ill person, if able, confirms the blessing with "Amen." The priest reads a passage of the holy scripture, recites a brief appeal to God, lays his hands on the sick person's head, and says a prayer of thanksgiving. (For a detailed version of the ceremony, see among the references: Right for the Anointing of the Sick, 2010.)

Lent

The ceremony known as Lent is neither a holy day nor a single occasion such as baptism or marriage. Rather, it is a period of time between two sacred days—Ash Wednesday and Easter. The original inspiration for such a rite was the story in the biblical gospels of Matthew, Mark, and Luke telling of Jesus enduring 40 days of fasting in a desert to prepare himself for launching his ministry. During his fast, he displayed his faith in God by resisting temptations posed by Satan. Thus, when Catholics observe austerities for 40 days prior to Easter (the day of Jesus rising from the dead), they are simulating the suffering that tested his faith. In effect, parishioners' denying themselves certain pleasures during Lent is intended to be a form of penance and mild suffering that strengthens their religious commitment. A typical Lent austerity is that of limiting one's daily food to a single full meal per day and of avoiding meat on certain days. Or, rather than sacrificing something pleasurable, a Catholic may observe the period of Lent by taking on an extra worthy task, such as aiding the sick or eliminating an undesirable personal habit.

Exorcism

The label *exorcism* refers to a ceremony intended to expel demons from a person, place, or thing. Lewis has proposed that:

> Jesus was the premier exorcist of his time. As much as one-quarter of Jesus' healings were exorcisms. The ability to cast out evil spirits was a sign of true discipleship among the apostles. At least twenty-six references to exorcisms by Jesus may be found in the bible, including, "Jesus preached and cast out devils," Mark 1: 39. "Jesus gave his twelve disciples the power against unclean spirits, to cast them out," Matthew 10: 1. "The evil spirits went out of them" Acts 19: 12. "Jesus rebuked the foul spirit, saying unto him, Thou deaf and dumb spirit, I charge thee, come out of him, and enter no more into him. And the spirit cried, and rent him sore, and came out of him: and he was as one dead, insomuch that many said, He is dead. But Jesus took him by the hand, and lifted him up; and he arose," Mark 9: 25–27 [Wickland, 1974]. In the exorcism of a madman Jesus had cast out the foul spirits; the spirits then entered

into a herd of pigs who in turn ran over a cliff and drowned in the waters below [Lewis, 1995].

The Roman Catholic Church continued developing the formal rite of exorcism during the medieval era. By 1614 the *Rituale Romanum* was complete; it is still in use today. (Bancroft, 1998)

Funerals

Traditional Catholic funerals involve several stages of procedure, extending from the time of the person's death to the internment of the body in a cemetery. The intention of the funeral is to offer spiritual support for the deceased's soul and to honor the body of the departed, as well as to provide solace and hope for the family and friends (Guidelines, 2012; Understanding Catholic Funerals, 2012).

The funeral process begins with a parish priest or other cleric going to the home or funeral parlor where the deceased's coffin is located. The priest sprinkles holy water on the coffin and then leads the procession of clerics and mourners who carry candles as they accompany the coffin to the church. The coffin is placed before the altar, hymns are sung, prayers are offered, and a requiem mass honoring the dead is held. The mass ends with the Gregorian chant *In Paradisum* (In Paradise) as the casket is carried from the church and transported to the cemetery. The graveside ceremony consists of the priest or the deacon blessing the grave, then committing the body to the grave with a prayer:

> Because God has chosen to call our brother from this life to Himself, we commit his body to the earth, for we are dust and onto dust we shall return. But the Lord Jesus will change our mortal bodies to be like His in glory, for He is risen, the firstborn of the dead. So let us commend our brother to the Lord, that the Lord may embrace him in peace and raise up his body on the last day. (The Rite of Committal, 2012)

Summary

Most Roman Catholic rituals originated from incidents in the Bible's New Testament, primarily from accounts of the life of Jesus in the gospels of Matthew, Mark, Luke, and John. The rituals evolved during the early centuries after the death of Jesus and, over time, were stabilized in written form, occasionally altered in their details to fit more compatibly into changing patterns of European-based cultures.

AFRICAN AND CATHOLIC CEREMONIES COMPARED

Ceremonies in traditional African faiths and in Catholicism are alike in several ways. Most important, both religions are founded on a belief in mediated causation—a conviction that significant events in people's lives result from the actions of powerful invisible spirits. The intent of prayers and rituals is to win the approval and aid of benevolent spirits and to thwart the efforts of evil ones.

In addition, African and Catholic belief systems are alike in their

- Advocating both individual and group prayers for appealing to the spirits
- Requiring devotees—or at least expecting them—to participate in communal rites, either as performers or as supportive observers
- Maintaining rites of passage from one stage of the lifespan to another—birth, puberty (age-of-reason), marriage, death
- Assigning particular ritual responsibilities and privileges to selected members of the community on the basis of those individuals' qualifications
- Including sacrifices in the rites
- Employing singing and instrumental music in rituals

In contrast to the similarities between African faiths and Catholicism are numbers of significant differences in their ceremonial practices.

From one community to another, African ceremonies vary in form far more than Catholic rites, principally because of the different organizational structures of the two religions. The age-old published rules of conduct of the worldwide Roman Catholic Church leave far less room for local variations in ceremonies than do the unwritten, orally transmitted practices of the thousands of African villages' belief systems.

In the main, African rituals are much livelier than Catholic ceremonies. Communal African rites feature loud, animated chanting, drumming, and dancing by masked and costumed performers. In comparison, Catholic ceremonies tend to be somber affairs, often accompanied by solemn choral and organ music.

The sacrifices in African ceremonies are likely to include bloodletting—killing an animal, such as a chicken or a goat—whereas sacrifices that are part of Catholic ceremonies are limited to the expenditure of money or the denial of privileges or the imposition of austerities. A typical, very modest sacrifice in a Catholic church is that of paying for a votive candle, that is, a candle lit in support of a prayer on behalf of a particular person or spirit.

VODOU/CHRISTIAN CEREMONIES

Haitian religious ceremonies combine African and Catholic traditions with local innovations that give the ceremonies a distinct Haitian character. The rites range from simple devotional acts, such as the lighting of candles with accompanying prayers, to family observances for the family dead, and to elaborate rituals enhanced by elaborate meals, drumming, singing, and exuberant dancing.

Prayer

Followers of Vodou/Christian religion pray not only to: (a) the Vodou deities and spirits of departed ancestors as derived from African traditions, but also to (b) the Christian Trinity (God, Jesus, the Holy Spirit) and Catholic saints. The purpose of praying can vary by the occasion (a holy day, bedtime, a mealtime, illness, a frightening event) and by the worshipper's intent. Typical intents of prayers to deities or ancestors include: (a) courting their approval, (b) seeking their help, (c) expressing gratitude for favors received, (d) pleading for their blessings, and (e) drawing their attention to people or endeavors that are worthy of divine support. Individual parishioners can differ from each other in when they pray and in the intentions that motivate their worship. For example, Professor Bellegarde-Smith, in his dual role as religious scholar and Vodou practitioner, explains that:

> I pray twice a day, when I arise in the morning and before I go to bed at night—and more often if I have a chance. What I pray about depends on what I am seeking guidance for. Also, who among family and friends need some guidance get remembered in my prayers on a daily basis. Vodou religious leaders pray individually in their homes and also during ceremonies in which there are dozens or hundreds of individuals. We Vodou leaders pray to African spirits, which are spirits also found in other parts of the world under other names. We don't need to pray to please the spirits, because the spirits are pleased by our actions, as one would please parents or friends. Nor would I would say that one prays to appease the spirits, because that brings to mind a vengeful spirit, and I don't think that any spirits I've ever dealt with were vengeful. (Bellegarde-Smith, 2011)

Types of Rituals

Like all religious rituals, those in Haiti are designed to establish communion between the individual or the community and the divine. Vodou/Christian rituals take different forms, depending on their intent. Private devotions may be made at small altars in the home or at elaborate altars in specially built rooms. Public rituals deriving from the African roots are usually held in temples (*hounforts*) or in outdoor *peristyles* (roofed sacred spaces), whereas rites associated with Catholic roots are conducted in churches. A hounfort includes an altar and is decorated with symbols (*veves*) of the lwa. Altars typically hold candles, cloth, herbs, decorated bottles, items associated with particular lwa and saints, along with offerings of food and drink. Individuals might sing and dance, light candles, make offerings, or simply pray quietly.

From the earliest years of colonialism until the end of the 20th century, Vodou was not recognized officially as a practice that deserved the status of a respected religion. However, in May 2003, President Jean-Bertrand Aristide issued a decree fully recognizing Vodou as an official faith with a status equal to that of Catholicism, Protestantism, Islam, and other religions. The decree qualified Haitian mambos and houngans to legally conduct baptisms, marriages, and funerals.

Vodou/Christian ceremonies are performed to celebrate special occasions in peoples' lives (birth, coming-of-age, marriage, death), to aid the poor and needy, to honor sacred children or ancestors, to initiate a Vodouisant into the religion, or to install ritual-assistants or members of the priesthood. In addition, more than two dozen holy days throughout the year are set aside for ceremonies, with many of the dates associated with traditional Catholic religious occasions. Each such celebration is dedicated to both a Vodou lwa and a Catholic saint (McAlister, 2012b; Idizol, 2011).

> January 6: The Erusiles and Lerois (the three kings' epiphany)
>
> March 17: Danbala and Saint Patrick
>
> July 16: Ezili Danto and Our Lady of Mount Carmel
>
> July 25: Ogou and Saint James
>
> November 1: Spirits of the Ancestors and All Saints' Day
>
> December 8: Erusile Freeda and the Immaculate Conception

A Household Ceremony

In the typical ritual carried out at home, the householder, as a Vodouisant or *servite/serviteur*, will have one or more tables set out as an altar honoring the ancestors and the particular deities that the householder serves. The items at the altar include pictures or statues of the spirits, perfumes, foods, and other items thought to be favored by the deities. The simplest altar may have only a white candle and a clear glass of water, and perhaps flowers. On a chosen spirit's special day, the Vodouisant lights a candle and intones a Catholic prayer—Our Father and Hail Mary—then salutes Papa Legba, guardian of the spirit world, and asks him to open the gate. The worshipper next addresses the selected deity. However, an ancestors' shade can be approached directly, without the permission of Papa Legba, because an ancestor is considered to be "in the blood."

A Public Ceremony

In a brief paragraph, Michael Rock has sketched principal features of a typical Vodou/Christian ceremony:

> After a day or two of preparation setting up altars, ritually preparing and cooking fowl and other foods, a Haitian Vodou [/Christian] service begins with a series of Catholic prayers and songs in French, then a litany in Creole and African "langaj" that goes through all the European and African saints and lwa honored by the house, including a series of verses for all the main spirits of the house. This is called the "Priye Gineh" or the African Prayer. Then songs for all the individual spirits are sung, summoning spirits to take possession of individuals to speak and act through them. Each spirit will give readings, advice, and cures to those who approach them for help. (Rock, 2004)

The conduct of the ceremony is supervised by a mambo or houngan who, early in the ceremony, honors Papa Legba—the guardian of the gate between the visible earthly world and the invisible spirit domain. Then, the congregation is led through the pre-ritual feast, and songs and dances are performed for the Rada, Ghede, and Petro spirit nations. The songs and dances at rituals are accompanied by drummers and other musicians. Frequently, a ceremony includes animal sacrifices.

> Generally, large amounts of food are offered to the loa during ceremonies, and in more traditional groups, the sacrifice of animals (mostly birds) may play a part. It is important to note that these animals have been pampered, are kept calm, and are killed quickly and with as little pain as possible. It is emphatically stated by houngans and mambos

that only people properly trained for this should commit such sacrifices, as an untrained person might cause the animals real pain and distress, which would be unacceptable. The blood of the animals is splashed on the altars, thereby "feeding" the loa the life-force of the animal, and the tremendous burst of lifeforce helps carry the prayers of the congregation to the loa. The animals are then cooked and shared among the congregation in a ritual meal. (Introduction to Vodou, 2004)

Spirit Possession

During a typical ritual, the act of possession within a trance state has derived from a centuries-old African religious tradition. Haitian possession practices have come principally from the African Dahomean kingdom in what is now the Republic of Benin. The possession trance is produced in various ways, encouraged by such motion as drumming, rattling, tapping a stick, and rhythmic chanting. The raising of hands and swaying can help. Possession and hallucinations can also be stimulated by drugs, sensory deprivation, physiological stress, or hypnosis or autohypnosis, which, in folk theory, cause the displacement of the soul (Walker, 1972, p. 3).

The houngan or mambo is the most likely person to become possessed, although possession can happen to anyone, even a noninitiate. Erin Hudson has offered a typical example of possession during a present-day Vodou ritual:

> The first instance of a manifested spirit that night occurred to the priestess. Spasms and convulsions shook the priestess's body. People surrounded her, helping her reach the ground gently, cushioning her fall, and a bit of rum from a bottle was sprayed on her face. As the night went on, spirits manifested themselves in more people, and the cycle of convulsions, a cushioned fall, and a bit of spray in the face happened each time. People rocked and swayed as those possessed by the spirit careened into crowded sections of the room. Sometimes there were breaks in the ceremony to air out the room. The drummers would take a rest, and the soft hum of voices would replace the rhythm of the drums. (Hudson, 2011)

> Some spirits are believed to be able to give prophecies of upcoming events or situations pertaining to the possessed one. . . . Practitioners describe this as a beautiful but very tiring experience. . . . The practitioner has no recollection of the possession and in fact, when the possessing spirit leaves the body, the possessed one is tired and wonders what has happened during the possession. It is said that only the lwa can choose who it wants to possess, for the spirit may have a mission that it can carry out spiritually. (Mizrach, 2014)

A Ceremony Set by the Calendar

An example of a ritual held at a particular time of the year is the Guede ceremony celebrated throughout November, the season of death and rebirth when Vodou/Christian practitioners offer a great feast for the Guede family of spirits. The Guede deities are from the lwa lineage of Baron Samedi (controller of cemeteries and death) and his wife, Maman Brigitte.

The feast opens with a lengthy Catholic prayer, followed by drummers playing syncopated rhythms to introduce chants and dances from Haitian folklore. During the festivities, the Guede spirits are offered rum, food, and grain to induce them to join in celebrating life after death.

> The attendees begin to dance around a tree in the center of the yard, moving faster and harder with the rising pulse of the beat. The priest draws sacred symbols in the dust with cornmeal, and rum is poured on the ground to honor the spirits. One woman falls to the ground, convulsing for a moment before she is helped back to her feet. She resumes the dance, moving differently now, and continues dancing for hours. It is perhaps no longer she who is dancing. She is in a trance, apparently possessed by Erzuli, the great mother spirit. (Guyup, 2004)

Devotees who have become possessed by the Guede lwa behave grossly, engaging in sexual banter with the Vodou priests and members of the audience, then soon turn serious and offer attendees advice about health practices and ways to solve problems of everyday life. During the ceremony, the supervising houngan or mambo sacrifices a sanctified chicken or other animal to the lwa.

Mystical Marriage

A distinct type of Vodou/Christian ritual is the *maryaj mistik* (mystical marriage) or *maryaj lwa* (spirit marriage) in which a devotee weds a deity. The preparations for the affair and the conduct of the rite are the same as in the wedding of two mortals "in a ceremony complete with bridal dresses, rings, cakes, and a priest" (Rock, 2002).

In Mambo Chita Tan's (2006) description of a specific maryaj lwa, the groom was a young man and the bride was the revered spirit Lwa Metres Mambo Ezili Freda Daomé, who is the Vodou equivalent of the Catholic Mater Dolorosa (Jesus' mother sorrowing over his death). The planning began weeks before the nuptials, with the main mambo assisted by two houngans. At the Vodou temple on the day of the ceremony, they prepared the altar with the bride's favorite foods, drinks, gifts, candles, lamps, and a picture of the Catholic saint, Mater Dolorosa. In preparation for the main ceremony, they invested several hours in singing rituals to drumbeats, and a houngan sketched Ezili Freda Daomé's *veve* (sacred symbol), a geometrically designed two-colored heart.

The wedding ritual opened with prayers and invitations to a variety of lwa from the Rada nation to join the festivities. Then, the bride appeared in the mind of one of houngans who, throughout the ritual, would be possessed to represent her. He left the room and soon returned as Ezili, garbed in wedding finery and acting the part of a delighted bride. The wedding ceremony was performed, the marriage contract signed and witnessed, and hugs and kisses exchanged. Following a reception, the houngan who had assumed the role of the bride left to change from the wedding attire into his own clothes.

Funerals

A typical Haitian funeral involves five main phases: (a) a parade through the streets from the deceased's home or mortuary, (b) a funeral service in a church, (c) a parade to the cemetery, (d) a graveside burial service, and (e) a wake after the funeral.

Funerary rites, which in Haiti take the form of a nine-day wake after the Catholic funeral, and rituals such as the *lave tet* (pronounced "Lav-AY Tet"), or washing of the head (a ritual of cleansing and purification) are all examples of these rituals (Introduction to Vodou, 2004).

RATIONALIZING VODOU/CHRISTIAN CEREMONIES

To explain why rituals in Haiti's Vodou/Christian faith qualify the religion as a cohesive worldview, we can identify many ways that African-derived and Catholic-derived ceremonies are quite alike. At the core of both traditions is a belief in mediated causation—the assumption that invisible spirits determine the outcome of major events in people's lives. In each tradition, rites are performed in individuals' homes as well as in sites for group worship—temples and churches that are often contain elaborately decorated shrines. Furthermore, the participants in public rituals include clergy—clad in special garb—who perform before an audience of devotees who respond to events in a defined fashion. The ritualistic activities include sermons by clerics, prayers to deities, singing, instrumental music, and an established routine of behavior for both the clergy and the audience. Many of the Vodou lwa to whom prayers are directed have their equivalents among the Catholic saints. During certain rituals, participants drink blood—either actual blood of a sacrificed animal (African origin) or a red beverage symbolizing Jesus' blood (the Eucharist of Christian origin).

These many ways that traditional African and Catholic ceremonies are alike prompt me to contend that, in terms of rituals, the Vodou/Christian faith qualifies as a coherent, unified worldview. To support such a proposal, I draw on two principles-of-accommodation from Chapter 1—*variations-on-a-theme* and *tolerance*.

- *The variations-on-a-theme principle:* Religions that share the same basic set of beliefs (same theme), but manifest that theme in different practices, can exist comfortably together.

Not only are the foundational beliefs of the African-based and Catholic religions quite alike in their Vodou/Christian form, but even the practices are highly similar in many instances. Observed differences are only in details that could be accepted under the tolerance principle.

- *The tolerance principle:* Religions can differ in the extent to which they accept add-on beliefs and practices. A more tolerant tradition will permit greater importation of add-ons than will a less tolerant tradition.

As explained in earlier chapters, during the centuries of French control of Haiti, colonial authorities and Catholic clerics developed a tolerance of Vodou practices in the slave population, a broadmindedness that has continued to the present day. For example, in recent years, the Catholic clergy have increasingly allowed their churches to be used for Vodou-related activities (Vodou, 2012). Such a permissive attitude on the part of Church personnel likely aids Vodou/Christian devotees to feel free of guilt for including African-based practices in their religious life.

CONCLUSION

The dual purpose of this chapter has been to (a) illustrate ways that ceremonies reflect religious devotees' belief in a mediated-cause interpretation of important events in the world—with invisible spirits serving as the mediators—and (b) identify how features of Haitian Vodou/Christian rituals have evolved from traditional African and Catholic rituals.

CHAPTER 8

Maxims and Tales

Maxims are concise wise sayings, such as proverbs or adages. Tales are stories, often in the form of parables or allegories. Religious maxims and tales are intended to teach moral lessons or to tell something about the philosophy, practices, or history of a belief system.

INDIGENOUS AFRICAN RELIGIONS

African folklore is replete with wise sayings and tales, but only a portion of them qualify as religious, that is, as adages and stories involving: (a) personified spirits that affect people's lives or (b) moral issues, in the sense of proper ways to behave toward spirits, fellow humans, and nature. The following examples are traditional aphorisms and fables with such a religious focus.

African Maxims

These wise sayings have been selected from a variety of tribal cultures. Each example is presented in two forms: (a) an English translation identified in italics and (b) an explanation of what the aphorism means in the culture from which it has been drawn (Weekly African Proverbs, 2004).

Kindness is seldom acknowledged. Explanation: When people don't thank you, God will thank you on behalf of the stupid people to whom you have been kind and who failed to acknowledge your generosity.

A stranger does not hold the head of a coffin. Explanation: Sometimes, the nature of a person's death dictates the place in which the body should be buried. The deceased person's friends at the head of the coffin know where that place is. A person new to a village would not know this.

Out of shame, the harlot does not appear on the village's main street. Explanation: In traditional society, prostitution is considered a social evil that causes harlots to suffer the punishment of guilt. They can avoid guilt by abstaining from such evil.

Whoever steals mushrooms will hear the evening announcement. Explanation: Villagers whose crops or personal belongings are stolen will have the theft announced publicly in the evening, when the thieves are told to return the stolen items or else a powerful god will punish them. Thieves therefore listen carefully to the evening announcement and dread the threat. Their fear and their guilty consciences urge them to return the stolen goods and avoid thievery in the future.

The vulture cannot cure baldness. Explanation: If someone claims to have the power to accomplish a task, he should demonstrate that skill in his own life before anyone is made to believe his claims of skill. In other words, don't be gullible. A vulture that brags about being able to cure baldness should first cure his own bald pate.

Acts of God are like riddles. Explanation: No one can accurately predict what will happen in the future.

The cow is God with a wet nose. Explanation: Just as humans were given life by God, so also villagers depend on cattle for their continued existence.

When a ghost is seen at a distance, it is frightening; but when it comes closer, you recognize it as one of your relatives. Explanation: Events that cause fear when seen from afar can become less fearsome when viewed up close.

African Tales

As illustrated with the following examples, traditional African stories have been intended to serve a variety of purposes, including those of (a) explaining the origin of phenomena, (b) teaching moral values, (c) validating people's social status, (d) rationalizing unusual events, (e) envisioning alternative realities, and (f) accounting for misfortune.

Explaining Origins

The intent of an origins tale is to explain how something came into being. That something could be any one of a great variety of objects—the world, humans, deities, plants, animals, mountains, lakes, items of daily living, and more.

Among the Tutsi of Rwanda, the origin of human life is traced from the supreme deity, Imaana, through woman. The story begins with the original woman and original man who were both sterile, so they could not produce children. When they begged Imaana for help, he responded by mixing clay with saliva to form a small human figure. He instructed the woman to put the figure into a pot and keep it there for nine months. Each morning and evening, she poured milk into the pot and was instructed to remove the figure from the pot only when it had grown limbs. She followed these instructions and after nine months, pulled from the pot a completed infant. Since then, Imaana has made all other humans by the same method.

Why the objects of nature acquired their characteristics is a question often answered in folk tales, as in the Yoruba story of the tortoise's shell. Ijapa the tortoise was desperately hunting for food when he learned that the all of the birds were preparing to attend their annual feast in the sky. Intent on jointing the guests, Ijapa visited each bird he could find and successfully begged for just one feather. He glued the collection of feathers to his back and became the most colorful bird anyone had ever seen. The birds that saw him asked his name. He told them he was named "All of Us." He now asked a group of birds to help transport him to the feast in the sky, which they did.

At the feast, the tortoise asked, "To whom does this food belong?"

When the birds answered, "All of us," Ijapa said, "My name is All of Us," and quickly consumed the whole meal, leaving nothing for the birds.

When the angry birds attacked Ijapa, his feathers came off, exposing him as a tortoise. To punish Ijapa, the birds threatened to leave him forever in the sky, whereupon he asked if they would give a message to his wife, asking her to lay out as many mattresses as she could find, so he would have a soft landing when he jumped to earth. The birds did send a message, but the message bid the wife to lay out all the wooden furniture from the house, and she did as asked. So, when Ijapa jumped, he crashed onto the furniture, shattering his shell. His wife collected the broken pieces and glued them together. That's why tortoises ever since have had rough shells in the form of geometric patterns (Omowunmi, 2009).

Teaching Moral Values

Many African folktales depict the wisdom of adopting moral virtues and of correcting character flaws. The following pair of West African stories teach the folly of greed and of disobeying the law.

The Tortoise, the Dog, and the Farmer: In the far distant past, a famine caused all creatures in the Kurumi region of Nigeria to turn weak and thin for lack of food—all creatures except Dog, who appeared very hale and healthy indeed. So, Tortoise asked Dog, "How do you keep so fit? Do tell me. I can keep your secret." Dog said, "There's no secret. Just work hard and lead a peaceful life."

But Tortoise didn't believe that, so during the night, he hid outside Dog's house; and early in the morning as the sun started to rise, Tortoise saw Dog come out carrying a basket. Tortoise followed Dog to a farmer's field, where Dog placed yams in his basket.

Tortoise shouted, "I've caught you. So that's your secret."

Startled, Dog cried, "Oh! Well, you can get some yams, too, but you must only come here with me, and we have to leave before the farmer rises from his sleep and comes to the field."

Thus, nearly every morning, the two stole more yams. But Tortoise took larger amounts each day, telling Dog, "I'm storing up yams for the future." This meant he had to spend longer in the field each day until the load became heavier than he could manage. Dog was leaving the field as Tortoise shouted for him to help carry the basket, but Dog hurried off. However, Tortoise's shouts alerted the farmer, who cried out, "Thief! Thief!" This drew a crowd of neighbors who captured Tortoise and brought him before the king, who decreed that the Tortoise be hanged in the market square.

Thus, thievery and greed are bound to lead to unwelcome results (Ohiomoba, 2009).

Kiigbo Kiigba and the Helpful Spirits: An ancient Yoruba village was inhabited by both people and spirits. To avoid disputes between the two, the village leaders passed a law requiring people to stay in their houses on designated days when the spirits would be about. However, one stubborn farmer named Kiibo Kiigba disregarded the law and went out to work in his field to plant yams the first day that the spirits roamed around. He'd not been planting long when he heard voices demanding to know "What are you doing?" Kiibo Kiigba replied, "I'm tilling my land." The voices shouted, "All right, we'll help you." Suddenly, hundreds of hoes appeared to quickly till the entire field. Kiibo Kiigba was delighted.

On the second day that people were ordered to stay home, Kiibo Kiigba went to his field. Once more, mysterious voices demanded to know what he was doing. He answered, "I'm planting my yams." The voices shouted, "All right, we'll help you," and immediately, all the yam seedlings were planted in neat rows all across the field.

The third time that people were ordered to stay home, Kiibo Kiigba went to his field, and once more, voices asked what he was doing. "I'm harvesting my yams," he answered. In an instant, the yams were out of the ground, piled in an enormous heap. When Kiibo Kiigba picked up a few yams, he realized they were not yet ripe for harvest, so his entire crop had been ruined by the helpful spirits. In despair, he started banging his hands against his head, and the voices called out, "What are you doing?" Kiibo Kiigba complained, "I'm hitting my head in anger." The voices shouted, "All right, we'll help you," and a hundred fists pounded him on the head.

So, refusing to obey the law is likely to invite misfortune (Kiigbo Kiigba, 2009).

Validating Social Status

Traditional stories frequently are designed to authenticate the divine origin of an individual's or a family's position in society.

According to the central myth of the Nri priestly caste among the Igbo, the supreme god, Chukwu, choose Eri, the archetypal ancestor of the Nri, as the chief of the Igbo ritual specialists. On that occasion, Eri and his wife, Namaku, had agreed to sacrifice their only son and only daughter to Chukwu in order to obtain food. Subsequently, the yam—the most precious of Igbo agricultural crops—sprouted from the grave of the son and the cocoyam grew from the grave of the daughter. Chukwu rewarded Eri and Namaku for obeying his order by bestowing on Eri and his descendants the privilege of being the traditional high priest with the exclusive right to cleanse all forms of abomination, especially those forms connected with the yam crop among the Igbo. Chukwu gave Eri the *Ofo* symbol so that he would be able to speak to Chukwu through the medium of the symbol. *Otonsi* became the ancestral symbol of authority, while the *Alo* signify the ritual authority of the high priest (Ejizu, 2001).

Accounting for Devious Events

Fables often depict animals as personified spirits, as creatures with human characteristics whose behavior accounts for perplexing—often incongruous— happenings. This type of spirit is found in numerous cultures in the role of a trickster, portrayed as a coyote, rabbit, or raven among American Indian tribes, and in African lore, as a spider named Anansi.

Anansi tales originated with the Ashanti people of West Africa, spread to other tribes, and were brought by slaves to the Caribbean. According to legend, Anansi began as the son of a sky god, Nyame, and married his own sister. On earth, he taught people how to sow grain and how to use a shovel in their fields. But most important, Anansi was a trickster—"crafty, sly, and villainous" (Smith, 2005).

In a tale typical of Anansi stories, the spider asked a favor of the sky god, Nyame, who agreed to grant the favor if Anansi would bring him hornets and a great python. So, Anansi, in order to capture the hornets, cut a small hole in a gourd, then filled a large bowl with water, which he took to the tree where the hornets nested. There, he dumped the bowl of water over the hornets and shouted, "You foolish folks, why don't you get out of the rain?"

The hornets pled, "But where can we go?"

Anansi showed them the hole in the gourd and said, "Climb into this dry gourd." When all of the hornets were in the gourd, Anansi plugged the hole with grass and delivered the gourd to Nyame.

He now prepared to outwit Onini, the python, by cutting a bamboo pole and then talking to himself as he walked past the python's home. Onini called out, "Why are you arguing with yourself?"

Anansi answered, "I have had a dispute with my wife. She says you are shorter and weaker than this bamboo pole. I say you are longer and stronger."

Onini said: "It's useless and silly to argue when you can find out the truth. Bring the pole and we will measure."

So, Anansi laid the pole on the ground, and the python stretched himself out beside it.

"You seem a little short," Anansi said. The python stretched further.

"A little more," Anansi said.

"I can stretch no more," Onini said.

"When you stretch at one end, you get shorter at the other end," Anansi said. "Let me tie you so you don't slip."

With a strong vine, he tied Onini's head to the pole. Then, he went to the other end and tied the tail to the pole. He wrapped the vine all around Onini until the python couldn't move.

By such guile, Anansi managed to deliver both the hornets and the python to the sky god and had the favor granted (The Story of Anansi, 2000).

Envisioning Alternative Realities

Tales sometimes depict imagined life conditions that differ from those of ordinary experience—novel conditions produced by beings from the world of such spirits as Eshu.

For the Yoruba of Nigeria, Eshu is the cunning but untrustworthy messenger between the gods and humans. He is a wandering, homeless shade, prone to spreading false rumors and fomenting conflicts among both the divinities and the people. In one tale, Eshu stole yams from the supreme god's garden, then used the god's slippers to make footprints in the garden, so Eshu could claim that the god himself had stolen the yams (Eshu, 2011). In the best-known Eshu story, Eshu decided to break up the lifelong friendship between the moon and sun, causing them to change places, thereby reversing day and night. He sought to accomplish this feat by walking down the road that separated the sun's farm from the moon's farm. Eshu wore a hat that was black on the left side and white on the right. He put his pipe at the back of his head and hung his walking cane down his back. After he had passed, the sun and moon quarreled over the color of Eshu's hat and over the direction he was walking. When the supreme god heard of the dispute, he summoned the sun and moon as each was calling the other a liar. Suddenly, Eshu appeared and said neither was a liar, but both were fools. The god, infuriated, ordered his men to catch the prankster Eshu. But Eshu, by trickery, evaded his pursuers (Frederick-Malanson, 1998).

Frequently, an alternative reality is one in which a physically weaker individual or one who is of lower social status triumphs by cleverness over a stronger or more prestigious rival. In Yoruba lore, a small antelope named Nala was drinking at a water hole when a hungry hyena suddenly appeared and announced to Nala, "I'm going to eat you."

The tiny antelope replied in a shaky voice, "Oh, no, you don't want to eat me, for I'm far too skinny. Instead, why not eat that big piece of cheese in the middle of the watering hole." She pointed to the reflection of the full moon in the middle of the pond.

Persuaded by such an inviting prospect, the hyena leapt into the pond, while Nala dashed off laughing into the forest (Bastian, 2008).

Accounting for Misfortune

Stories are often designed to explain why bad things happen to people. Such tales may include actions people can take to defeat the evil spirits that are assumed to be the source of tragic events. Here is one from Yoruba tradition.

Ajíja was a medicine man who lived in the sky with Arámfè, the father of the gods, until Ajíja came to earth in a whirlwind—a dust devil—along with another medicine man. Together, they made nostrums, including one which, when Ajíja pronounced a series of magic words, would kill any person that he selected. Ajíja could also kill with his walking stick. When Ajíja wanted to make trouble, he could wander through a village, setting fire to houses by casting a firebrand onto the thatched roofs. It is also said that he was a one-legged devil who threw people to the ground and broke their ankles. He sometimes assumed the form of a large lizard.

When a man meets Ajíja, he should protect himself by putting pepper in his mouth and saying, "Ahanríyen, Fágada Shaomi" (names of Ajíja), "ki íru re bómi" (put your tail in water). The man should then spit the pepper at Ajíja (Wyndham, 1921).

Summary

Over the centuries, maxims and tales have served as essential instruments for conveying African religious beliefs from one generation to the next. The fact that wise sayings and stories were passed on orally rather than in written form allowed taletellers to refashion their narratives in ways that resulted in a host of alternative versions of religious lore.

CATHOLICISM

Wise sayings and stories in the lives of present-day Catholics include hundreds drawn from religious sources over the past 2,000 years. Those sources include the Bible, the writings of influential Catholic clerics throughout the ages, and present-day purveyors of the Catholic faith.

Christian Maxims

Two abundant sources of Catholic aphorisms are the Bible and the sermons of priests and evangelists.

Adages from the Bible

The chief compendium of Christian wise sayings is the Bible. The most frequently quoted adage from the New Testament is the verse known as the Golden Rule, a moral principle that Jesus recommended: "As ye would that men should do to you, do ye also to them likewise" (Luke, 6: 31, 1611). Additional virtues that he advocated were:

Mercifulness: Love your enemies, do good to them which hate you. Bless them that curse you, and pray for them which despitefully use you. (Luke 6: 27, 1611)

Tolerance: Judge not, and ye shall not be judged: condemn not, and ye shall no be condemned; forgive, and ye shall be forgiven. (Luke 6: 37, 1611)

Generosity: Give, and it shall be given unto you. . . . For with the same measure that you mete withal it shall be measured to you again. (Luke 6: 36, 1611)

The advice Jesus offered included nine Christian beatitudes:

Blessed are the poor in spirit: for theirs is the kingdom of heaven.

Blessed are they that mourn: for they shall be comforted.

Blessed are the meek: for they shall inherit the earth.

Blessed are they which do hunger and thirst after righteousness: for they shall be filled.

Blessed are the merciful: for they shall obtain mercy.

Blessed are the pure in heart: for they shall see God.

Blessed are the peacemakers: for they shall be called the children of God.

Blessed are they which are persecuted for righteousness' sake: for theirs is the kingdom of heaven.

Blessed are ye, when men shall revile you, and persecute you, and say all manner of evil against you falsely, for my sake. Rejoice, and be exceeding glad: for great is your reward in heaven. (Matthew 5: 3–12, 1611)

The most frequently cited Jewish and Christian guide to proper human behavior is the set of Ten Commandments (the Decalogue) in Chapter 20 of the book of Exodus in the Jewish Torah and the Christian Old Testament. Those 10 rules—said to have been dictated by God to Moses—include three ways people should act and seven ways they should not act. Thus, people should: (1) worship only the one true God, (2) respect one's parents, and (3) respect the Sabbath day by not working. People should not (4) use God's name in an insulting fashion, (5) worship idols, (6) kill, (7) steal, (8) commit adultery, (9) tell lies about others, or (10) yearn for anyone else's property or spouse.

In the Bible's Old Testament, the richest source of adages is the book of Proverbs, which offers 30 chapters of such advice as:

Mercy and Truth: Let not mercy and truth forsake thee: bind them about thy neck; write them on the table of thy heart. So shalt thou find favor and good understanding in the sight of God and man. (Proverbs 3: 3–4, 1611)

Wickedness: Enter not in the path of the wicked, and go not in the way of evil men. . . . The way of the wicked is as darkness: they know not at what they stumble. But the path of the just is as the shining light, that shineth more and more unto the perfect day. (Proverbs 4: 14, 18–19, 1611)

Tattling: A talebearer revealeth secrets; but he that is of a faithful spirit concealeth the matter. (Proverbs 11: 13, 1611)

Obedience to God: The fear of the Lord is a fountain of life to depart from the snares of death. (Proverbs 14: 27, 1611)

The Role of Punishment in Child Rearing: He that spareth his rod hateth his son: but he that loveth him chasteneth him betimes. (Proverbs, 13: 24, 1611)

Jesus often cast his advice in similes, illustrating principles of behavior by comparing people's actions to such events as house-building.

Whosoever cometh to me, and heareth my sayings, and doeth them, I will show you to whom he is like: He is like a man which built a house, and digged deep, and laid the foundation on a rock; and when the flood arouse, the stream beat vehemently upon that house, and could not shake it; for it was founded upon a rock. But he that heareth, and doeth not, is like a man that without a foundation built a house upon the earth; against which the stream did beat vehemently, and immediately it fell; and the ruin of that house was great. (Luke 6: 47–49, 1611)

Adages from Catholic Sages

Advice to Catholics about the proper way to lead their lives is often drawn from counsel offered by such revered clerical luminaries as the following.

Saint Augustine: Your first task is to be dissatisfied with yourself, fight sin, and transform yourself into something better. Your second task is to put up with the trials and temptations of this world that will be brought on by the change in your life and to persevere to the very end in the midst of these things.

Saint John of the Cross: The more we are afflicted in this world, the greater is our assurance in the next; the more sorrow in the present, the greater will be our joy in the future.

Saint Isadore of Seville: Whenever anything disagreeable or displeasing happens to you, remember that Christ suffered crucifixion, and be silent.

Saint Ambrose of Milan: The rich man who gives to the poor does not bestow alms but pays a debt.

Saint Thomas Aquinas: We can't have full knowledge all at once. We must start by believing; then afterwards we may be led on to master the evidence for ourselves.

Saint Isidore of Seville: Confession heals, confession justifies, confession grants pardon of sin, all hope consists in confession; in confession there is a chance for mercy. (Quotes from the saints, 2011).

Adages from Sermons

Preachers frequently include maxims in their sermons. A very popular style of preaching consists of a priest first quoting a verse from the Bible to serve as a theme that will be elucidated in detail in the body of the sermon. Non-biblical aphorisms can also serve as the focus of a sermon when the origin of the maxim is a popular saying, the title of a book or song or movie, or the preacher's own invention. The intent of including an adage in a sermon is often to cast a religious belief in a concise form that members of a congregation can easily remember. The following are maxims extracted from a selection of modern-day sermons.

At the point of greatest despair in life, when we feel that we cannot go on, that is the moment of opportunity in which we can open up for moments of profound transformation.

The heroes are the ones that quietly do not give up. They just gently persist through life when all seems to be lost.

Scatter your wealth around the world. We flourish by causing others to flourish.

As Christians, we are deeply committed to doing God's will. God will show us when his plans conflict with ours. We need to listen for God's guidance.

There can be no truthfulness among friends without judgment—without that risky, sometimes painful willingness to confront a friend. Judgment—the assignment of right and wrong, the acknowledgement of genuine injustice, the naming of real hurt, the telling of truth—can be an act of deepest love.

Catholic Tales

For convenience of discussion, Christian stories can be divided into two types—examples from the Bible and tales told by people engaged in religious instruction.

Stories from the Bible

Catholic tales, like African religious stories, serve a variety of purposes, such as: (a) chronicling historical events, (b) encouraging faith in a deity, (c) illustrating wise decision-making, (d) proving that the Lord can be trusted, (c) teaching moral precepts, (e) validating an individual's social status, and (f) illustrating a deity's power.

Teaching History: According to the Bible's Old Testament (the Hebrew Torah), people from Israel in ancient times had migrated south from their homeland on the eastern border of the Mediterranean Sea to settle in Egypt. As the decades passed, the immigrants "increased abundantly, and multiplied, and waxed exceeding mighty; and the land was filled with them" (Exodus 1: 7, 1611). This worried the Pharaoh of Egypt, who complained that the Israelites were "more and mightier than we." So, the Pharaoh ordered the Hebrews into hard labor and decreed that newborn Hebrew males be put to death. He also refused to let the people of Israel leave Egypt. When the oppression of the Israelites grew unbearable, God told a young leader named Moses that God would punish the Egyptians for tyrannizing the Hebrews. The punishment would consist of a plague designed to kill "all the firstborn" Egyptians. But to avoid making the mistake of killing Israelites as well, the residents of each Hebrew house were to mark the door lintel and doorposts with the blood of a lamb.

> For the Lord will pass through [at night] to smite the Egyptians: and when he seeth the blood upon the lintel, and on the two side posts, the Lord will pass over the door, and will not suffer the destroyer to come in unto your houses to smite you. (Exodus 12: 23, 1611)

Thus, the Passover event served as a first step in freeing the people of Israel from bondage in Egypt, enabling them to escape through the Red Sea and trek north to "the promised land." Ever since ancient times, Jews have annually celebrated the Passover in gratitude for God's arranging their ancestors' flight from Egypt. Some Christian denominations also deem the tale of the Passover a significant historical incident.

Encouraging Faith in a Deity: The importance of bravery, skill, and faith in God is illustrated in the Old Testament story of a confrontation between Israel's army and an army of Philistines. The two armies had been facing each other in a standoff for 40 days when a giant Philistine named Goliath came onto the battlefield to challenge the Israelites. The Bible lists his height at six cubits and a span, making him over 11 feet tall. (A cubit is the length of a man's arm from elbow to fingertips—about 21 inches. A span is the distance from the tip of the thumb to the tip of the little finger when the hand is spread out—about 9 inches.)

[Goliath] had a helmet of brass upon his head, and he was armed with a coat of mail. . . . And he had greaves of brass upon his legs, and a target of brass between his shoulders. And the staff of his spear was like a weaver's beam; and his spear's head weighed six hundred shekels of iron. And he stood and cried unto the armies of Israel and said unto them . . . Choose you a man of you and let him come down to me. If he be able to kill me, then will we be your servants; but if I prevail against him, and kill him, then shall ye be our servants, and serve us. (Samuel I, 17: 4–9, 1611)

No soldiers in Israel's army accepted the challenge, which they saw as a form of suicide. At that moment, a young shepherd named David was bringing food to his three brothers who were in Israel's army. And David, upon hearing Goliath's challenge, volunteered to confront the giant. David's brothers scoffed, pointing out that he was a mere youth with no military experience. But David said he had killed a bear and a lion that had attacked his sheep, so "The Lord that delivered me out of the paw of the lion and out of the paw of the bear will deliver me out of the hand of this Philistine." Finally, King Saul, the head of Israel's army, agreed, "Go and the Lord be with thee." David refused the heavy coat of armor, helmet, and sword he was offered, and instead, picked up five smooth stones from a nearby brook.

When Goliath saw the lad who intended to do battle, he invited David to "Come to me, and I will give thy flesh unto the fowls of the air, and to the beasts of the field." David replied,

Thou comest to me with a sword, and with a spear, and with a shield; but I come to thee in the name of the Lord of hosts, the God of the armies of Israel, whom thou hast defied. This day will the Lord deliver thee into mine hand; and I will smite thee, and take thine head from thee; and I will give the carcasses of the host of the Philistines this day unto the fowls of the air, and to the wild beasts of the earth; that all the earth may know there is a God in Israel. And all this assembly shall know that the Lord saveth not with sword and spear: for the battle is the Lord's, and he will give you into our hands. (Samuel I, 17: 45–47, 1611)

As the giant approached to slay the youth, David slipped a stone into his slingshot and slung it at Goliath, striking the giant in the forehead, just below the helmet. As Goliath fell to the ground, mortally wounded, David ran forward, grabbed the giant's great sword, and severed the Philistine's head from his body.

The men of Israel and Judah arose, shouted, and pursued the Philistines. And the wounded of the Philistines fell down by the way to Shaaraim, even unto Gath and unto Ekron. And the children of Israel returned from chasing after the Philistines and spoiled their tents. (Samuel 1, 17: 52–53, 1611)

Therefore, faith in the Lord saved the day, and David would grow to be a man and become Israel's greatest king.

Illustrating Wise Decision-Making: Upon King David's death, his son Solomon became king of Israel. Solomon's wisdom was demonstrated in the case of two prostitutes, each of whom claimed to be the mother of a particular infant son. Solomon thus faced the task of deciding which of the claimants was the true mother of the child. When the two women appeared before Solomon, one said,

Oh, my lord, I and this woman dwell in one house; and I was delivered of a child with her in the house. And it came to pass the third day after I was delivered, this woman was delivered also. . . . This woman's child died in the night, and she arose at midnight and took my son from beside me while I slept and hid it in her bosom and laid her dead child on my bosom. And when I rose in the morning to give my child suck, it was dead. But when I had considered it in the morning, behold, it was not my son which I did bear. (Kings 1, 3: 17–21, 1611)

But the second woman protested and swore that the live infant was indeed her own. To solve the conflict, Solomon asked a servant to bring him a sword, and he ordered, "Divide the living child in two, and give half to the one [woman] and half to the other." In response, the first woman, horrified at the prospect of the child being killed, told Solomon to give the child to the second claimant "and in no wise slay it." But the other [woman] said, "Let it be neither mine nor thine, but divide it," whereupon Solomon gave the infant to the first woman for "'she is the mother thereof.' And all Israel . . . feared the king, for they saw that the wisdom of God was in him to do judgment" (Kings 1, 3: 25–28, 1611).

Thus, the tale of the two harlots served to illustrate how God's wisdom can be channeled through a revered religious figure to affect events in the world.

Proving That the Lord Could Be Trusted: The Old Testament book of Job opens with Satan debating with God over whether Job, a wealthy member of God's earthly devotees, truly loved and honored God. When

God assured Satan that Job was indeed "perfect and upright, fears God, and eschews evil," Satan replied that if God took away Job's riches (extensive lands, thousands of sheep, camels, oxen, and donkeys), Job would no longer venerate the Lord. God accepted Satan's dare by removing Job's worldly goods. When Job, now impoverished, still honored God, Satan challenged the Lord to further test Job's loyalty by afflicting Job with physical ailments. God responded by burdening Job with painful boils from head to toe. When three of Job's friends came to help their despondent companion, they spent days arguing with Job as he bemoaned his fate. The tale then continues, chapter after chapter, with Job claiming injustice ("Why me, Lord?") and his friends giving advice. Finally, God spoke to Job, describing the wonders that God had performed in the world. As a result, Job reaffirmed his faith in the Lord's infinite wisdom and power, and he admitted to God that:

> I know thou canst do every thing, and that no thought can be withholden from thee. . . . I uttered [things] that I understood not; things too wonderful for me, which I knew not . . . but now mine eye seeth thee [as thy true self]. Wherefore I abhor myself and repent in dust and ashes. (Job 42: 2, 5–6, 1611)

Following this declaration of faith, humility, and loyalty, God restored Job's health and gave him twice the riches he had held before Satan's challenge. "After this, Job lived 140 years" (Job 42: 16, 1611).

Thus, a lesson Catholics have been taught through the story of Job is that unwavering trust in God during troubled times will eventually be rewarded in great measure.

Teaching Moral Precepts: During Jesus' three-year ministry before his death, a favorite device he used to teach moral lessons was the parable or allegory. The following are two moral lessons from Jesus.

When a group of Pharisees (religious scholars who adhered to strict laws inherited from Moses) criticized Jesus for welcoming sinful people and dining with them, Jesus told his critics a tale of lost sheep. When a lone sheep was lost out of a flock of 100, the shepherd went to great lengths to find the lost one.

> And when he hath found it, he layeth it on his shoulders, rejoicing. And when he cometh home, he calleth together his friends and neighbors, saying unto them, "Rejoice with me, for I have found my sheep which was lost." (Luke 15: 5–6, 1611)

Then, Jesus interpreted for the Pharisees the significance of this tale to explain his own habit of consorting with sinners whom the Pharisees held in contempt.

> I say unto you, that likewise joy shall be in heaven over one sinner that repenteth more than over ninety and nine just persons which need no repentance. (Luke 15: 7, 1611)

Apparently Jesus did not trust one parable as sufficient for making his point about tolerance and compassion, so he followed the story of the lost sheep with two additional anecdotes. The first concerned a woman who lost one of her 10 silver coins, then went to great trouble hunting until she found it. Like the shepherd, she collected her friends to rejoice in retrieving the coins. And again, Jesus, in his effort to instruct the Pharisees, drew a parallel between the recovered coin and the significance of remorseful souls.

> Likewise, I say unto you, there is joy in the presence of the angels of God over one sinner that repenteth. (Luke 15: 10, 1611)

The third anecdote was about a son—a spendthrift, prodigal son—who begged his father to give him the inheritance he would receive upon his father's death. The indulgent father did so, only to have the son leave home to waste the funds in riotous living in a far country. Years later, the son, now reduced to poverty, returned home to tell his father,

> I have sinned against heaven and in thy sight, and am no more worthy to be called thy son. (Luke 15: 21, 1611)

In response, the father neither rejected nor admonished the son but, instead, ordered servants to

> Bring forth the best robe, and put it on him; and put a ring on his hand and shoes on his feet. And bring hither the fatted calf and kill it, and let us eat and be merry. For this my son was dead, and is alive again; and he was lost and is found. And they began to be merry. (Luke 15: 22–24, 1611)

Judging People's Worth: When Jesus was about to send his disciples off to teach the gospel throughout the world, he created a parable illustrating the virtue of mercy and the importance of judging people by their deeds, not by their positions in society.

A certain man [a Jew] went down from Jerusalem to Jericho and fell among thieves which stripped him of his raiment and wounded him, and departed, leaving him half dead. And by chance there came down a certain [Jewish] priest that way; and when he saw [the wounded man], he passed by on the other side. And likewise, a Levite [a temple assistant] came and looked on [the robbery victim] and passed by on the other side. But a certain Samaritan [not a Jew], as he journeyed, came where [the victim lay], and . . . had compassion on him. And went to him, and bound up his wounds, pouring in oil and wine, and set him on his own beast, and brought him to an inn, and took care of him. And on the morrow when [the Samaritan] departed, he took out two pence and gave them to the host, and said unto him, "Take care of [this fellow]; and whatsoever thou spendest more, when I come again I will repay thee." (Luke 10: 30–35, 1611)

Then, Jesus asked his disciples, "Which of these three [men] thinkest thou was neighbor unto him that fell among the thieves? {It was] he that showed mercy. Go and do likewise" (Luke 10: 36–37, 1611).

Validating an Individual's Social Status: Religious leaders profit from stories that invest themselves with magical powers—with abilities to perform feats beyond the talents of ordinary mortals. Such feats are usually referred to as miracles. They are unnatural events, in that they defy the laws of nature. Therefore, individuals who perform miracles typically claim to wield divine power, for only an omnipotent god-like being could breach natural law.

The Bible's New Testament attributes a host of such amazing feats to Jesus, thereby serving to verify that, indeed, he was the divine Son of God. Among the miraculous events were his walking on the sea (Matthew 15: 25, 1611), reviving Lazarus, who had been dead four days (John 11: 43–44, 1611), restoring a blind man's sight (John 9: 1–7, 1611), curing a leprosy victim (Mark 1: 40–42, 1611), healing the lame and deaf (Matthew 11: 5, 1611), turning five loaves of bread and two fish into enough food to feed a crowd of 5,000 that had followed Jesus into the desert (Matthew 14: 17–21, 1611), and, finally, his raising himself from the dead two days after he had been crucified (Matthew 28: 1–20, 1611).

Stories Embedded in Sermons

Just as Catholic sermons can contain nonbiblical adages, so also can homilies and Sunday school lessons include tales of everyday life. The stories may be descriptions either of actual past happenings or of imagined, make-believe, what-if situations, usually told by priests in connection with mass or by

Catholic brothers, sisters, or members of the laity when giving instruction in the faith.

As demonstrated in the following examples, stories can serve diverse purposes, including those of: (a) explaining a religious process by means of nonreligious analogies, (b) illustrating exemplary Catholic behavior, (c) proposing how to cope with adversity, and (d) interpreting religious lore through imagined events.

Offering Nonreligious Analogies: In a sermon entitled *Wicked and Righteous Commingled,* a preacher sought to illustrate the need for people to be cleansed of the ungodly wickedness that was mixed with blessed virtues in their original character structure. The pastor first cited a passage from the book of Genesis, then told a brief story of a metallurgical process.

> Genesis 2:7—"And the Lord God formed man of the dust of the ground, and breathed into his nostrils the breath of life; and man became a living soul." This is equally true of all precious metal. In its original condition it is mixed with earth, which can only become separated out by the refining process. This is a symbol of the process God uses to remove the dross. Precious metals are found in the hills and in the ground and are from the dust, just as we were created. The refining process is used to separate those metals from the dust. (Wicked and Righteous, 2007)

Illustrating Exemplary Christian Behavior: The emphasis of a many sermons is on Christian morality—on how to behave toward fellow humans. Such a sermon typically consists of the priest reading a passage from the Bible, then illustrating how the moral principle in that passage should be applied in the parishioners' daily lives. Consider the following two examples.

Proper Business Practices: To begin his sermon, the priest read a brief tale from the Bible's book of Leviticus (25:35) in which God is quoted as saying, "If you lend money to my people, to the poor among you, you shall not deal with them as a creditor; you shall not exact interest from them." The priest then interpreted the passage to mean

> When a loan was made to one's countrymen, no interest was to be expected in return. But, when a loan was granted to a foreigner, interest could be charged. That way, the nation increases its wealth from the interest that was charged to the immigrants and tourists. . . . Today, this law would be similar to a brother, a sister, a parent, a child, or

a relative asking for a loan. In love, the loan should be given with joy without asking anything in return. Spiritually speaking, this law goes beyond the biological family. It would also apply to the spiritual family that we belong to, the Body of Christ, the Holy Catholic Church. It would mean that when another Christian is in need, we should joyfully help him out without asking any [financial] interest in return. In love, we should lend or give from our hearts. (Love Your Neighbor, 2011)

Obedience to God's Authority: The sermon began with the priest reading from the Bible [Matthew, 21:28–32], describing Jesus' story of a man who directed his two sons to work in the vineyard. Both agreed, but only one actually worked; the other broke his promise and wandered off. The pastor then compared the dishonest son to "God's chosen people of the Old Testament who broke the Old Covenant. [The errant son] was no different than the people within the Church today who break the new Covenant of God by turning away from His righteous ways." To illustrate a present-day application of the parable, the priest continued,

[There was] a man who had a real bad reputation. While in prison, he found the Lord Jesus in his life. Upon his release, he headed to his small town to settle down, found himself a good girlfriend and moved in with her. On the following Sunday, he got up early in the morning so he could attend a Christian service. During the sermon, the preacher was kicking up a storm while speaking of the sin of fornication. . . . The new convert said to himself, "Boy, those dudes must be real bad sinners to have displeased the Lord God so much. I will never be a fornicator like them." After the service, he went to introduce himself and congratulated the preacher for his excellent sermon. Having done so, he asked the preacher, "By the way, what is a fornicator?" Having been told that it is one who lives in a common-law relationship, the new convert rushed home, packed his girlfriend's baggage and literally threw her out of the house. He did not want to have to face God for having lived the life of a fornicator. . . . Such a sin totally disregards the sacredness that God has placed within the marriage. Jesus asked, "Which of the two did the will of his father?" I ask who is doing the will of the Father, "Is it the fornicator?" "Is it those who take birth control pills contrary to the teachings of the Holy Catholic Church?" "Is it those who approve of abortions?" "Is it those who constantly use the Most Holy Name of Jesus in vain?" (Perfect Obedience, 2011)

Proposing How to Cope with Adversity: Preachers often introduce their lectures with an anecdote that captures the congregation's curiosity and also leads into the sermon's theme. In this case, the theme is an approach that people might profitably adopt when facing difficult times.

> According to Greek myth, there was once a young woman named Pandora who was both beautiful and deceitful. She was taken into the household of Epimethus where stood a large box. Inside this box stood all of the evils of the world. Despite warnings, Epimethus left this woman into his household. The woman opened the box and let out all kinds of evils upon the world. Thus it was known as Pandora's Box. . . .
>
> In the story of Pandora's Box, the world is filled with all kinds of evil things when the lid is opened. What I didn't mention was that inside of the box, after all the other bad things had flown out, lay hope. In the midst of all kinds of evil, hope is the only thing that we can cling to.
>
> We place our hope in the fact that one day Jesus will return and will make all things perfect. Until that time, we must simply wait patiently, enduring all things because we have to. (Stine, 2006)

Interpreting Scripture Through Imagined Events: The tales preachers include in their sermons are often intended to illustrate ways religious lore can be interpreted through hypothetical happenings. A priest on Christmas Day told the following story to explain what he considered to be the significance of Jesus' birth.

> To give some idea about what happened on the first Christmas, I offer a comparison. Imagine a boy doing his homework with a dog sitting at his feet. The dog seems perfectly content even though he has no idea what the boy is up to. The boy, with his books and pencils and writing paper, is in different world from the dog, but still the two have a deep affection for each other. This happy state of affairs between humans and dogs did not always exist. The dog's ancestors used to fear humans and hide from people. But at some point, a very brave person approached the wolves. Maybe he just saw an abandoned wolf pup and took him in. Whatever he did, he bridged the enormous distance between the two species, and dogs began to live together with people. Now, the distance between us and God is infinitely greater than the difference between a human being and a wolf. We know less about God's purposes than a wolf or a dog knows about a boy. God created the universe, and you and I are only a tiny speck in it. Moreover, because of our sins and guilt,

we try to hide from God. But now, because of Christmas, we no longer need to live in fear. God has reached down to us. He has become one of us [by the birth of Jesus]. (Bloom, 2009)

AFRICAN AND CATHOLIC MAXIMS AND TALES COMPARED

The following comparison of African and Catholic traditions begins with likenesses and then turns to differences.

Similarities

The themes of African tales and Bible stories are often alike. There are plots in both traditions that focus on such matters as death, life after death, loving kindness, bravery, generosity, friendship, self-sacrifice, vanity, pride, greed, hate, and revenge. Maxims in African and Christian traditions are also similar in teaching morality (truthfulness, bravery), constructive action (diligence, caution, high work standards), and prudence (filial piety, humility, respect for authority).

Differences

Identifying differences between African and Christian tales can include analyzing each tradition's (a) quantity of stories, (b) diverse versions of tales, and (c) roles assigned to animals.

Quantity of Stories

African religions include far more tales than does Catholicism. The number of stories that can reasonably be considered an established part of Christian doctrine is limited chiefly to the ones in the Bible. That number probably doesn't exceed 100, or 200 at most. However, if anecdotes that clerics insert in their sermons are included in the Catholic count, the total becomes far larger. However, those stories are ephemeral, soon forgotten, and thus not part of the Christian canon.

The quantity of African tales that are permanent elements of religious belief extends into the thousands. Whereas some stories may be no more than passing fantasies, a great many have become lasting components of African worldviews, repeated time and again in storytelling sessions, rituals, chants, and dances.

Alternative Versions

Among African tribes, the same basic story can appear in different variations, suggesting that the narrative may have come from a single source, then transformed over the centuries as it filtered into different groups' oral literature.

However, in Christian tradition, tales remain essentially the same over time and from one place to another. This is primarily due to the Bible stories having been in printed form for centuries, with the Bibles used in one society the same in content as those used in other societies. Inconsistent versions of Bible stories are rare. One such exception appears in the story of Noah (Genesis 7: 2–9) where verses 9 and 10 explain that Noah took two of every living species aboard his ark while verses 2 through 5 say that Noah obeyed God's order to take along seven members of each clean species and two of each unclean species.

Animals' Roles

The characteristics and roles assigned to animals in African religious tales differ markedly from animals' traits and roles in Christian stories. Not only are animals extremely frequent in African narratives, but animals display human qualities (spoken language, complex thinking) and such magical skills as the ability to prophesy the future, flit about the world at will, and change themselves from one sort of beast or bird into another sort. In effect, Africans' animals are typically envisioned to be mundane forms of incredibly accomplished invisible spirits that deserve center stage in religious stories.

In contrast, animals in Catholic accounts not only lack such human attributes as language, complex intelligence, and eternal souls, but they are assigned only passive roles in tales. Lambs in the Old Testament are objects of sacrifice or devices that serve human purposes, as in lambs' blood being used to mark Jewish homes in the Passover tale (Exodus 12: 3–11,1611). Job's 7,000 sheep, 3,000 camels, 5,000 oxen, and 500 "she assess" are not portrayed as personalities, but are merely Job's possessions, symbols of his wealth (Job 1: 3,1611). And the donkey in the story of Jesus riding through the streets of Jerusalem is nothing more than a beast of burden (John 12: 14–15, 1611).

VODOU/CHRISTIAN FAITH

There appears to be no general agreement about the origin of the many dozens of maxims and tales in Haitian culture or about which ones qualify as religious. As for the adages, those that refer to a supreme being—God or

Bondye—are obviously religious and could derive from either African or Catholic roots. Furthermore, maxims focusing on wise, moral behavior are religious in the definition of religion that we have adopted in this book. Those maxims could have been drawn from either African or Catholic traditions, or in some cases, created by Haitians themselves. The same is also apparently true of the tales that hold a prominent place in Haitian oral culture.

People who study these matters recognize that Haitians have traditionally known such stories from the Bible as those of Jonah-and-the-whale and David-and-Goliath. In Bellegarde-Smith's opinion, there have been two principal sources of the Bible tales—slave masters in the distant past and missionaries in more recent decades.

> People know such stories because the slave owners always made sure the slaves knew all those stories. And then when a white pastor would come from some such place as Boise, Idaho, to bring tons of shoes and used clothing, he would tell the stories to the people. Otherwise the people would not know the stories. . . . The Catholics in Haiti didn't teach Bible tales; they taught the catechism. (Bellegarde-Smith, 2011)

In addition, it is apparent that throughout the world, Catholic priests and catechists have always included in their sermons tales drawn from both the Bible and everyday experiences of clerics. As a result, a large body of stories and anecdotes has been compiled over the decades for priests and catechists to use (Roman Catholic Homilies for Holy Days, 2012). Vodou/Christian adherents would be expected to hear such narratives when attending mass.

Vodou/Christian Maxims

Each of the following examples of Vodou/Christian sayings begins with a Haitian Creole expression followed by an English translation in *italics*. The adages focus on the nature of Vodou/Christian deities and on moral/wise behavior (Corbett, 1983; *Haitian Proverbs*, 2004; Literature, 2012).

Bondye Bon (God is good). Explanation: Whatever happens is what God does for the best.

Kreyon Bondye la pa gen gonm (The pencil of God has no eraser). Explanation: God's actions are proper, final, and irreversible.

Neg di san fe. Bondye fe san di. (People talk and don't act. God acts and doesn't talk.) Explanation: What people say they will do can't be trusted, whereas God's actions can be trusted.

Bondye do ou. fe pa ou, M a fe pa M. (God says do your part and I'll do mine.)

Kreyol pale; kreyol komprann. (Speak plainly; don't try to deceive.)

Bèl antèman pa vle di paradi. (A beautiful funeral does not guarantee a place in heaven.)

Moun mouri pa konnen valè dra blan. (The dead do not know the value of white sheets.) Explanation: Funerals and their accouterments are for the benefit of the living, not for the benefit of the deceased.

Malè pa gen klaksonn. (Misfortune has no horn.) Explanation: Trouble occurs without warning.

Nan pwen mouta jezi pa deplase. (There is no mountain that Jesus cannot move.) Explanation: Place your faith in Jesus, for he can accomplish anything.

African-Derived Tales

The fact that the themes and characters in Haitian stories are often similar to those of African folklore suggests that African traditions significantly influenced the nature of fables in present-day Haitian culture.

Storytelling in Haiti is typically introduced by a raconteur shouting "Krik." If listeners want to hear the tale, they shout back, "Krak!"

> Tales are told outside at night, usually on a porch, to an assembly of adults and children. The outlines of such stories are minimalistic. . . . For the storyteller, the fun is in the invention of the embellishments and variations that will hook an audience well familiar with the tale. Indeed, the story can never be the same. As one might expect, the storyteller's freedom is not absolute. For example, one is not permitted to change the simple and haunting melodies of folk-tale songs. (Chery, 2011)

> The tales are meant to be told and dramatized rather than read. The narrator impersonates his characters, mimics their actions, moves around, gestures, dwells on and expands elements that seem to intrigue his audience, and generally treats his performance as a production. In some regions the accomplished story-teller is called a *maît' conte*—a "story chief" or master of ceremonies—and elsewhere he is called a samba. (Courlander, 2002)

Haitian folktales are typically lengthy narratives, too long to be related in their entirety in this chapter. Therefore, the versions in the following pages are abstracts, limited to identifying each story's principal characters and events. As illustrated with the following examples, imported African folk stories and their Caribbean alternatives have been intended to serve a variety of purposes, including those of: (a) teaching wisdom and moral values, (b) explaining the origin of phenomena, (c) rationalizing societal conditions and (d) accounting for good and bad fortune.

Wisdom and Its Opposite

The following pair of tales have clearly been borrowed from African tradition, then modified when reproduced in the Caribbean.

An example of an entire literary genre imported from Africa that became widespread throughout the Caribbean is the collection of tales about Anansi (Ananse), the trickster spider.

> Anansi is the hero of children and the champion of the little guy and the powerless. Like them, he often gets in trouble and must use his intelligence to save himself. Anansi's stories spread his fame among the Akan people of West Africa and their neighbors. In the Americas he was adopted by enslaved Africans from different ethnic groups. Anansi stories are both entertaining and instructional. Listeners are sometimes advised either to follow Anansi's example or beware of his folly. Anansi pits his cunning (usually with success) against superior strength; he also symbolizes greed and envy. Some stories include a proverb at the end or may incorporate a song. In one tale he may be a bachelor in search of a bride or the hand of the king's daughter. In another story he may have his wife, Aso, and his son, Intikuma. (Auld, 2012)

When slaves brought Anansi narratives to the Caribbean, both the spider's name and tales of his antics were often altered. The variations in the spelling and pronunciation of his name reflect a cross-cultural change from his African Ghanaian origin into English, French, Dutch, creole, and patois. In the English colony of Jamaica, *Anansi* was changed to *Anancy*. In Curaçao, he became *Nansi*, and in the French colony of Haiti, he would be known as either *Ti Malice* (Uncle Malis) or the less common *Ti Jean* (Uncle John). When France held the islands of Saint Lucia and Grenada, *Anansi* became *Compe Czien* (Brother Spider) (African Legend of Ananse, 2012).

Thus, in Haiti, the personality characteristics of the African *Anansi* are found in stories about *Ti Malice*. Courlander (2002, p. 60) accounted for the intent of the name by proposing that "Haitians would roughly translate the name *Malice* as meaning *mischief*. But the *Ti* in the name could well have come from *tio* which means *Uncle* in Spanish."

When transported to the New World, Anansi—in his various guises—was joined in Haiti by a dull-witted dupe named Bouki to produce tales that featured mischievous cleverness and guile (Ti Malice) and the opposite—gullible stupidity (Ti Bouki). The word *bouki* has been traced to the West African Wolof ethnic group where the term means hyena, a beast portrayed in folklore as a dunderhead. The quality of Bouki's thought process is illustrated in a conversation that Corbett (1983) cites between Bouki and Malis (Malice). Malis was amazed when he saw Bouki playing dominoes with Bouki's dog, and Malis remarked, "What a brilliant dog. He can play dominoes." Bouki replied, "He's not all that smart. I beat him three out of five games today."

The following are two Malice and Bouki tales contrasting cleverness and simple-mindedness.

Bouki Goes Shopping: Malis could not go to the market, so he asked Bouki to go instead to buy charcoal, vegetables, rice, beans, and tasty beef—a delicacy that Malis knew Bouki adored. Malis warned, "Don't eat that piece of beef, or I'll give you a beating." So, Bouki shopped at the market and put the items in his basket, saying to the beef, "I'll not eat you, because if I do, Malis will say Bouki is bad." As Bouki walked quickly home, he turned a corner and looked back to see a little man following him. So Bouki began to run, then called out, "Are you chasing me to get the charcoal. Then here it is!" Bouki threw the charcoal at the little man and ran on. But the little man wouldn't stop. Bouki was so frightened that he threw the whole basket of food at the chaser. When Bouki reached home, he ran inside and hid under the bed. When Malis discovered Bouki, he asked what had happened. Bouki replied, "A man chased me. Come outside and see." When they stepped into the sunlight, Bouki pointed to where the little man was directly under Bouki's foot, still in pursuit. Malis shook his head in despair as he told Bouki, "The little man is your own shadow" (Louis & Hay, 1999, pp. 45–46).

Bouki Gets Whee-ai: One morning, when Bouki was on his way to the market to sell yams, he chanced upon an old man happily eating by the roadside. Bouki wanted to learn what delicacy the aged fellow was enjoying, so he asked, "What is the name of that fine food?" The old man, being deaf, didn't understand the question, but at that moment, he bit down on a hot red pepper and shouted in pain, "Whee-ai"! Bouki thanked him and set off to the market where he asked the tradespeople he met where he could buy whee-ai, but they only laughed at him. Distressed, he started to return home and met Ti Malice, who listened to the sad story and said, "Don't fret, I'll get you whee-ai." Ti Malice went to his own house to fetch a sack into which he put sharp cactus leaves, then covered them with potatoes, oranges, and a pineapple. He returned to Bouki and handed him the sack. Bouki reached in, pulled out a potato, and complained, "That's not whee-ai!" Next, he took out the pineapple and complained again, then voiced the same disappointment when he withdrew an orange. Finally, at the bottom of the sack, he grabbed the cactus leaves and screamed with pain, "WHEE-AI!" Ti Malice said, "You wanted *whee-ai*, now you got it" (Chef de la Patrie, 2010).

Explaining Origins

Two examples of narratives designed to explain how something began are *A Piece of Fire* and *Ti Jean's Waist*.

A Piece of Fire: Ages ago, Legba, the messenger god, reported to an assembly of gods that a great chunk of fire had fallen from the sky and was scorching the earth. In response, Agwé, god of the sea, surrounded the fire with ocean to prevent it from destroying the world. Ogoun, god of iron-smiths, encircled the fire with a great chain. Shango, god of lightning, used a thunderbolt to cast the chained fire into the nearby city. Then, the three gods began to argue over who now owned the fire until they were interrupted by Nananbouchlou, the mother of all the gods. She settled the dispute by declaring that the fire was a beautiful treasure, but it had caused dissension among the gods, so "We will continue to live with it among us, but peace-fully." With that, she flung the brightly burning stone high into the sky, where we see it today as the evening star (Courlander, 1964).

Ti Jean's Waist: The following anecdote was designed to account for the origin of a physical feature of the spider Anansi (oft known as *Ti Jean* in Haiti). Spiders did not always have thin waists but instead were quite rotund. One day, while walking in the forest, Ti Jean remembered that it was harvest festival day, so every village would be having a grand feast. He lived between two villages and hoped to dine at both, so he ordered his two sons to each tie a rope around their father's middle. Each son grabbed his rope and went into his assigned village to pull the rope when the feast was ready. But both feasts occurred at exactly the same time. When each son tugged on his rope, Ti Jean's middle was squeezed tight, so Ti Jean failed to attend either feast. And to this day, spiders have had thin waists (Anansi Legend, 2012).

Rationalizing Societal Conditions

One bright day, the animals gathered to hear Zandolit, the tree lizard, pro-pose that "Each of us animals looks out for himself, not for the good of all. Our lives would be better if we had a king who looked out for everyone." This set off a host of suggestions about which animal was best suited to be king. But in response to each suggestion, there were objections. Bull was rejected for being undiplomatic, too prone to anger and fighting. Donkey was criti-cized for being merely a beast of burden instead of a bold leader. Rooster's skinny red legs would make him a laughing stock. Turkey's lack of wisdom was obvious to everyone. Rabbit's hiding in the grass and twitching his nose were obviously not kingly habits. Snake's crawling on his belly and dwelling in a hole disqualified him. Horse's carrying a bit in his mouth and a man on his back eliminated him as a candidate. But finally, when Dog's name was submitted, everyone applauded. Dog was then clad in royal garments with a crown on his head. At the great feast prepared for Dog's inauguration, Dog's mouth watered when he smelled the cooking meat, and he couldn't resist. He dashed to the cooking pit, snatched the roast in his mouth, and bolted away, with crown and robes flying off. The crowd of animals shouted, "Dog is not our king. He's a thief." Zandolit, the tree lizard, sadly concluded, "All the proposed candidates for king were rejected because they were judged by their weaknesses, not by their strengths. If the animals had considered the strengths of our fellow creatures, we would have a king. Instead, we have none" (Suranyl, 2008).

Accounting for Good and Bad Fortune

In the tale of *The Fortunate Farmer,* Di Dim is described as a descendent of slaves from Africa. He had recently been robbed of his farm by a white businessman, and since then, had lived by chopping fruit from forest trees. One day, he was a passing a cave in the forest when he heard a hissing sound, and a white snake slithered out to greet him with "I'm Sister Snake. I've heard that you are a man of magic. I have always wanted to be a beautiful princess. If you use your magic to turn me into a beautiful princess I promise that I will marry you and you will become the Prince of Haiti and be a very wealthy man." Such a prospect pleased Dim mightily, so by magic, he changed the snake into a beautiful princess, clad in gold with shoes made of diamonds. However, when Dim said, "Now marry me and make me the Prince of Haiti," the princess refused, complaining that Dim had "bad teeth. When you have good teeth, I'll marry you." Again, Dim worked his magic. But now, despite his handsome teeth, the princess objected to Dim's black, kinky hair and demanded that he have blond hair before they were wed. Again, by magic, Dim fulfilled her demand. Again, she refused, now requiring more changes—blue eyes, white skin, and great wealth. As Dim sought to comply, he was told by the King of Magic that the only magic he could not perform was that of making Dim rich. The angry princess, now in a fury, set out to marry the man who had cheated Dim out of his farm. Dim, in an effort to retaliate for such ill-treatment, worked his magic to turn the princess back into a snake, who was then forced to live once more in the forest cave. When the King of Haiti learned of such a feat, he thought that Dim must be a very powerful fellow who could bring to Haiti great riches. So the king made Dim the Prince of Haiti who would wed a beautiful princess and at last become a truly happy man (Fleury, 2012).

RATIONALIZING VODOU/CHRISTIAN MAXIMS AND TALES

In support of my belief that the maxims and tales of the Vodou/Christian faith are part of a cohesive worldview, I draw on three of the principles-of-accommodation described in Chapter 1—*in-name-only, nonconflicting-add-ons*, and *tolerance.*

The *in-name-only* principle, as applied to maxims, states that when adages from two religions have the same meanings but may be phrased differently, they can compatibly coexist within such a combined belief system as the Vodou/Christian faith. Many of the adages from African traditions teach the same moral/ethical beliefs as do Catholic precepts that bear on such matters as honesty, bravery, sacrifice, diligence, trust, faith, obedience, prudence, and wisdom.

The *nonconflicting-add-ons* principle means that if an adage or tale from Religion A does not contradict or violate a basic belief of Religion B, then the adage or story can be accepted by members of a faith—such as Vodou/Christianity—that is sufficiently tolerant to combine the two belief systems. For example, the Bible does not include stories that invest animals with the ability to entertain human emotions or express themselves in speech, but neither does it deny such possibilities. Thus, Vodou's amazing Ti Malice and talking lizard, Zandolit, can be accepted alongside the Bible's wondrous Jonah who, for a time, lived in a whale without suffering harm.

CONCLUSION

As illustrated throughout this chapter, African, Catholic, and Vodou/Christian beliefs have been taught to devotees over the centuries in the form of wise sayings and stories. The adages and tales have served as convenient mnemonic devices to help adherents understand and recall theological and moral doctrine.

CHAPTER 9

Symbols and Sacred Objects

Religious symbols are words, numbers, or graphic representations of a religion, its beliefs, or its adherents. Sacred objects are revered items, either reminiscent of important people or events in a religion's history or used in the practice of the religion.

INDIGENOUS AFRICAN SYMBOLS AND OBJECTS

African religions are replete with spoken and visual symbols as well as carved, sculptured, painted, and woven objects intended to enrich and clarify devotees' understanding of their faith.

Symbolic Representations

Symbols in African traditional belief systems include numbers, gestures, and drawn figures.

Numerals and Actions

Some African traditions assign sacred meanings to numerals. In one version, zero (0) signifies the supreme god—the source of all life, the sum total of life and death. The number 3 represents creation, 5 stands for religion, and 7 for spirituality (Spiritual Numerology, 2001).

Common to most African religions have been various styles of drumming, dancing, clapping, and chanting that convey sacred meanings to villagers and function as prayers to deities and spirits of ancestors.

   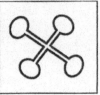

Figure 9.1 Adinkra Symbols: God Reigns, Kola Nut, Mother Earth, and Immortal Soul. (Adapted from MacDonald, 2007)

Graphic Symbols

Across the centuries, scores of visual symbols have been created by West African religious adepts to convey sacred meanings. Frequently, the venerated signs have been displayed on placards, fabrics, pottery, woodcarvings, paintings, leatherwork, and beadwork.

Typical graphic symbols are illustrated in the Adinkra designs from Akan ethnic groups in Ghana and the Gyaman in the Ivory Coast.

The kola (cola, palm) nut is one of the most revered cultural symbols in West Africa, particularly in Nigeria, where the kola tree has been considered the earth's first tree and the emblem of life. The tree produces embryonic leaves that botanists call cotyledons in the form of seeds. The nuts are a source of caffeine, chewed for their flavor and mild narcotic effect. Spiritual meanings have been attributed to the number of seeds a kola contains. According to one interpretation, a kola containing a single seed is regarded as belonging to a sacred spirit, and thus, is forbidden to mortals, so people do not chew it. A kola with three seeds signifies bravery and is reserved for mighty warriors and consecrated members of the community. The most typical kola has four cotyledons that represent peace and blessing. "Kola with six cotyledons (seed leaves) indicates communion with ancestors. . . . The smallest part or cotyledon is not eaten but is thrown away for the ancestors to eat. . . . [Among the] Igbo, kola is always accompanied by wine or drink because the Igbo say that 'One who gives a deity kola has to give him water with which to help him swallow it' " (Ukaegbu, 2003).

African Sacred Objects

The visual arts in West Africa were created chiefly for decorating shrines, manipulating supernatural forces, and promoting divination. Art has been used to celebrate abundant harvests, to solicit the aid of spirits in time of need, and to praise divine forces working on people's behalf. The objects invested with sacred meanings have included masks, textiles, woodcarvings, metalwork, beadwork, leatherwork, and ceramics.

Masks

In West Africa, masks have been used in religious ceremonies for depicting spirits and ancestors and for communicating with them. The masks are usually created by artisans trained by a master carver, with the skill often passed within a family from one generation to the next. Mask makers enjoy a respected position in tribal society because of the talent that the work requires and the spiritual and symbolic knowledge it involves.

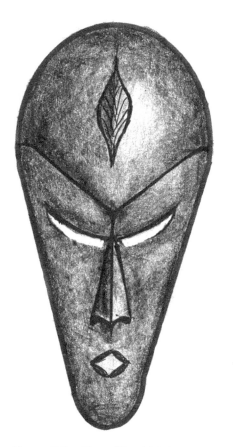

Figure 9.2a Ghana Ritual Mask.

Particularly famous as mask makers are the Ashanti of Ghana, who have produced highly diverse styles. In Ghanaian religious rituals, masks serve two principal functions. First, they are intended to appease and please minor deities and the shades of ancestors so as to court those benevolent spirits' aid in time of need. Second, masks are expected to frighten away evil powers that may hover about and do harm at any moment. Frequently, the wearer of the mask during a religious ritual is an initiate "who absorbs the evil forces inhabiting the place to be purified or, instead, accumulates an emotional charge, destined to touch the beneficent divinity" (Masks of Ghana and Africa, 2009).

Most masks worn during tribal rites by the Biombo of the Congo are carved from wood, then colored with red tukula powder—a dye made from the camwood tree. The eyes are typically a coffee-bean shape, with a

Figure 9.2b Biombo Ritual Mask.   **Figure 9.2c** Yohure Ritual Mask.

checkerboard design decorating the eyebrows and the cheeks. The shafts rising from at the back of the head represent a Biombo hairstyle (Biombo mask, 2011).

Among the Yohure of the Ivory Coast, funeral masks are worn on two occasions. First is the *je* celebration, when a ritual is conducted to purify the village after a death and to help the deceased's soul on its way to a final resting place. Painted masks are mainly worn by dancers during this ceremony, while for the second ritual—the *lo* ceremony—masks covered with black pigments are worn. Both types of masks are intended to influence supernatural powers—the *yu* spirits—which can either harm humans or promote their welfare (Yohure mask, 2011).

Although West African masks may be made from a variety of materials (including cloth, raffia, leather and more recently plastic), the majority are carved from softwood. The process of carving and making masks for masquerades is ritualized, comprising a prescribed series of steps that have to be learned through years of apprenticeship. Woodcarvers choose their wood carefully, preferring to carve a green, moist wood with the right physical and spiritual qualities, the latter of which are determined through a private divination ritual and adjusted with an offering. The decoration stage is also ritualized; for example, nobody other than the maker could be present when the skin was put onto a wooden Ekoi mask. (Douglas, 2002)

Textiles

Over the ages, woven fabrics—garments, table coverings, drapes, and wall hangings—have played an important part in African religious life. Weaving methods and the fibers used have varied from one ethnic group to another. Consider, for instance, three West-African fabrics—*asoke, adinka,* and *kente.*

The Yorubas' asoke cloth is a sturdy, practical material used primarily in religious rituals, especially during funerals. Some asoke cloths are notable for their openwork (holes) and inlaid designs which, in modern times, have been made with rayon threads on a background of silk or cotton. The cloth is woven in four-inch strips of varied lengths that are sewn together so as to make each fabric unique. Three varieties of asoke have been the: (a) *etu,* a dark-blue indigo-dyed cloth, (b) *sanyan,* a brown fabric woven from the beige silk of the Anaphe moth, (c) and *alaari,* woven with silk from the Sahara region.

Adinkra cloth from Ghana is made by embroidering wide panels of dyed cotton fabric and stamping them with gourds that have been carved with traditional symbols reflecting the thoughts and feelings of the wearer of the garment. Dark colors—brick-red, brown, black—have been associated with death and worn for such somber events as funerals, whereas white, yellow, and light blue have been used on festive occasions.

Kente cloth is a ceremonial fabric of the Asante people of Ghana. It is handwoven on a treadle loom in four-inch-wide strips that will be sewn together to form a garment. The term kente means basket in reference to the ancient practice of weavers using raffia to create a textile whose appearance resembled a *kenten* (basket). In modern times, kente garments have been created in a diversity of colors and designs to be worn during important social and religious events.

Traditional African textiles are often enhanced through hand-stamping, stenciling, dyeing, painting, or embroidery. Different shades of soil are used to make paint. Dyes are created from herbs, leaves, bark, nuts, fruits, vegetables, and grasses that are mixed with water or other chemicals such as zinc, sulfur, or iron to create diverse textures and hues. Fabrics' colors can be assigned meanings in different tribes' traditions. In some areas of Nigeria, red is a protective color worn by chiefs to ward off evil, while red is used for mourning robes by the Akan in Ghana. Among the Fante of Ghana, red symbolizes death or bloodshed, green stands for fertility and vitality, white for purity, yellow for glory and maturity, gold for long life, blue for love, and black for spirituality and maturity (History of African Textiles and Fabrics, 2011).

Wood Carvings

Figure 9.3a Wood Reliquary Figure.

In virtually all West African ethnic groups, woodcarving has been a highly developed art form. For example, the variety of carved wooden objects created by the Igbo artisans of Nigeria have included musical instruments, doors, stools, mirror frames, trays for offering kola nuts to guests, fertility dolls, and small figures used in divination.

The Fang, Kota, and Hongwe people in Gabon have sculpted figures to serve as guardian statues protecting the remains of ancestors that are kept in reliquary baskets or bark boxes. Parts of the carved images have typically been covered with thin strips of copper or brass.

Divination is the art of interpreting signs and symbols, especially as used by a shaman to determine the cause of disease or the treatment of illness. In southwest Nigeria, the palm nuts used by a Yoruba shaman are stored in a divination bowl called an *adjella-ifa*. The Yoruba god of divination is Ifa, who is believed to have taught methods of healing to humans (Divination Bowl, 2011).

Figure 9.3b Wood Divination Bowl.

A kneeling woman with breasts exposed, pregnant, or with a child strapped to her back denotes maternity/fertility and the power of *ase*, which is the energy that can be used either to create or destroy.

Metalwork

Over the centuries, West African artisans have fashioned religious objects from iron, brass, bronze, copper, silver, and gold. A wide variety of articles has been created by the region's smiths. Neck rings, anklets, and bracelets have been made of forged iron or of cast brass to serve as dance paraphernalia during rituals. The Nupe metalworkers of Nigeria have been recognized for vessels manufactured with embossed and etched designs. Silver and gold, as well as semiprecious metals, have long been used for creating jewelry of religious significance.

Since ancient times, the Yoruba have produced religious objects in copper and brass by the lost-wax method in which a cast is made of a sculptured figure; then, the figure is removed and a thin coating of wax is applied to the inside of the cast. Next, molten metal is poured into the cast, resulting in a metal duplicate of the original figure (Yoruba Ancient Art, 2006).

In the nation of Benin, a ritual honoring past kings (*obas*) features dancers wearing brass helmets. To prepare for the rite, courtiers would place a

Figure 9.3c Wood-Carved Maternity Spirit.

bronze head on an altar in an open courtyard of the royal palace (Figure 9.4). The head represents a former revered oba.

The altar is in the form of a semicircular mud platform packed hard and rubbed smooth. On this occasion, the palace courtyard provides the setting for the most important rite of divine kingship in Benin. During the ceremony, the currently reigning oba "honors the spirit of his late father and performs sacrifices to the royal ancestors and to the earth in which they are buried. . . . The rite expresses the continuity of divine kingship, and the altar before which it takes place provides the means by which the connection between the living king and his predecessors is made" (Benin Bronze Altar Head, 2006).

The process of using fire to transform ore into metal, and metal into an object, was widely seen in Africa as a dangerous act of creation. As such, it was susceptible to interference by ancestral spirits and by acts of sorcery, or spells, from other members of the community. Secret rituals, symbols, rules, and taboos were therefore seen as essential to counteract these malevolent forces, and they were viewed as of equal importance to a successful smelt as were the ore and fuel. . . . Acts of sorcery were often blamed for smelting failures. Preparing medicines to protect the furnace from these spells was therefore considered an essential part of metalworking. Because metalworkers knew how to make offerings and sacrifices to the spirits and ancestors, and how to protect their work from malevolent spirits

Figure 9.4a Brass Helmet.   **Figure 9.4b** Bronze Altar Head.

and magic, they were often regarded by the rest of the community with a mixture of fear and awe. (Douglas, 2002)

Beadwork

Among the Yoruba, beadwork displays an established color symbolism. For example, *fun-fun* is a white, blue-silver, or icy color associated with cool personalities, such as those of the spirits Obatala and Yemoja. In contrast, the hue *pupa* consists of shades of red that express passionate fiery personalities, such as those of the deities Oya, Sango and Osun. The *dudu* palette includes earth tones—browns, moss greens, leafy greens—that evoke visions of stable, grounded personalities, such as those of the spirits Ogun and Ochosi.

For the Yoruba, beading is not merely a practical folk art. Rather, it is "a spiritual experience, with each bead strung to create something with meaning, as exemplified in the beaded crowns worn by *obas* (kings), footstools, leather pouches, and chair cushions" (African Shapes of the Sacred, 2007).

In Cameroon, diverse objects are covered with beads—gourds, jewelry, wooden stools, sculptures, flywhisks, toys, baskets, and sculptures. To prepare the objects for a beaded surface, cloth is first sewn to the surface of the item. Then, beads are sewn onto the cloth, several at a time. In addition to glass beads, seeds, and cowry shells are used to decorate the object (Ventura & Gutek, 2011).

Ceramics

Pottery in West Africa has assumed a variety of forms, including large storage and water containers; mid-sized vessels to hold personal belongings, to serve food, and to brew beer and palm wine; and small bottles and embellished containers for religious and ritual use. Decorated jars and bowls have been prominently displayed at shrines and on family altars.

Studies of traditions in Nigeria suggest that "ceramic arts in this region are conceptualized as active participants in maintaining and legitimating social relationships not just in this world, but between the living and the ancestral dead. There is no easy division between sacred and profane; thus the symbolism of figurative vessels embedded in ritual contexts is inseparable from the material symbols of daily life" (Frank, 2011).

Figure 9.5a Ceramic Embossed Vase (Nigeria).

Figure 9.5b Terracotta Head (Ghana).

The creation of pottery and ceramics in West Africa has been a craft traditionally dominated by women.

Once a vessel is formed and dried to a leather-hard state, a potter has a series of choices. She may cut intricate designs into the clay surface with a wooden or metal blade; create a roughened, textured surface by impressing patterns with a roulette; burnish the surface to a high sheen; or alter the original form by adding handles, clay pellets, or strips. She may color the entire surface or apply a slip (colored, clay wash) to highlight

Figure 9.5c Clay Jar (Mali).

the decorative areas, which often appear on the most visible parts of a vessel. (Ceramic Arts, 2011)

Summary

Across the centuries, a wide selection of objects in indigenous African cultures have served as religious art, symbolically honoring deities and revered ancestors. The articles used for expressing religious concepts in graphic form have included masks, costumes, statues, furniture, doors and windows, bowls, jars, cutlery, jewelry, weapons, altars, garments, wall hangings, flags, and more.

The media employed for such endeavors have ranged from wood, metals, and clay to textiles and beadwork.

Two-dimensional symbols (printed on fabrics, drawn or painted on articles, or etched into wood or metal) have usually been highly stylized images, such as the Adinkra figures earlier in this chapter, rather than attempts to depict images in realistic detail. Three-dimensional symbolic objects, such as woodcarvings and clay sculptures, have typically represented humans or animals with bodily proportions intentionally simplified and certain dimensions exaggerated rather than cast as photographic realism. The purpose has been to accentuate certain human and animal characteristics while diminishing attention to others.

CATHOLIC SYMBOLS AND OBJECTS

Catholicism in the 21st century continues to be distinguished by symbols and sacred articles from the past that represent a long history of lasting traditions.

Symbolic Representations

Numbers, gestures, words, phrases, and graphic representations have figured prominently in Catholic life for more than two millennia.

Numerals and Gestures

Christians have often assigned religious meanings to numbers. For example, 3 has signified the trinity (God, Jesus, and the Holy Spirit), 5 has symbolized the five wounds Jesus suffered on the cross (hands, feet, and side), 6 has represented the number of days God took to create the universe, and 7 has stood for perfection, as God rested on the seventh day of creation, satisfied with his accomplishment. In addition, Saint Paul cited seven gifts from the Holy Spirit, and Jesus issued seven utterances from the cross. Finally, the number 7 figures prominently in the Book of Revelation, which was originally in the form of an epistle written to seven churches in Asia Minor, with the message including many references to the quantities of seven.

A gesture signifying Catholic belief is that of making the sign of the cross—moving one's hand vertically from forehead to waist, then moving it horizontally across one's chest from left to right.

Certain words and phrases have also represented the Catholic faith. Whereas some expressions have a positive connotation and are encouraged, others are deemed vile and their use prohibited. Esteemed language includes such statements as:

> The Lord be with thee.
> Christ, the Redeemer.
> Hail, Mary, full of grace.
> Jesus saves.
> Amen.

Among the Bible's Ten Commandments, the one that warns people to avoid using the Lord's name in vain refers to such offenses as uttering the names of venerated biblical figures as curse words or in jest.

Graphic Symbols

The most popular Christian visual symbol throughout the centuries has been the cross, signifying the crucifixion of Jesus who died to atone for the sins of all who would follow his teachings. There are numerous versions of the cross. The one most widely recognized in modern times is the Latin cross, which apparently first came into use during the second or third centuries CE.

The Celtic cross is said to have originated in Ireland in the early years of the Christian era, then carried in the sixth century by Colomba to the nearby island of Iona, thus accounting for the symbol's alternate name—Cross of Iona.

The three-bar Russian Orthodox cross has been adopted by many Eastern Orthodox churches and Eastern (Byzantine-rite) Catholic churches. One popular Eastern Orthodox interpretation of the bars on the cross proposes that the top bar symbolizes the sign that was placed above Jesus' head reading "King of the Jews." The bottom, slanted bar on the right side (from the vantage point of Jesus on the cross looking out) points up to Barabas, the thief crucified on Jesus' right, whom Jesus told, "Today you shall be with me in paradise." The left side, pointing down, is said to signify the death of the unrepentant thief crucified to the left of Jesus.

The Maltese cross—four spearheads pointing to the center—was the emblem of the Order of Hospitallers during medieval crusades to the Christian holy land. Eventually, the Hospitallers established their headquarters on the island of Malta, which accounts for the present-day name of their emblem.

The anchor cross originated in ancient Egypt and was used by Christians when they hid in Rome's catacombs. Over the centuries, the anchor cross has served as the guardian symbol for seafarers.

The graded cross is erected atop three steps, with the highest step signifying *faith*, the middle step *hope*, and the bottom step *charity*.

The Greek cross, consisting of two simple bars of equal length, is the earliest of the Christian crosses.

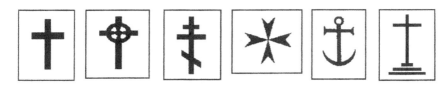

Figure 9.6 Christian Crosses 1: Latin, Celtic, Russian, Maltese, Anchor, and Graded.

Figure 9.7 Christian Crosses 2: Greek, Fleur de Lis, Tau, Cross & Crown, and Lorraine.

The *fleur de lis* (literally in French, *flower of the lily*) is not a cross as such but has served the purpose of a cross by representing the Trinity (Father, Son, Holy Spirit) and by its association with Jesus' resurrection after he was crucified. According to legend, a lily sprang from the tears of Jesus' mother, Mary, as she wept at the foot of his cross.

The cross in the form of the Greek letter *tau* predates the Latin cross and is often associated with the Old Testament (the T is envisioned as the shape of the pole on which the brazen serpent appeared to Eve in the Garden of Eden) just as the Latin cross is associated with Jesus' death in the New Testament. The T-shaped symbol is also known as the Egyptian cross and Saint Anthony's cross. Saint Anthony was a fourth-century ascetic who established the first Christian monastery in the Egyptian desert.

The cross-and-crown is often interpreted as symbolizing the reward in heaven (the crown) after Catholic devotees' trials during their earthly life (the cross).

The cross of Lorraine is of ancient origin, dating back to the deified kings of Sumeria, the region surrounding the Tigris and Euphrates rivers in what is now Iraq. During the medieval Christian crusades to the holy land, the double-bar cross was adopted as the emblem of the Knights Templars (*Poor Fellow-Soldiers of Christ and of the Temple of Solomon*).

Among Christian graphics, the image of a fish has become a distant second in popularity to the cross. Fish symbols today are often displayed on Christians' autos and jewelry.

One popular form of the symbol features the Greek word fish, *ichthus*, encased in a fish outline. In Greek letters, the word *fish* is spelled *Iota Chi Theta Upsilon Sigma*.

Christians have often interpreted *ichthus* as an acrostic "which has many translations in English. The most popular appears to be 'Jesus Christ, Son of God, Savior'—**I**esous (Jesus) **CH**ristos (Christ) **TH**eou (God) **U**iou (Son), and **S**oter (Savior)" Variations of the sign include the simple outline of a fish,

Figure 9.8 Ichthus.

the outline with the name *Jesus* inside, and the outline standing vertically and surrounding a cross (Robinson, 2006).

Over the centuries, the cross and fish have been joined by other Christian symbols, including the skull and crossbones, lamb (Saint Agnes), sheep (12 apostles), stag (Saint Aidan), ship (Jude), Bible (Saint Paul), sea shell (Saint James), tree (Saint Bride), harp (Saint Cecilia), and more.

Catholic Revered Objects

For convenience of analysis, sacred objects can be divided into two types— relics of historical significance and objects currently used in the conduct of religion.

Venerated Relics

Three of the most highly valued Christian relics over the centuries have been the Crucifix, the Holy Chalice, and Jesus' Shroud.

The Crucifix is either a statuette or a painting of Jesus nailed to the cross when the magistrate Pontius Pilot condemned him to death. Today, crucifixes are commonly seen in Roman Catholic churches, schools, and hospitals. In Italy, a law issued by Mussolini in 1924 required that each public school classroom and every hospital room display a crucifix. Recent lawsuits challenging that practice have been denied by the highest Italian courts, thereby demonstrating the continued strength of a religious convention in an ostensibly secular state.

In Catholic tradition, the Holy Chalice is the vessel Jesus used at the Last Supper to serve wine to his disciples the evening before he was crucified. According to the Bible, "He took the cup when he had supped, saying, 'This cup is the new testament in my blood' " (1 Corinthians 11: 25). Medieval legends declare that the chalice was later used to catch Jesus' dripping blood when he was nailed to the cross. That chalice was the Holy Grail pursued by Sir Galahad in the King Arthur tales. Since Jesus' time, conflicting accounts have led to confusion about the nature of the chalice and its whereabouts. One version holds that Saint Peter kept the vessel after Jesus' death and transported it to Rome where Peter became the first pope. The grail was then said to be guarded by succeeding popes until sent to Spain in the third century. Today, at least three cathedrals claim to house the authentic chalice.

One vessel is the jewel-studded golden Chalice of Saint Gozlin, now in the treasury of the cathedral in the French city of Nancy. The relic in Genoa, Italy, is a green-glass dish rather than a cup. The one in Valencia, Spain, is a cup fashioned out of agate. Whether any of those vessels was used by Jesus at the Last Supper is doubtful, yet each is apparently honored by many Catholics as the original one (Chalice, 2006).

Equally uncertain is the authenticity of a shroud publicized as the cloth used to cover the crucified Jesus when he was placed in a tomb. Present-day

Figure 9.9 The Christian Crucifix.

debate continues over an ages-old, blood-stained linen cloth—14.5 feet long and 3.7 feet wide (436 by 110 centimeters)—displaying the shadowy image of a man. The cloth, currently at the cathedral in Turin, Italy, has been the recent subject of forensic study that has led some investigators to label it a clever medieval forgery made from a fabric created sometime between the years 1260 and 1390. However, other investigators have deemed the Turin shroud authentic (Trivedi, 2004).

Three additional relics are: (a) a blanket and a cloak in Aachen, Germany, that are claimed to be Jesus' baby blanket and his mother Mary's garment and (b) pieces of wood in various locations—most notably Santo Toribio de Liébana in Spain—that supposedly are from the cross on which Jesus died (Relics in Christianity, 2006).

Figure 9.10 Chalice of Saint Gozlin.

Centuries-old Catholic memorabilia whose authors and locations are not in doubt include such art works as: (a) Michelangelo's statue of youthful King David and the artist's painting of the creation of Adam on the ceiling of the Sistine Chapel in Rome, (b) Leonardo da Vinci's painting of the Last Supper, (c) Raphael's portrait of *Madonna and Child,* and (d) El Greco's painting titled *Assumption of the Virgin.*

Sacred Objects in Current Use

Not only do Catholics admire relics from the past but they also honor objects used in present-day religious ceremonies. The Bible is perhaps the most cherished item. Others include:

Wine and bread (blessed by a priest as the symbolic blood and flesh of Jesus that communicants ingest during the Eucharist ceremony)

Statuettes and portraits of Jesus, his mother, and saints

Pendants, prayer beads, necklaces, rings

Church fonts for baptizing neophytes

Vestments of priests (tunic, hat, stole, and others)

Figure 9.11 Face Segment of the Turin Shroud.

Summary

The symbols and revered objects of Catholicism range from ancient signs and relics to present-day emblems and articles used in the daily practice of the religion.

AFRICAN AND CATHOLIC SYMBOLS AND OBJECTS COMPARED

Religious symbols and artifacts in traditional African faiths and in Catholicism are alike in at least two important ways. In both belief systems, invisible spirits are the foci of symbols and revered objects. The intent of a faith's devotees is to honor spirits and to seek their approval and support. Furthermore, the two systems are similar in many of the forms in which the creations are shaped: (a) numerical and graphic symbols and (b) sculptured, painted, woven, cast, and printed objects.

However, in a variety ways, portrayals of indigenous African beliefs and Catholicism differ. For example, African religions have provided far greater quantities and varieties of symbols and objects than has Catholicism, particularly because African faiths were never part of an overarching administrative structure as Catholicism has been. Each African region, or indeed, each village has been a separate entity, free to identify its own deities and ancestral shades and to represent them in whatever visual forms the artists chose.

Most Catholic objects are limited to relics, pictures, statuary, and jewelry depicting events associated with biblical characters and saints—particularly events related to Jesus. In marked contrast, the symbols and realia of African faiths have concerned a great diversity of deities and revered ancestors, including actual and imaginary animals. Whereas no animals in Catholic lore have been accorded human personality traits, African traditions have often attributed human traits to animals—crocodiles, spiders, lions, turtles, and more.

Furthermore, in Catholic tradition, most artists who painted or sculpted images of humans or of spirits (such as God or angels), sought to depict their subjects as photographically realistic or as idealized images. This classical tradition was especially dominant in the past. In modern times, artists of Catholic subject matter have been more willing to portray biblical characters in varied styles—impressionism, cubism, surrealism, pop art. On the contrary, African artists have always felt free to depart dramatically from visual realism in the figures they drew or molded.

African artists have also been less constrained than Catholic painters and sculptors in depicting human figures in the nude.

SYMBOLS AND OBJECTS IN THE VODOU/ CHRISTIAN FAITH

Haitian culture is richly supplied with visual arts. Bellegarde-Smith (2011) has suggested that "Haitian art's foundation is religious, the most grandiose religious art to be found anywhere in the Caribbean and elsewhere."

In my search of the literature, I found a host of evidence to support the observation that symbols and objects in the Vodou/Christian faith have derived from three main sources—African religions, Catholicism, and creativity generated within Haitian culture itself. Haitian art has assumed a variety of forms, including drawings, paintings, crosses, metal art, sequin-embellished flags, ceremonial rattles, drums, and dolls.

Objects are not sacred unless they've been sacrilized through rituals. The bottles of rum, the bottles of wine, the bottles of perfume on altars are not sacred until they've been used in a religious service. (Bellegarde-Smith, 2011)

Drawings (Vévés)

Reminiscent of the symbols of deities in African art and of events in Catholic history are Vodou/Christian designs on objects or as ephemeral finger-drawn sketches in corn meal, sand, or ashes. Printed Vodou *vévés* are typically more delicate and complex than their African forbearers, as illustrated in Figure 9.12, where three favorite Haitian lwa are portrayed.

- Papa Legba is the gatekeeper to the spirit world and guardian of the crossroad that is symbolized in the pair of alternative vévés representing his nature.

- Damballah-Wedo is depicted as a serpent with twisting snake-like movements as he slithers across the ground, flicking his tongue and climbing tall objects. He is the world's loving father and the source of peace and tranquility

- Ogoun is the lwa of blacksmithing, associated with power, war, and politics. He has been credited with stimulating the slaves' 1804 revolution that established Haiti as an independent nation.

Figure 9.12a Vodou Vévés: Papa Legba First Variant.

Figure 9.12b Vodou Vévés: Papa Legba Second Variant.

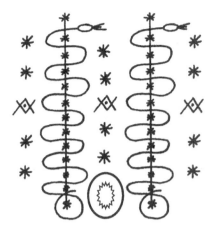 

Figure 9.12c Vodou Vévés: Damballah Wedo.

Figure 9.12d Vodou Vévés: Ogoun.

A ubiquitous symbol in Haitian culture is the Catholic cross, either in printed form, worn as an amulet, or displayed on altars.

> Haitians do wear Christian crosses, and that's part of the colonial history. Also, the cross signifies the crossroad in African tradition—the interaction between the physical plane in which we live and the metaphysical world of the spirits. You do not have to die to contact the spirit world; the spirits are there at the crossroad. (Bellegarde-Smith, 2011)

Paintings

Recent decades have witnessed a prolific flow of Haitian paintings in oils and acrylics, with the style of most of the works qualifying as naïve, folk, or primitive, featuring

> strong use of pattern and a lack of realism, particularly when it comes to dimension and perspective. This type of art reflects everyday life and is often primitive in nature. Most folk artists do not have formal training, and the works of art they create are often for household use or to decorate family objects, [representing] an art form that comes from the traditions and experiences of the common people. (Corbett, 1997)

Corbett has agreed that most Haitian paintings do fit the description of naïve art, but he questions the notion that all such works are by individuals unschooled in academic art.

It is a fact that virtually all the "first" generation painters of the 1940s boom in Haitian art were self-taught. However, the term *self-taught* refers to the painters and not the style of painting. There is nothing to prohibit a trained painter from adopting the naive or primitive style (terms that refer to the genre, not the artist) of painting. Many later Haitian "primitives" have indeed been formally trained in classical art. (Corbett, 1997)

The syncretic character of much of modern-day Vodou/Christian painting is illustrated in the murals that decorate the Episcopal Saint Trinite Cathedral in Port-au-Prince, where 15 artists contributed to the venture in 1949. The murals contrast Vodou art with traditional biblical scenes.

Only one [of the artists] was a member of the same church, another a Protestant, and the remainder Catholics and/or Voodoo believers. Two

Figure 9.13a A pen and lithograph crayon simulation of a typical modern-day Haitian painting.

Figure 9.13b A pen and lithograph crayon simulation of a typical present-day Haitian sequin drapo.

of the most famous survivors are in the current exhibition. Wilson Bigaud's "Marriage at Cana" and Prefete Duffaut's "Temptation of Christ," depicting the devil and a surreal vision of his birthplace, Jacmel, express their individuality as well as the uniqueness of Haitian views in a reverent, humorous, and earthy manner. The people depicted are Haitian—God's all-seeing eye observes, police chase thieves, football is played, an oil drum serves as pedestal for Christ's baptism. The animals seem human as one almost hears the native music or feels a tropical breeze stir the lush vegetation. Indeed, Episcopal Bishop Alfred Voegeli took justifiable pride as the murals became world famous in the 1950s. . . . Andre Dimanche's "Damballah Virgin" is linked to Erzulie, a multi-faceted lwa that has ties to Aphrodite, Mater Dolorosa, health, and an angry Madonna. This rediscovery of African gods in the symbolism of Christian images provides syncretistic views of saints, angels, sirens, mermaids, healers, the cult of twins, spirits of the graveyard, and others. (Brictson, 2001)

Sequined Flags (Drapos)

An art form unique to Haiti is the *drapo*—a flag-shaped satin, velvet, or rayon cloth adorned with sequins, beads, or appliqués. Altar drapos are placed on a sacred table during ceremonies to invoke the lwa, with drapo designs often including vévés of the lwa whose favor is being sought. Portrait drapos are intended to personify lwa through images of Catholic saints.

> Vodou appropriation of this imagery was both a way to fool the Catholic missionaries, and a sincere recognition of traits shared between the saints and the [Vodouisants'] own lwas. A drapo artist would very often make use of the saint's image as a template for the elaborate beadwork. This unusual remnant of the attempt to Catholocize Haiti is evidence of the tolerant nature and essentially open structure of Haitian Vodou. . . . [Recently] a young generation of artists is employing new techniques, and taking on new themes. The drapo of these artists are larger and more elaborate than ever before. They depict Vodou ceremonies, weddings, and other interactions of the lwas, with increasing detail and depth. (Drapo Vodou: Spirit Flags, 2012)

Metal Art

The introduction of Haiti's steel-drum art has been traced to Georges Liautaud, a blacksmith who began his artistic career by fashioning intricate steel cemetery crosses in the town of Croix-des-Bouquets. In the 1950s, at the urging of art experts who admired his work, Liautaud expanded his range of subject matter by creating many styles of metal sculpture, "expressing artistic interpretations of voodoo spirits and daily life", thereby launching Haiti's unique metal-drum art form that was also adopted by other Haitian sculptors.

> The raw material for most of Liautaud's sculpture is the [55-gallon] steel oil drum. Cutting the sides in half, he flattens it to a three-by-six-foot sheet and then transfers the patterns, which he had previously drawn on paper, to the metal with a piece of chalk. He uses different sizes of chisels and dies and a large hammer to cut and mold the designs. He smoothes out the steel's rough edges, beats out the convex and concave shapes, and when the highly intricate sculpture is completed and thoroughly satisfying to the artist, he signs his name boldly with a small chisel in the most prominent place. (Russell, 2012)

Asson Rattles

During a Vodou ceremony, the mambo or houngan who directs the ritual shakes a rattle to attract the power of the loa. The rattle is called an *asson*, a type of religious object originated in Africa, where such instruments have been fashioned from dried oval-shaped gourds with beads on the outer surface.

Inside the dried calabash are sacred stones and serpent vertebrae, considered bones of African ancestors. Eight stones in different colors are used to symbolize eight ancestor gods. Chains of colored beads symbolize the rainbow of *Aida-Wedo*, and more snake vertebrae encircle the round calabash. When the vertebrae rattle, making the asson "speak," the spirits come down to the faithful through *Danbhalah*, the oldest of the ancestors. Once the houngan or mambo

Figure 9.14a Metal Cross.

Figure 9.14c Asson Rattle.

Figure 9.14b Snake-Motif Metal Art.

has attracted the loas through the deity's veve, has appealed to *Legba* for intercession, and has performed the water rituals and prayers, the veve releases the power of the loas and brings them into the ceremony. (A.D.H., 2012)

The asson in Figure 9.14 consists of a coconut covered with beads. When the priest shakes and twists the asson, the beads roll back and forth over the rough coconut shell, to produce "a great shoop-shoop sound" (Asson Sacred Rattle, 2012).

Drums

Diverse kinds of drums, so important in African religious ceremonies, have been equally vital to the conduct of Haitian Vodou/Christian rites. The doctrine governing drums and their proper use is detailed and complex, requiring drummers to abide faithfully by the rules if the loa are to respond to the rhythmic summons. The types of drums and their rhythm patterns can vary from one locality (*lakou*) to another and from one Vodou sect (*nachon*) to another.

Figure 9.15a Wood-Carved Drummer.

Figure 9.15b Rope-Decorated Drum.

Figure 9.15c Carved Wooden Drum.

Figure 9.15d Death-Mask Drum.

Lakou Souvenance is a Vodou community that celebrates its Rada (ancient kingdom of Dahomey) heritage, [whereas] Lakou Badjo has Nago (Yoruba) roots, and Lakou Soukrie is where the Kongo (Central/Southern Africa) traditions are preserved. In each of these communities, the ritual prayer language, drums, songs, rhythms, and dances are unique, direct descendants of the ancestral and spiritual line to which that particular Lakou is dedicated. In Souvenance, one finds Rada Dawòmen drums, dances, and songs all performed in honor of the Rada Lwa (spirits of Haitian Vodou). At Soukrie, the Kongo lwa are served with their own specific Kongo instruments and repertoire, and at Lakou Badjo, Nago drums, rhythms and songs are used. (Schwartz, 2003)

Dolls

The question of types of dolls, their origins, and their functions in Vodou has been an issue of contentious debate over recent decades. The matter rose to international public attention in the mid-20th century through Hollywood

Figure 9.16a Wooden Doll.   **Figure 9.16b** Doll in Beaded Vase.

horror movies and pulp-fiction novels that featured zombies and vengeance dolls. Ostensibly, a Vodou conjurer would construct a doll in the rude image of a distant enemy, then stick pins in the doll, an act designed to cause the enemy excruciating pain, misfortune, and possibly death. However, critics of the practice contend that such myths are not part of traditional Vodou, as derived from African roots, even though

> some Vodouisants, primarily in New Orleans, have adopted them, often [in order to sell dolls] to tourists. Tales of similar puppets have existed in European witch folklore for centuries. It's certainly possible that Europeans, knowing very little about Vodou and commonly decrying it as evil and Satanic, merged rumors of Vodou with witchcraft rumors from back home. (Beyer, 2012a)

Among serious Haitian Vodouisants, dolls may portray a lwa as a wooden image embellished with raffia and cloth garments or as a papier-mâché model of a lwa atop a beaded or sequined bottle.

Summary

The types of art described in this section have illustrated an assortment of popular versions of Haitian religious art but have failed to reveal the full range of Vodou/Christian symbols and objects. Additional art forms include papier-mâché masks, wood carvings, jewelry, pottery, leatherwork, and bottles swathed in cloth or covered in beads, sequins, or images intended to protect the mystic secrecy of the contents.

RATIONALIZING VODOU/CHRISTIAN SYMBOLS AND OBJECTS

I estimate that the motley array of sacred objects associated with present-day Vodou/Christianity can be defended as forming an internally consistent collection by dint of two principles-of-accommodation offered in Chapter 1, those of *nonconflicting-add-ons* and *tolerance*.

Figure 9.16c Beaded Beer Bottle.

There has been nothing in biblical tradition that prohibits Catholicism from accepting new forms of religious expression as add-ons in literature, music, or the visual arts. It is true that conservative forces within the Church have often resisted adopting new media. In music, the organ and harp have been preferred to drums and the accordion. In art, oil painting and stone sculpture have been considered more blessed than folk murals on abandoned buildings or images of saints carved from discarded steel oil drums. However, within the tolerant religious environment that evolved in Haiti during and after the Spanish and French colonial periods, such add-ons have been welcomed in Vodou/Christianity.

Not only have African and Catholic traditional media breached the barriers between the two faiths, but the resulting cross-fertilization has expanded the varieties of sacred objects available in Haitian religious culture. For example, Catholicism's oil painting has expanded Haitian artists' ways of depicting lwa, and African metal art has provided an innovative means of depicting Christian saints on cemetery crosses.

CONCLUSION

The merging of African religious traditions with Catholicism has resulted in a far more diverse and symbolically rich collection of sacred objects than existed in either of those sources alone. Furthermore, the resulting array of objects has been significantly augmented in recent decades by the creativity of Haitian artists themselves, especially as evidenced in folk-style paintings, metal sculptures, sequined flags, and decorated bottles.

CHAPTER 10

Sacred Sites

T he expression *sacred sites* is intended to mean places in which adherents of a religion conduct rituals or else where adherents believe invisible deities or ancestors dwell. Some sites are mundane, perceptible locations—shrines, churches, and revered geographical areas, such as mountains, forest glades, lakes, rivers, and the like. In contrast, other venerated places are unseen, ethereal locations. Whereas mundane sites can be directly viewed and verified, the ethereal, other-worldly sites cannot be observed, and thus, must be accepted on the basis of one's own intuition and visions or else on the word of a trusted authority, such as holy scripture or a seer capable of extrasensory awareness. In effect, other-worldly, intangible locations are imagined, not seen. They are often thought to be where people's spirits or souls live after their bodies die.

TRADITIONAL AFRICAN RELIGIOUS SITES

Among the multitude of indigenous African faiths there are thousands of visible sacred sites to visit and a host of invisible, other-worldly realms in which devotees believe spirits reside. All of these places exist within an overall religious universe. According to the Kenyan theological scholar John Mbiti (1969/1999, pp. 56–57):

> Nature in the broadest sense of the word is not an empty impersonal object or phenomenon: it is filled with religious significance. . . . God is seen in and behind these [natural] objects and phenomena: they are

His creation, they manifest Him, they symbolize His being and presence. . . . The invisible world presses hard upon the visible: one speaks to the other, and Africans "see" that invisible universe when they look at, hear, or feel the visible and tangible world.

Viewable Locations

As explained by Mbiti:

> People have set apart places as sacred, including mountains, caves, waterfalls, rocks, groves, trees, rainmaking stones, and certain animals, and made objects that they regard and use as sacred, such as altars, sacrificial pots, masks, drums, and colors. Communities observe and treat some places as sanctuaries in which no human beings or animals may be killed, and where no trees may be felled. The community or individuals make sacrifices, offerings, prayers and rituals there. Some homesteads have family altars or graves that serve as sacred spots where family members make prayers, offerings, and small sacrifices. African religiosity has often personalized nature in order that humans may communicate and live in harmony with it. This is not worship of nature, but an acknowledgement that nature deserves to be respected, to be held sacred and used responsibly. If humans hurt nature, nature hurts them. Humans are the priests of nature, indeed of the universe. This is a sacred trust given to them by God, who endowed them with more abilities than other creatures on earth. African religiosity is very sensitive towards the relation between nature and persons, even if today this sensitivity is getting lost in the money-oriented exploitation of natural resources. (Mbiti, 2001)

Prominent among revered places in African religions are geographical areas, shrines, altars, and cemeteries.

Geographical Areas

Such sites can be specific, identifiable locations—one's home, a clearing in the forest, a mountain, a valley, a river. Or, they can be rather vague, somewhat amorphous regions, such as the sky or earth or water.

Specific sites can vary markedly in size. An example of a very large sacred area is Tanzania's Mount Kilimanjaro, the highest mountain in Africa, traditionally revered by the Chagga people who worshipped the god Ruwa in the centuries before most of the Chagga adopted Christianity under European colonialism. Ruwa was not viewed as the creator of the universe, but rather, as a liberator of people from bondage and a provider of sustenance, treating his devotees in a merciful, tolerant manner.

A far smaller revered location is the Osun Sacred Grove—75 hectares (three square miles) of dense forest on the outskirts of the city of Osogbo in southern Nigeria. The grove is what remains today of a centuries-old sanctuary featuring 40 shrines and nine riverside worship stations dedicated to Osun, the goddess of fertility, and to other Yoruba deities. In recent decades, a group of religious artists has restored the shrines by replacing deteriorating wooden structures with more permanent sculptures in iron and cement that are designed in the spirit of the originals. In 2005, the grove was inscribed as a UNESCO World Heritage Site (Osun-Osogbo Sacred Grove, 2011).

Shrines

These are locations in which a religion's devotees honor divinities and ancestors with objects symbolizing those spirits and with rituals designed to please the spirits and solicit their support.

Shrines assume a variety of forms—wooden huts, stone buildings, forest glades, natural caverns, dug caves, and stone sepulchers. Some shrines are simple in design. Others are large and elaborate. The traditional shrine house of the Asante in Ghana includes rooms for an orchestra and for the officiating priest. The large *mbari*-style house of the Owerri Igbo of Nigeria is a square, open-sided shelter containing multiple life-size painted clay figures dedicated

Figure 10.1 West Africa Shrine.

to Ala, the earth goddess. Additional sculptures depict craftsmen, officials, Europeans, animals, and imaginary beasts.

> Among the structures significant to the Dogon of Mali are rounded sanctuaries dedicated to the ancestors, covered with rectilinear check-erboard designs; granaries with wooden doors and locks carved with multiple human figures; and the men's meeting house, or *togu na*, a low structure with a stacked millet roof and structural posts. (African Architecture, 2011)

Objects displayed in shrines include wooden or stone effigies of gods and ancestors.

Altars

An altar is a structure or elevated place, such as a mound or platform, where religious rites are performed or where sacrifices are offered to deities or to spirits of ancestors. Altars in Africa have been very popular, in both communal and household forms. A communal altar is one used by villagers as a group, typically located in a village square or in the forest nearby where spirits are thought to reside. A group altar is often a mound of packed soil that serves as a component of a shrine. A household altar is placed within, or adjacent to, an individual family's home.

As prayer sites designed to honor cherished divinities and ancestors, altars are decorated with objects that worshippers invest with meanings characteristic of their favorite spirits. Among the Yoruba, items that are white—such as shells, porcelain, chalk, or beads—symbolize Oshu, the goddess of love and of the ocean and streams. Among the Edo, such objects as clay water pots, white cowry shells, and miniature ladders are symbols of Olokon, the male god of the sea who promotes prosperity and fertility. Edo altars dedicated to deceased fathers and grandfathers include a bell for calling the ancestral spirit from the realm of invisible beings. Altars to mothers and grandmothers display a carved wooden hen to symbolize the protection a hen provides for her chicks. Because Iemanja is the goddess who protects children and fertility, she is represented on altars by objects from the sea, such as seashells. Following a successful hunt, the Edo leave offerings of food for the spirits of the forest, with the food placed in the crook of a tree or lain on a leaf on the ground.

Thus, a diverse collection of objects can be found on altars, including ceramic and wooden bowls, seashells, stones, roots, twigs, candles, statuary, precious oils, coins, trinkets, and more—with the items assigned sacred meanings by the sites' worshippers in their effort to solicit the favor of spirits from the occult world (African Shrines, Altars, and Ancestors, 2011).

Burial Places

Among African faiths' most significant sites are places in which the dead are interred.

> Death, although a dreaded event, is perceived as the beginning of a person's deeper relationship with all of creation, the complementing of life and the beginning of the communication between the visible and the invisible worlds. The goal of life is to become an ancestor after death. This is why every person who dies must be given a "correct" funeral, supported by a number of religious ceremonies. If this is not done, the dead person may become a wandering ghost, unable to "live" properly after death and therefore a danger to those who remain alive. . . . Although there is recognition of the difference between the physical person that is buried and the nonphysical person who lives on, this must not be confused with a Western dualism that separates "physical" from "spiritual." When a person dies, there is not some "part" of that person that lives on—it is the whole person who continues to live in the spirit world, receiving a new body identical to the earthly body, but with enhanced powers to move about as an ancestor. There are many different ideas about the "place" the departed go to, a "land" which in most cases seems to be a replica of this world. For some it is under the earth, in groves, near or in the homes of earthly families, or on the other side of a deep river. (Anderson, 2001)

> Death does not constitute a hope for a future and better life. To live here and now is the most important concern of African religious activities and beliefs. Even life in the hereafter is conceived in materialistic and physical terms. There is neither paradise to be hoped for nor hell to be feared in the hereafter. (Mbiti 1969/1999, pp. 4–5)

It is customary in most African religions for the dead to be interred in the ground, either in a formal cemetery or else under or near the family house so the deceased can easily return home. The funeral ceremony typically includes sacrificing an animal—an act intended to show respect for the dead by providing food for the deceased's journey to the beyond. Africans are also buried with their personal possessions for use in the hereafter (Kovach & Robert, 2007).

Many African peoples have a custom of removing a dead body through a hole in the wall of a house, and not through the door. The reason for this seems to be that this will make it difficult (or even impossible) for the dead person to remember the way back to the living, as the hole in the wall is immediately closed. Sometimes the corpse is removed feet first, symbolically pointing away from the former place of residence. (Anderson, 2001)

Particular spirits are assigned the task of overseeing burial sites. Among the Yoruba, the goddess Oya is the cemetery guardian and wife of Shango, the orisha of rebirth. In the Congo, Mariwanga is a female deity who rides on the wind and is in control of cemeteries.

Invisible, Other-Worldly Sites

Followers of African faiths are convinced that they know the location of certain spirits—a particular house, shrine, altar, tree, forest glade, lake, mountain, animal, or the like. However, the places where other spirits live are obscure. Perhaps some phantasms just hover about, their presence only vaguely sensed. Other spirits are thought to reside in the unknown but can be summoned by a diviner who assumes a trance state, or else, an unseen divine may be found and visited by means of a devotee's dream.

The term *trance*, as intended here, refers to a person entering an altered state of consciousness that involves abandoning one's customary mode of thought and behavior and replacing them with unusual personality traits. As noted in Chapter 3, techniques that facilitate this altered state of consciousness range from (a) inhaling vapors of medicinal preparations, to (b) drinking potions, and to (c) engaging in rhythmic chanting, drumming, and dancing. The assumption is that the entranced individual's usual self has abandoned the body, with the body now inhabited by the spirit of a divinity or dead ancestor that has been summoned from the unknown to deliver messages to individuals or to the general populace.

People's dreams can include the impression that the dreamer is visiting distant sites and encountering departed family members, friends, enemies, or strangers. People who experience such a slumber-time sensation may interpret it as more than a just curious trick of the mind. Instead, they may envision their dream trips to be their self or soul exiting their body and traveling through space to places where divinities or the shades of deceased individuals reside. Thus, a dream may be interpreted by devotees as a vehicle for transporting the dreamer to the presence of otherwise invisible spirits.

SIGNIFICANT CATHOLIC SITES

As in African religions, the Catholic belief system includes both viewable places and invisible locations.

Viewable Locations

Mundane locations in Catholicism include places mentioned in the Bible, ones associated with individuals who were canonized as saints over the past two millennia, sites of worship (churches, cathedrals, chapels), and burial grounds.

Some viewable sites are large expanses in which important events occurred over an extended period of time. Such territories include Egypt, where early Israelites were held in bondage, and Sinai, the mountainous desert region through which the Israelites wandered for 40 years after escaping from Egypt.

Other noteworthy locations are towns and cities where battles were fought or critical incidents occurred. One example is the city of Jericho, whose walls Joshua's followers allegedly blew down, thereby demonstrating how God-given powers could promote the welfare of the Lord's chosen people. Another significant place was Jerusalem, the center of Jewish culture under King David. In the Bible's New Testament, Bethlehem was notable as the birthplace of Jesus.

Perhaps the most controversial biblical description of a place is the portrayal of the universe in the first chapter of Genesis—with the world represented as a flat Earth under a dome-shaped sky referred to as a firmament in which the sun, moon, and stars were embedded. It is difficult today for many Christians to accept this conception of the universe because it is a far cry from modern-day science's version of a ball-shaped earth revolving in endless space.

Places of note in the evolution of Catholic tradition since Jesus' day are locations associated with miracles attributed to saints. Lourdes, France, is visited by thousands of pilgrims each year for healing that is credited to Saint Bernadette Soubiroux, who had visions of the Virgin Mary at Lourdes in 1858. Catholic pilgrims

Figure 10.2 Catholic Cathedral.

in search of cures also visit Mugnano, Italy, the town of Saint Philomena's martyrdom at age 14 in 1802. Saint Peter's Basilica in Rome is built where Jesus' disciple, Peter, was martyred. In the Italian town of Assisi, a basilica holds artifacts from the life of Saint Francis (1182–1226), including "the crucifix from which Jesus spoke to St. Francis, asking him to rebuild His church" (*Shrines of Italy*, 2006).

Places of worship are usually churches, cathedrals, chapels, and a devotee's own home. When European colonists settled foreign lands—such as Africa and Haiti—they erected churches as the community's most important meeting place. When towns grew to become cities, and as immigrants from diverse Christian denominations arrived, a greater variety of churches appeared. When city congregations became increasingly affluent, churches became more elaborate colonial copies of ornate European cathedrals.

Burial Sites

Catholics traditionally have interred their dead in graves or tombs regarded as sacred places to be revered. Devotees memorialize the life of the deceased by marking the burial site with a grave stone or tomb that displays the name and the birth and death dates of the departed.

Invisible, Other-Worldly Sites

In contrast to viewable, earthly places are those invisible locations whose description is accepted from a trusted source—a document or a respected person—or from personal extrasensory revelation not accessible to other people. Four such locations in Christian tradition are heaven, hell, purgatory, and limbo. Each is a place to which a person's soul might go after death.

Heaven

The Bible speaks often of heaven and identifies its location—high in the sky—but rarely describes heaven's contents and living conditions. Although Jesus said that in heaven ("in my father's house"), there "are many mansions" (John 14: 2), the precise nature of those mansions and their surrounds was not made clear.

The biblical book of Revelation, attributed to a devotee named John, envisions heaven as featuring God on a throne.

And he who sat there appeared like jasper and carnelian, and round the throne was a rainbow that looked like an emerald. Round the throne were twenty-four thrones, and seated on the thrones were twenty-four elders, clothed in white raiment; and they have on their heads crowns of gold. And before the throne burn seven torches of fire, which are the seven spirits of God; and before the throne there is as it were a sea of glass, like crystal. And round the throne, on each side of the throne, are four living creatures, full of eyes in front and behind: the first living-creature like a lion, the second living-creature like an ox, the third living-creature with the face of a man, and the fourth living-creature like a flying eagle. And the four living-creatures, each of them with six wings, are full of eyes round about and within, and day and night they never cease to sing "Holy, holy, holy, is the Lord God Almighty, who was and is and is to come!" (Revelation 4: 1–8; 7: 9–17, 1611)

Ever since early Christian days, theologians—and particularly saintly ones during the Middle Ages (Saint Gregory the Great, Saint Ambrose, Saint Augustine, Saint Jerome, Saint John Chrysostom, Saint Basil, Saint Gregory Nazianzen)—have offered their own versions of heaven, versions apparently discovered through divine inspiration. One example of the present-day inheritance of such views is this segment from the *Catholic Encyclopedia* (2008).

In heaven there is not the least pain or sadness; for every aspiration of nature must be finally realized. . . . [The souls of the deceased] delight greatly in the company of Christ, the angels, and the saints, and in the reunion with so many who were dear to them on earth. (Heaven, 2008)

Among well-known depictions of heaven, perhaps the most complex is the version in the third part of the epic Italian poem, *The Divine Comedy,* written by Dante Alighieri in the early 14th century. The parts of the poem are titled *Inferno, Purgatory,* and *Paradise.* In Dante's vision, heaven or paradise consists of nine spheres, ranging from the least desirable to the most desirable in recognition of the fact that people arriving in heaven can vary in their degree of holiness, that is, in their ability to love God. The first level is for good people, but ones who renounced their vows, such as a nun who left her convent. The second level is for individuals who did good on earth out of a desire for fame. The third level is for those who did good out of love. The fourth is for the wise, the fifth for ones who fought for Christianity, the sixth for the just, the seventh for the contemplative, and the eighth for the blessed, such as saints. The ninth sphere is occupied by angels. "Thus, there is a heavenly hierarchy, but everyone is satisfied with his post, because he understands the fact that he is not capable of any greater experience" (Dante Alighieri, 2014).

Hell

Whereas heaven is a joy-filled, pain-free destiny for souls after death, hell (*hades* or the Hebrew *Shoel*) is quite the opposite. By long tradition, hell is said to exist in the depths of the earth where deceased sinners suffer eternal torment

The most detailed, best-known estimate of conditions in hell is found in the *Inferno* section of Dante's *Divine Comedy*. Dante's hell is composed of nine circles, each inflicting punishment in keeping with the arriving soul's chief sin when on earth. The first circle (Limbo) is for virtuous people who had no chance to accept Jesus, either because they were not baptized (as in the case of new babies) or were pagans, such as the Greek authors Homer, Aristotle, and Plato who lived before Jesus' time, and Roman authors Vigil, Horace, and Ovid, who were Jesus' contemporaries but were not among his followers. Occupants of limbo are not actively punished. Instead, they suffer psychologically by regretting that they were not Christians when alive (Dante Alighieri, 2014).

In the second circle, souls that were lustful on earth are whipped about by violent storms. In the third, gluttons lie in the mud under constant rain and hail. In the fourth, people who spent life greedy for worldly wealth are forced to move enormous weights. In the fifth, souls of chronically angry people fight each other in swamp water while slothful souls gurgle beneath the water. In the sixth, heretics are trapped in fiery tombs. In the seventh, the violent, the suicidal, and the blasphemous are immersed in a river of boiling blood, transformed into thorny bushes, or cast into a desert of flaming sand. The eighth circle is for souls that were intentionally evil when on earth—flatterers, sorcerers, false prophets, corrupt politicians, hypocrites, thieves, troublemakers, counterfeiters, perjurers, impersonators, and simonists who sold sacred objects for profit. They suffer punishments ranging from snakebites and boiling pitch to horrible diseases and immersion in human excrement.

The ninth circle is entirely ice. Satan is frozen into the center of a pit. His companions, also encased in ice, are the souls of people who were traitors on earth—traitors to their kin (such as Cain who killed his brother, Able, in the biblical book of Genesis) or traitors to their city or country, to their guests, or to their benefactors. Dante portrays Satan as a beastly, six-winged, three-headed giant chewing on the bloody bodies of traitors (Dante Alighieri, 2014).

Purgatory

In Roman Catholic doctrine, the souls of Christians may, upon death, still be stained with sin, unworthy of immediately entering heaven. Those souls are thus obliged to spend time at a way-station called purgatory, where they will be cleansed of sins before deserving eternal heavenly bliss.

As with heaven and hell, Dante's version of purgatory continues to influence Christians' ideas about life after death. According to *The Divine Comedy*, purgatory is a terraced mountain, with each of the seven terraces representing one of the deadly sins—pride, envy, wrath, sloth, avarice, gluttony, and lust. The terrace that a soul occupies is suited to the most prominent of the sins the person committed while alive. On that terrace, the soul must suffer a suitable punishment until repentance permits the soul to ascend to the mountain summit that represents the Garden of Eden from which the first man and woman, Adam and Eve, had been ejected for disobeying God. The purged soul is then permitted to pass from the garden into heaven (Dante Alighieri, 2014).

Limbo

As noted earlier, limbo is the afterlife lodging for souls of good people who did not have a chance to become Christians because they either died before being baptized or else lived before Jesus' time. Because limbo is occupied by virtuous souls, it is a happy place, with the joy of the residents marred only by feelings of distress over their not qualifying as Christians.

AFRICAN FAITHS AND CATHOLICISM COMPARED

In several ways, the two religious traditions—African and Catholic—are similar in the treatment of sites they revere. Both faiths assign spiritual power to locations where devotees worship, and both insist that people respect the sacredness of those sites. The desecration of shrines, altars, churches, or other consecrated places is forbidden, and steps are taken to punish the abusers.

However, the conceptions of sites in African and Catholic worldviews also differ from each other in significant respects. Rarely, if ever, does Catholic doctrine propose that such objects of nature as trees, mountains, rivers, and the like are the habitations of deities or of deceased ancestors, as is typically believed by adherents of African faiths. Notions about where the shades of departed humans are located also differ between the two traditions. Whereas the Catholic belief system includes such entities as heaven, hell, purgatory, and limbo as highly significant places, no such sites are included in African religions. In effect, African traditions do not envisage souls of the dead being rewarded in a paradise, tormented in an infernal region, or forced to inhabit a way station throughout eternity. Deceased ancestors, in African belief, simply continue to lead their regular lives after death, but in an other-worldly condition.

IMPORTANT VODOU/CHRISTIAN SITES

Like African religions and Catholicism, the Vodou/Christian faith includes both viewable and invisible locations.

Viewable Places

Significant mundane locations include natural phenomena, temples, altars, and burial places.

Natural Phenomena

From African forbears, Vodou/Christianity inherited a belief that every feature of the natural world is imbued with spiritual meaning and is associated with particular lwa—such features as a tree, the sea, a river, a mountain, special days of the week, a specific color, a song, a particular ceremony.

> All knowledge presupposes a fundamental holism grounded in the idea of oneness and unity of all forces of nature, in the idea of interdependence and interconnectedness of these forces, and in the premise of supremacy of totality over individuality. The universe is a seamless cosmos where every force of nature has meaning, and a connection with other entities. Creating dissonance in nature's polyrhythms, disturbing the harmonious flow of energy, bringing about division in the community, are all acts which represent moral transgression in the Vodou world. (Michel, 2012)

When Strongman (2011) was asked to identify sacred sites in Haiti, he suggested cemeteries—Bois Caïman (the site of the Vodou ceremony presided over by Dutty Boukman on August 14, 1791, which set off the overthrow of French rule in Haiti), the waterfall Sout d'Eau (Sodo), the giant tree at La Souvenance, and such sacred rural hamlets (lakou) as Nan Soukri, Badjo, and Nan Campêche. He also mentioned mythical places, such as the bottom of the sea.

Temples and Shrines

Devotees of a combined Vodou/Christian faith can be expected to engage in religious devotions in both Vodou and Catholic sites.

The Catholic church that members attend will feature the basic trappings of virtually every Catholic worship site in the world: (a) rows of seats for

members of the audience who face (b) a table-like altar where the priest offi-
ciates during the Eucharist ceremony, (c) a pulpit at the left side of the altar,
where the priest preaches, amidst (d) a surrounding of decorative regalia, of
statuary, and of painted or stained glass biblical scenes, including images of
the Virgin Mary and of Jesus impaled on the cross.

In contrast to the church, the form and contents of typical Vodou temples
or shines derive from both African and Catholic traditions as well as from
innovations introduced by Haitians themselves over the centuries, thereby
providing a unique setting in which to worship the lwa and saints. The name
for such a place of worship is *hounfour*, *humbo* or *oun'pho*. Temples assume
many forms, ranging from elaborate, formal structures to a simple designated
area behind a home.

A typical formal temple consists of a building within a courtyard that may
be surrounded by a low wall. The building contains an altar and perhaps
rooms in which initiates can meditate.

> The walls and floors are decorated in elaborated colored designs, called
> *vèvès*, symbolizing the gods. These drawings can be permanent or cre-
> ated in cornmeal, flour, powdered brick, gunpowder, or face powder
> just before a ceremony. They are quite beautiful and incorporate the
> symbols and occult signs of the *loas* being worshipped: the symbol for
> *Legba* shows a cross; one for *Erzulie*, a heart; *Danbhalah* a serpent; and
> for *Baron Samedi*, a coffin. Usually drawn around the center post, or
> the place of sacrifice, the vèvè serves as a ritual "magnet" for the *loa's*
> entrance, obliging the loa to descend to the earth. (A.D.H., 2012)

In the courtyard outside the main temple is a *paristyle*, an open-air, roofed
structure featuring a center post (*poteau-mitan*) supporting the roof. The
post—usually made of wood and set in a masonry base—symbolizes the
revered lwa "*Legba Ali-Bon* ('wood of justice' or Legba Tree-of-the-Good)"
who acts as the guardian of the crossroads leading to all Vodou knowledge
and communion with the deities. The *poteau-mitan* is often decorated with
divots in which candles are inserted and perhaps with a brightly painted snake
twined about the post. The paristyle floor is hard-packed earth without pav-
ing or tile (A.D.H., 2012; Hudson, 2011).

> Outside the paristyle, the trees surrounding the courtyard serve as
> *reposoirs* or sanctuaries for gods. Vodou devotees believe that all things
> serve the loa, and are by definition expressions and extensions of God,
> especially the trees. Trees are revered as divinities themselves, and

receive offerings of food, drink, and money. Like cathedrals, tree groves are places to be in the presence of the holy spirit; banana trees are particularly revered. (Vodou: Art and Cult from Haiti, 2012)

Altars

In Catholicism, the term *altar* identifies "the table on which the Eucharistic Sacrifice is offered. Mass may sometimes be celebrated outside a sacred place, but never without an altar, or at least an altar-stone" (Altar, 1912, 1996). In the linked Voudo/Christian faith, an altar is a location in a Vodou temple or in a devotee's home dedicated to the worship of especially revered lwa and saints.

> Within the temple . . . the altar stone, called a *pe*, is covered with candles and *govis*, small jars believed containing spirits of ancestors. Offerings of food, drink, and money may also grace the altar, as well as ritual rattles, charms, flags, sacred stones, and other paraphernalia. Years ago, the sacred snakes symbolizing *Danbhalah* lived in the *pe's* hollow interior, but no longer. (A.D.H, 2012)

For altars in Vodou/Christian followers' homes, worshipers assemble images of the lwa and saints, along with offerings that include jewelry, mirrors, liquor, perfume, cigarettes, sunglasses, beaded bottles, sacred stones, bits of wood, and the like. The objects are intended to please the worshipper's favorite deities. The deities, in return, are expected to answer prayers for health, love, or good fortune.

> An altar is like a symbolic representation of the world, of situations and contexts. Altars can be so many things, too. It's like the lwa. It's an attempt to grasp the totality. Also, they are sometimes miniaturized versions of grand narratives. If we are going to make a comparison to Christianity, it reminds me a lot of nativity scenes because they are sort of a way to make visually and three-dimensionally perceptible a reality that's mysterious and very grand in a nontextual way—in a very powerful performative way—to ourselves and to other people. (Strongman, 2011)

Each altar has a particular identity, with lwa and objects grouped according to a devotee's spiritual nation. For instance, a Rada nation altar honors lwa inherited from West Africa and uses many images borrowed from Catholic

worship. A Petwo/Kongo altar is dedicated to creolized lwa, featuring asser-
tive imagery derived from a Kongo heritage. A Bizango altar contains objects
reflecting the judicial and policing function of the Bizango secret society
(Bizango Altar, 2012).

Altars are intended not only for spiritual purposes, but they serve as artistic
creations as well, representing found art, that is, objects fortuitously discovered and now united to create spiritual symbols. Individual items on the altar
are appreciated for both their spiritual significance and their visual elegance.
For example, an altar's decorated bottles illustrate a duality of religious function and artistic form. They are *travay maji*, or magic works (McAlister,
1995, p. 318).

In both temples and devotees' homes, altars form a point of connection
between earthly human life and the ethereal spirit realm.

Burial Places

Traditionally, the deceased in Haiti have been interred in a cemetery following an elaborate funeral that is a mixture of Vodou and Christian elements. In each cemetery, because of frequent flooding, the dead are placed
in above-ground tombs rather than underground graves. As in African tradition, Vodou lore assigns the care of burial sites to one or more lwa.

> In every major cemetery in Haiti, Papa Baron Samedi, "lord of the
> dead", is represented by a black cross mounted on a small tomb. Guede,
> the keeper of the cemetery, is the primary contact with the dead. In the
> event that a person wishes to petition or contact the dead, he or she
> must first appeal to Guede/Baron Samedi to make the connection with
> ancestral spirits. Guede is generally a good and generous spirit; both
> Papa Baron and Gran Brigitte [female guardian of graves and wife of
> one of the Barons] have healing power. According to Vodou priests,
> Guede can decide the fate of a person near death by allowing him or her
> to recover or make the transition to the afterlife. (Baron Samedi, 2012)

In 2010, the country's earthquake that killed an estimated 300,000 people forced the violation of time-honored Vodou/Christian burial practices.
Survivors of the disaster could not arrange funerals for so many victims, nor
could cemeteries come close to accommodating such a cascade of dead bodies. Consequently, in the weeks following the cataclysm, an estimated 70,000
corpses were dumped into mass graves in open fields (Haiti Earthquake,

2010). Such treatment of the deceased enraged Vodou leaders who complained to the nation's president, Rene Preval, that "The conditions in which bodies are being buried is not respecting the dignity of these people" (Delva, 2010).

Invisible, Other-Worldly Sites

When the belief system of Vodou/Christian adherents includes such invisible places as heaven and hell, their conviction has derived from the Catholic source rather than the African. Such imagined locations are not part of African-derived Vodou. For example, Bondye, the supreme being in Vodou, does not occupy a particular place, but is assumed simply to be remote from humans. Vodou's lesser deities are imagined to be either in an ethereal nothingness (until summoned to possess some human's body during a ceremony) or are inhabiting such objects of nature as trees, mountains, streams, and such.

RATIONALIZING VODOU/CHRISTIAN SACRED SITES

As in previous chapters, I propose in Chapter 10 that a Vodou/Christian faith represents a consistent, reasonable belief system when viewed in terms of principles-of-accommodation described in Chapter 1. Three precepts that justify Vodou/Christian religious sites being seen as a unified collection are the principles of *in-name-only, nonconflicting-add-ons,* and *tolerance.*

Consider, first, *in-name-only.* African-derived Vodou and Catholicism both have communal places of worship (temples, shrines), ones called *hounfour, humbo* or *oun'pho* in Vodou tradition—the equivalent of *église* in French and church in English. Likewise, both Vodou and Catholicism have a place for revered objects, a place called altar in English, *autel* in French, and *lotèl* in Haitian Creole. In both Vodou and Catholic traditions, the deceased are buried in a grave (English), *tombe* (French), and *tonm* (Creole). Thus, Vodou and Catholicism share types of sites that differ only in their names and details.

Furthermore, I suggest that those differences in details have been accommodated by the tolerance that evolved over the centuries on the part of Vodou adepts and European colonialists (Spanish and French plantation owners, their descendants, and Catholic clergy). As a result, nonconflicting-add-ons could become part of a combined Vodou/Christian worldview. For example, Vodou devotees have attended Catholic churches and included on their altars such Christian symbols as crosses and pictures of the Virgin Mary. Catholic clerics, in turn, have endured parishioners' beliefs that spirits inhabit such objects of nature as trees, ponds, and mountains.

CONCLUSION

The dual purpose of Chapter 10 has been to (a) describe types of sacred sites in African traditional religions and Catholicism and (b) identify ways those traditions have combined with historical events in the island nation to produce the Vodou/Christian faith that continues to be the dominant world-view in Haitian society.

CHAPTER 11

Religious Societies

The expression *religious societies* identifies organizations that promote the aims of the religions with which the organizations are associated. African religions and Roman Catholicism have both maintained such societies, and derivative forms of them have emerged in Haiti over the centuries. In this chapter, a selection of typical ones are analyzed in terms of their names, purposes, organizational structures, membership, activities, and breadth of influence. These organizations have sometimes been called secret societies, so I also note what it is that religious societies keep secret and why.

INDIGENOUS AFRICAN RELIGIOUS SOCIETIES

In the following section, five illustrative West African societies are the focus of attention—the Poro, Sande, Ekpe, Ogboni, and Zangbeto.

The Poro Society

Poro is a secret men's fraternal organization with member groups in Sierra Leone, Ivory Coast, Liberia, and Guinea. The primary function of this Kpelle sodality is to initiate youths into social manhood. The society is secret in the sense that certain of its beliefs can be revealed only to initiated members. The brotherhood is organized as a series of status levels, with men of higher rank privy to more of the society's knowledge and activities than are members of lower rank.

The intent of Poro is social control, which is maintained by the organization regulating the sexual, social, and political conduct of all members of the wider society, a goal pursued by high-status members who impersonate powerful supernatural figures by donning masks and performing in public. Uninitiated residents of the community are not informed that the masked figures are actually people and not sacred spirits.

Bellman (1984) has contended that the Poro initiation rite is mainly aimed at teaching initiates to keep secrets. Among Nigeria's Kpelle peoples, "knowing when, how, and even whether to speak about various topics" is a valued virtue among all mature members, so that practicing secrecy is a significant lesson to learn.

> For the Kpelle, initiation is a ritual process that takes place about every sixteen to eighteen years, about once each generation. One of the Poro's forest spirits, or "devils," metaphorically captures and "eats the novices", only for them later to be metaphorically reborn from the womb of the devil's "wife." Marks incised on the necks, chests, and backs of initiates represent the "devil's teeth marks." After this scarification, initiates spend a year living apart from women in a special village constructed for them in the forest. (Lavenda & Schultz, 2011)

The Sande Society

Paralleling the men's Poro lodges in West Africa are Sande chapters for women, designed to guide girls into adult status. Sande initiates undergo an experience similar to that of Poro youths during a year of initiation. Neophytes in a Sande lodge not only study the group's doctrine but must also pay an entrance fee, with further training and an additional fee required upon their ascent to each higher tier in the organization's structure. Wherever Poro and Sande groups are strong, "authority is divided between a sodality of mature women and one of mature men. Together, they work to keep society on the correct path. Indeed, the relationship between men and women in societies with Poro and Sande tends to be highly egalitarian" (Lavenda & Schultz, 2011).

Ekpe—The Leopard Society

In the languages of the Efiks, Orons, and Igbos of West Africa, the word *ekpe* means leopard, a term identifying a men's initiation society which, in the 18th and 19th centuries, served as the principal body for organizing regional trade among ethnic groups throughout the Cross River Basin of Nigeria and Cameroon. The society was also known by other local terms for leopard, such as Ngbè and Obè.

Each community maintained an autonomous Ekpe chapter that not only governed trade but controlled the general behavior of the citizenry by means of councils, masked policemen, and ceremonies that featured costumes, music, and dance. Ekpe members were initiated into the local lodge around the age of puberty, obliged to pay an entrance fee, and bound by an oath of secrecy about the organization's beliefs and activities.

An Ekpe lodge comprised a series of tiers—usually seven to nine—that represented different degrees of prestige, power, and the society's secret doctrine. New initiates entered at the bottom tier, then endeavored over the years to work their way to higher levels of influence and access to the society's tenets and rules. Promotion to each higher level was accompanied by an initiation ritual, fees, and oaths.

Ekpe activities centered around an oblong, clay-wall building decorated with painted designs and usually located in the village center. Wooden figures inside the hall represented spirits to whom society members paid homage. The ceremonies formed a

> complex mélange of religious survivals of remote cultural origin, languages, music, instruments, dances, songs, traditions, legends, arts, games, and folkways. . . . The teachings required to maintain [the tenets of correct living] were passed from one generation to the next in the form of philosophical insight, moral values, and aesthetic mastery. The ceremonies were often symbolic reenactments of cultural history, a form of theater used to teach participants past events and bring their meanings to the process. The legends were understood as historical events by their gifted performers. Across the African continent, ritual performances proceeded in various ways, each with the ultimate goal of "opening the eyes" of initiates, of giving them a "second birth," so that they could be taught incrementally the esoteric mysteries of their civilization to prepare them for community leadership. (Miller, 2009, pp. 4, 9)

The Ogboni Society

The Ogboni is an elite religious and fraternal organization among the Yoruba of Nigeria, Togo, and Benin. The society's membership consists of both men and women drawn from affluent and socially influential families. Each Ogboni lodge is headed by an Elders Council that supervises the worship of the Earth Goddess, *Ilè* or *Odua*. The council also regulates the conduct of the society's political and social service activities. In both the past and present, Ogboni has been known as a social club as well as an enforcing agency that members use to ensure that affairs are favorable to people with money and power. Ordinary people often fear the society, believing that its members can use sorcery to impose their will (Immigration and Refugee Board of Canada, 2005).

Candidates for Ogboni membership are selected from established upper-class families or from among individuals who have proven to be leaders in political, religious, or economic affairs. Because a high fee is charged to join the society, membership is limited to people of wealth. The Ogboni initiation ceremony features "the splitting of a kola nut on the *image eda* (a pair of tongs, the handles of which bear a human image) on which the mystery of the society centers, and the blood of a killed fowl drops on both kola and image" (Offiong in Zeiger, 2008). Each new member accepted into the society receives a pair of carved Edan Staves that symbolize the secrecy that every member is committed to honor. A person's possessing the staves proves that the bearer is a trusted Ogboni member.

Before the arrival of European colonial governments, the Ogboni played an important role in determining who governed a region or community.

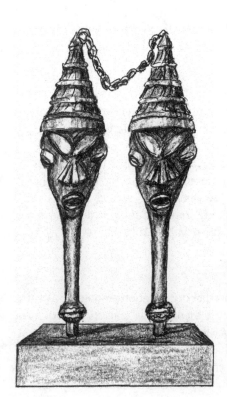

Figure 11.1 Ogboni Society Edan Staves.

It was the duty of the Ogboni society to check the excesses of the Oba (King) whenever he was becoming despotic or misusing his powers. Based on this vital role, every Yoruba town or village had one form of Ogboni society or the other to check on the Baale (village chief) whenever he was wielding his power arbitrarily. (Adeleke in Zeiger, 2008)

In each community, prominent Ogboni members have filled the dual role of religious leader and public magistrate. In modern times, a distinction is drawn between the traditional Ogboni religious society and a secularized variety that serves as a support network for members in important social positions. Thus, the Ogboni continue to be known as power brokers in political, judicial, religious, and economic matters.

The Zangbeto Society

In Benin, Togo, and parts of Nigeria, the word *zangbeto* means "watchers of the night" and identifies the principal purpose of the secret Zangbeto society's chapters that serve as vigilante forces in towns and villages. The history of Zangbeto reaches back centuries, with the society especially active during the past three decades in response to social disorder in parts of West Africa.

One version of the society's origin holds that several centuries ago, a man was pursued by his enemies and needed to flee from his hometown unnoticed in the night.

Using supernatural powers, he disguised himself by covering his body with dried leaves and raffia [giving him the appearance of a miniature hay stack] and by making scary sounds with the horn of an animal. Thus he was eventually able to leave the town unharmed and undetected by his enemies. He later founded a settlement, which he named Hugbonu (in modern Porto Novo, Benin) and subsequently had the men with him dress in a similar manner and keep watch over the new settlement by night to ensure that his enemies did not attack him in his new home. Since then, Zangbeto has been used to keep watch over settlements and towns. (Hunsu, 2011)

Over the decades, Zangbeto members, when on duty as night watchmen, have garbed themselves in raffia, an act believed to cast them into a trance, thereby transforming them from humans into powerful spirits who can detect wrongdoers in the dark and turn them over to the authorities or, through sorcery, inflict excruciating punishment. The watchmen envision themselves as personified spirits of deceased ancestors, responsible for maintaining cultural

Figure 11.2 Zangbeto Vigilante.

traditions. The Zangbeto society continues in modern times to supplement the official police. The Zangbeto also function as a masquerade troop, periodically staging public performances, with the actors dancing about in elaborate, multi-colored simulated haystacks.

CATHOLIC SOCIETIES

Throughout the past two millennia, the Roman Catholic Church has accumulated many dozens of societies. Some are international, some are national, some are confined to a diocese (district), and others are confined to a parish (particular church). One way to classify such organizations is to divide them into religious orders and fraternal organizations. Members of religious orders make service to the church their life profession, a dedication that includes celibacy—the rejection of marriage and sexual intimacy. In contrast, fraternal organizations consist chiefly of Catholic devotees whose main occupations are not within the church, but who, as laypersons, seek to promote the Catholic cause. The laity, unlike members of Catholic orders, can wed.

The typical nature of different types of Catholic societies is illustrated in the following section with four orders and two fraternal organizations. The discussion extends beyond a description of Catholic societies worldwide to note the place of such orders in Haiti, past and present.

Catholic Orders

There are numerous categories of Catholic orders, with each category distinguished by the central mission to which its members are dedicated and to the lifestyle members adopt.

For example, mendicant orders are societies whose members own no property, so they members exist solely on the support of the people to whom they preach the gospel and whom they serve. They seek to model their lives after that of Jesus who lived his life of service as a penniless almsman. Prominent mendicant orders include the Augustinians, Carmelites, Dominicans, Franciscans, Mercedarians, Servites, and Trinitarians.

Members of monastic orders withdraw from the general population to live among fellow monks, friars, or nuns who dedicate their lives to prayer and contemplation. Examples of monastic societies are the Benedictines, Camaldolese, Carthusians, Cistercians, Pauline Fathers, and Trappists.

Clerics regular are priests in charge of a specific church. Their work consists of preaching to, counseling, and saving the souls of members of their parish. Typical of clerics regular orders are the Barnabites, Jesuits, Piarists, and Somascans.

The aim of missionary orders is to convert nonbelievers or heathens to Catholicism. By the 21st century, there were nearly three dozen official Catholic missionary societies bearing such titles as Society of Mary (Marists), Paulist Fathers, Columban Fathers, Maryknoll Sisters, and the Catholic Medical Missionary Society.

Catholic orders and fraternal societies that continue today to pursue their mission work in Haiti include Franciscan Friars Minor, Sisters of Saint Francis of Sylvania, Christian Brothers, Congregation of Daughters of Wisdom, Daughters of Mary, Daughters of Charity of Saint Vincent de Paul, Daughters of Mary Immaculate Queen, Grey Nuns of Saint Hyacinthe, Holy Cross Fathers, Society of Jesus (Jesuits), Little Brothers of Saint Teresa, Little Sisters of Saint Teresa, Montfort Missionaries, Salesians, Sisters of Saint Anne, Spiritan Fathers, Congregation of Daughters of Wisdom, Clerics of Saint Viator, Missionaries of the Sacred Heart, Missionary Oblates of Mary Immaculate, Sisters of Charity of Saint Louis, Dominican Sisters of Charity of the Presentation of the Blessed Virgin, Religious Sisters of Jesus and Mary, Society of the Sacred Heart, Marianists, Scheut Missionaries, Salesian Sisters of Don Bosco, Brothers of the Sacred Heart, Sisters of Saint Francis of Assisi, Sisters of Saint Joseph of Cluny, Missionaries of the Immaculate Conception, Sisters of Charity of Saint Hyacinthe, and Sisters of Christ Marie Alphonse.

According to 2004 statistics, the Archdiocese of Port-au-Prince had some 2.5 million Catholics, which was 74 percent of the total population. Haiti's capital city was served at that time by 277 priests, along with 387 men and 1,200 women in full-time Catholic religious work (Forty-seven Religious Counted, 2010).

The typical nature of such groups can be illustrated with four orders—Franciscans as mendicants, Benedictines as monastics, Jesuits as clerics regular, and Marists as missionaries.

Franciscans

In the year 1209, an Italian priest named Francis in the city of Assisi was inspired by a vision to found a holy society dedicated to the virtues of humility and poverty. As so often happens with religious movements, the group soon divided into the three independent branches that today represent the dominant Catholic Franciscan orders. All three are guided by rules created by Saint Francis.

The most prominent of the trio is the Order of Friars Minor, usually referred to simply as The Franciscans. They are men dedicated to the lifestyle of poverty and service to the poor envisioned by Saint Francis. From the beginning, the friars divided their time between study, prayer, and moving about the country to preach, as they continue to do today.

The second branch is the Order of Saint Clare, composed of nuns referred to as Poor Clares. The society was founded by a young noblewoman who, inspired by Saint Francis' preaching, left home to become a member—and eventually the abbess—of the Order of San Damianoi, a nunnery that was renamed the Order of Saint Clare after her death in 1253. According to Franciscan lore, when Clare first dedicated herself to an austere, monastic life of poverty, Saint Francis had "cut off her hair and gave her a rough brown habit to wear, tied with a plain cord around her waist", thereby establishing the traditional habit of the order (Saint Clare, 2012). The original Poor Clares confined themselves to the nunnery, engaging in manual labor and prayer. In modern times, Poor Clares not only follow a regimen of prayer and austere living but provide social service and education as well.

The third Franciscan branch is the Brothers and Sisters of Penance, established for laypersons by Saint Frances in 1221 "as a sort of middle state between the cloister and the world for those who, wishing to follow in the saint's footsteps, were debarred by marriage or other ties from entering either the first or second orders" (Franciscan Order, 2012). As in the past, the order's leaders today portray the society as

> a demanding lifestyle of prayer, penance, and increasing simplicity and poverty, but the rewards are sweet, vast, and eternal for those who persist. It is a gift we bring to God. The life of penance is to be lived quietly, so as to be virtually invisible to those around us. (Brothers and Sisters of Penance, 2012)

At the time of the 2010 earthquake in Haiti, 16 brothers of the Franciscan Friars Minor continued their educational activities in three convents (Haiti: Franciscans Survive Quake, 2010).

Benedictines

The Order of Saint Benedict was created in the sixth century by an Italian nobleman's son who rejected an aristocratic lifestyle and chose instead to become a contemplative hermit. Later, he would found a series of monastic communities of monks living under the authority of an abbot. Benedict not only founded separate monasteries for men and women but also inspired the development of additional orders that follow his set of rules—such orders as the Congregation of Cluny, the Cistercians, and the Trappists. The rules, which continue to guide the behavior of Benedictines today, stressed the importance of humility, silence, and obedience, and provided directives for daily living. In modern times, some Benedictines follow an enclosed life with little involvement in local churches or the society outside of the monastery's walls, while others offer various degrees of education, evangelization, publication, and healthcare for the public (Theisen, 2007).

In Haiti, the Benedictine monastery Morne Saint Benoit, north of the capital Port-au-Prince, is a dependent monastery of an abbey in France.

Jesuits

The Society of Jesus, whose members are referred to as Jesuits, was founded in 1534 by Ignatius of Loyola, a Spanish soldier inspired to model the order along military lines that included vows of poverty, chastity, and obedience, particularly obedience to the pope. The society's founding document, *Formula of the Institute* (Aldama et al., 1982) committed members to "strive especially for the propagation and defense of the faith and progress of souls in Christian life and doctrine." In the Spanish conquest of the Americas, the Jesuits were among the first societies to arrive in the islands of the Caribbean.

In contrast to such monastic orders as the Benedictines and Trappists, Jesuits have been social activists. Originally, they ministered to the sick and defended the Catholic faith, then over the centuries, expanded their activities to include operating large numbers of schools and colleges around the world and conducting scholarly research, thus becoming the largest single Roman Catholic order. By 2007, the number of Jesuits in the world was 19,216, of which 13,491 were priests, 3,049 scholastic students, 1,810 Brothers, and 866 novices (Curia, 2007).

Marist Brothers

Missionary organizations within Roman Catholicism include a large number of orders known as Marian Societies whose inspiration derives from Jesus's mother, Mary. One of these organizations—the Marist Brothers—includes affiliated lay people. The order was created in France in 1817 by a young priest of the Marist Fathers. Today, the society's work involves more than 3,700 Brothers operating primary and secondary schools, academies, industrial schools, orphanages, and retreat houses for needy young people in the Americas, Africa, Asia, and Oceania, including three teaching communities in Haiti. The society's announced mission is that of

> making Jesus known and loved through the Christian education of youth, especially the most neglected. We guide the young toward a

future rich in knowledge, service to others, and strong spiritual values. We are educators, mentors, counselors, social workers, youth leaders, missionaries, and friends. We come together to live simple lives in communities that serve others. (Real Brothers, 2012)

They share their mission with more than 40,000 lay Marists worldwide, affecting the lives of an estimated 500,000 children and youths.

Fraternal Societies

There are numerous Catholic societies whose members are chiefly laypersons. Some priests, deacons, and nuns may also belong to such groups. The intent of most Catholic fraternal organizations is to encourage widespread, active support for the Catholic cause throughout the populace. To illustrate the nature of such groups, the following paragraphs describe two that enjoy mass membership throughout the world—Marianist Lay Communities and Opus Dei.

Marianist Lay Communities

Among the scores of societies within the Roman Catholic Church are the four members of the Marianist Family that trace their origin to a French priest, William Joseph Chaminade, who, in 1817, founded the Society of Mary. The matron saint of the society is Jesus' mother, Mary, with the group's priests and brothers referred to as Marianists. A second section of the Family is the Alliance Mariale, composed of consecrated lay women. A third section—Daughters of Mary Immaculate—is for nuns. The fourth section is titled Marianist Lay Communities, whose members are either married or are single men and women pursuing a mission that:

embodies the Marianist charism in their lives and responds generously to God's call, as Mary did. They are concerned about self-knowledge, discernment, and spiritual growth. They make an ongoing commitment to personal and community prayer, listening to the Word, openness to spiritual guidance, and celebrating their faith through the Eucharist. Lay Marianists' approach to works of mercy and justice is framed by Mary's attitudes of listening to the Word of God, openness to God's spirit, acceptance of the will of God [Do what He tells you], simplicity, hospitality, and fidelity. They ally themselves with Mary in her faith, in her love for Christ, and in her mission. Lay Marianists ordinarily express their commitment of bringing Christ to the world in the midst of their community or other public setting. (Lay Marianists and the Spiritual life, 2012)

Marianist Lay Communities were established in Haiti in the year 2000.

Opus Dei

The Latin term *Opus Dei* means God's Work and identifies a Catholic institution founded by Saint Josemaría Escrivá in 1928. The sodality's announced mission is "to help people turn their work and daily activities into occasions for growing closer to God, for serving others, and for improving society. Opus Dei complements the work of local churches by offering classes, talks, retreats, and pastoral care that help people develop their personal spiritual life and apostolate" (What is Opus Dei, 2012).

By 2012, there were 87,000 members of the society worldwide. About 1,900 members were priests. The remaining 85,100 were laypersons, divided about equally between women and men. Around 50,000 members lived in Europe, 30,000 in the Americas, 5,000 in Asia and the Pacific, and 2,000 in Africa.

There are several categories of Opus Dei members, including that of numeraries who pledge to remain celibate; they usually live in an Opus Dei house where they commit their entire salaries to the society and practice forms of corporal punishment, such as wearing a cilice (spiked chain) around their thigh, whipping themselves with a knotted rope, sleeping without a pillow, sleeping on the floor, fasting, or remaining silent for certain hours during the day. Such self-mortification is intended to: (a) simulate Jesus' pain when he was nailed to the cross, (b) please God by self-sacrifice, and (c) cause suffering as compensation for one's sins. The importance of unquestioning obedience is spelled out in the society's Maxim 941 that enjoins members to practice "Blind obedience to your superior [as] the way of sanctity, . . . for in a work of God, the spirit must be to obey or to leave" (What is Opus Dei, 2006).

Other types of Opus Dei membership permit individuals to be wed, live with their families, and practice austerities. In addition to members, the society includes cooperators who engage in all sorts of daily occupations. They support Opus Dei financially and need not be Catholic. Cooperators are estimated to number as many as 700,000 individuals. Strong supporters of the society in various countries have been identified as "priests, middle and upperclass businessmen, professionals, military personnel, and government officials" (Catholic Secret Societies, 2011).

Recent examples of Opus Dei activities in Haiti include periodic service provided by nurses from the United States, medical doctors from Spain treating earthquake victims, and college students from Trinidad taking supplies to earthquake areas (Ribnek, 2010; Lafuente, 2010; Egwin, 2010).

Opus Dei and a similar Catholic society called The Knights of Malta have been highly controversial organizations, both of them criticized for maintaining too much secrecy regarding their membership, their true aims, and their activities. Father Andrew Greeley, a Catholic priest and professor of social sciences at the University of Chicago, was quoted as charging that:

Opus Dei is a devious, antidemocratic, reactionary, semi-fascist institution, desperately hungry for absolute power in the Church and quite possibly very close now to having that power. . . . Opus Dei is an extremely dangerous organization because it appeals to the love of secrecy and the power lust of certain kinds of religious personalities. It may well be the most powerful group in the Church today. It is capable of doing an enormous amount of harm. It ought to be forced to come out into the open or be suppressed. (Greeley in Catholic Secret Societies, 2011)

Opus Dei has also been criticized by former members for alleged demeaning treatment of women within the organization.

However, some journalists who investigated Opus Dei discounted such criticism, proposing that critics were simply opponents of the Catholic faith. Representatives of Opus Dei contend that its members are completely free to lead their personal, professional, and political lives as they choose, with the society playing no role in members' or cooperators' personal decisions. Opus Dei representatives contended that the society could not be held responsible for such decisions (Top 10 Secret Societies, 2011).

AFRICAN AND CATHOLIC SOCIETIES COMPARED

African and Catholic religious societies are alike in a variety of ways. Both are intended to propagate and defend the faith they represent. Both set standards that individuals must meet in order to become members. Both are organized as hierarchies, with their members differing among themselves in the responsibilities they bear, the power they wield, and their knowledge of the society's doctrine.

Within both the African and Catholic traditions, religious societies can vary in their intended functions. For example, in West Africa, the Poro and

Sande societies initiate youths into adulthood, while the Ogboni protects the favored social position of the wealthy, and the Zangbeto serves as a night watchman corps. In Catholicism, Benedictines concentrate on monastic self-improvement, Marists educate the young, and the Carmelite Sisters for the Aged and Infirm nurse the elderly.

Finally, both African and Catholic groups are, to some degree, secret in that only their members—in contrast to nonmembers—are privy to certain of the society's dogma and activities.

However, indigenous African religious groups also differ from Catholic societies in important ways. Roman Catholic orders and sodalities are all sheltered under the worldwide administrative umbrella and sanctions of the Church in Rome. However, African societies have been autonomous, each operating under the aegis of a single village's or a limited region's religious leaders. Furthermore, public rituals in African religions typically contrast dramatically with those of Catholic societies. A traditional African ceremony features highly animated dancing and chanting to drum beats by costumed, masked performers, cheered on by the audience. In addition, African ceremonies often include blood sacrifices of such animals as chickens and birds—an act intended to appease angry spirits or promote prosperity. But Catholic rituals, quite unlike African rites, are typically sedate ceremonies conducted by robed priests, brothers, or nuns. Somber music is provided by an organ, piano, or orchestral instruments that frequently accompany a choir. An essential element of nearly every Catholic ritual is the Eucharist, the rite in which attendees drink a bit of wine or fruit juice and chew a bread wafer to symbolize their ingesting Jesus' blood and flesh.

SECRET SOCIETIES AND HAITI'S VODOU/ CHRISTIAN RELIGION

The origin of Haiti's secret religious societies can be traced to three principal sources: (a) African vigilante and political control groups, (b) Roman Catholic orders and sodalities, and (c) Freemasonry.

African Vigilante and Political Control Groups

Earlier in this chapter, I described types of African secret societies that have played a strong role in maintaining control in African villages by placing their members in powerful leadership positions and by patrolling the streets at night to keep the peace. Such were principal activities of the Leopard, Ogboni, and Zangbeto societies. Slaves imported to the Americas from Africa in the 16th through 18th centuries brought those traditions to Haiti.

Although the official control of public life in Haiti during colonial times was in the hands of the Spanish and French rulers, throughout the slave population, the vestiges of African societies provided an undercurrent of expectations and tactics that would burst into action at the opening of the 19th century in the form of the slaves' revolt that won them political independence from France in 1804.

> With their rigid structure and military organization, these societies were perfectly suited to the *maroon* communities: small groups of fugitive slaves from the plantations. From 1791 to 1804, the secret societies played a key role in the slaves' resistance against the French. The struggle was fought with both tangible and magic weapons, as the priests of the societies invoked the most aggressive, hottest spiritual powers to their cause. (Vodou: Art and Cult, 2010)

From those early times until the present day, chapters of the secret Bizonga and Sanpwel societies have been distributed throughout the nation, serving as vigilante police during the times of near-anarchy that periodically have characterized Haitian history.

> According to one present-day Sanpwel member (Mambo Racine, aka Kathy Grey), Sanpwel is not a Vodou religious phenomenon, it is a secular organization affiliated with Vodou, much as the Knights of Columbus are affiliated with the Roman Catholic Church, [and] functions as a law-enforcement agency, taking sanctions against people who violate one or more of the "Seven Conditions" [which include such violations] as disrespect for parents or siblings, slander which deprives someone of their livelihood, stealing a woman, and speaking ill of the Sanpwel. (Racine, 2012)

The societies maintain temples where members attend Vodou ceremonies supervised by a houngan or mambo. The facade of a typical Sanpwel temple has been described as:

> painted predominantly in red and black, beautifully decorated with pink and green figures. A crowing black rooster with a bright red crest surmounts the front entrance. The massive double doors are ornamented with geometric figures composed of four red triangles within white circles, within black squares. [Inside, the walls of the peristyle] are painted with multicolored images of lions and dragons, and various loa such

as Erzulie Dantor. La Sirene is represented as a mermaid several times. There is a wrought-iron enclosure for the drums, and an elevated dais for the master's throne. Across the peristyle, opposite the entrance, is another set of double doors. They are made of a beautiful dark wood, masterfully carved with intricate figures of people, plants, and animals. (Racine, 1990)

In contrast to such descriptions of the Bizonga and Sanpwel as benevolent peacekeeping bodies is documented evidence of the societies' cruel tactics in support of oppressive political regimes. Particularly during the era of the Duvalier presidencies (François "Papa Doc" and Jean-Claude "Baby Doc"), members of the secret societies were reported to have terrorized critics of the Duvaliers.

Additional societies that do not assume a policing or judicial role are "local hierarchies of priestesses or priests (*mambo* and *houngan*), 'children of the spirits' (*ounsi*), and ritual drummers (*ountògi*) who comprise more formal 'congregations' (*sosyete*). In these congregations, knowledge is passed on through a ritual of initiation (*kanzo*) in which the body becomes the site of spiritual transformation" (McAlister, 2012b).

Roman Catholic Orders and Sodalities

As described earlier in this chapter, a host of Catholic religious orders have worked in Haiti over the past four centuries and continue to maintain a strong presence there today. In addition to the priests, brothers, and sisters whose professional lives are dedicated to promoting the Church's mission, there are also lay groups furthering the Catholic cause.

Across the centuries, the relationship between the Roman Catholic Church and the Haitian government and people has varied with the current political environment. But in the main, the influence of the Church has been very strong, with the Catholic hierarchy enjoying a bond of mutual support with both the government and the well-to-do mulatto gentry. This bond was broken in the 1960s, when Papa Doc Duvalier expelled all Catholic bishops from Haiti and was thus excommunicated from the Church. However, in the 1980s, Church authorities in Rome adopted a radically new stance in Haiti. Rather than continuing to support an oppressive government and a wealthy mulatto elite, the Church officially addressed issues related to peasants and the urban poor.

Reflecting this change was the statement by Pope John Paul II, during a visit to Haiti in 1983, that "Things must change here." Galvanized by the Vatican's concern, Roman Catholic clergy and lay workers called for improved human rights. Lay workers helped develop a peasant-community movement, especially at a center in the Plateau Central. The Roman Catholic radio station, Radio Soleil, played a key role in disseminating news about government actions during the 1985–86 crisis and encouraging opponents of the Duvalier government. The bishops, particularly in Jérémie and Cap-Haïtien, actively denounced Duvalierist repression and human-rights violations. (Haggerty, 1989)

This concern for the common people has marked much of the behavior of Catholic orders over recent decades.

In addition to the continued key role of Catholic clergy in the island nation, the religion's lay societies have furnished additional support for the Catholic cause. An example of such sodalities is the Order of the Knights of Columbus, an organization launched in the United States in 1882 by a group of Catholic laymen who

> sought strength in solidarity and security through unity of purpose and devotion to a holy cause: they vowed to be defenders of their country, their families, and their faith. These men were bound together by the ideal of Christopher Columbus, the discoverer of the Americas, the one whose hand brought Christianity to the New World. The Order has been called "the strong right arm of the Church." (Knights of Columbus, 2006)

By the early 21st century, worldwide membership in the Knights of Columbus exceeded 1.8 million. The society's recent work in Haiti has consisted of raising over one million dollars and providing several million volunteer hours of work to aid victims of the 2010 earthquake. The group's contribution included providing 1,000 wheelchairs for the "Healing Haiti's Children" program that made rehabilitation and prosthetic care available to children injured in the quake (Rael, 2011).

Freemasonry

The origin of Freemasonry is obscure, but apparently, the movement began within stone mason guilds in Europe during the Middle Ages. The oldest known document referring to the Masons "is the *Regius Poem*, printed about 1390, which was a copy of an earlier work. In 1717, four lodges in London formed the first Grand Lodge of England, and records from that point on are more complete. Within thirty years, the fraternity had spread throughout Europe and the American Colonies" (History of Freemasonry, 2012).

Freemasonry is a mutual-help brotherhood binding members together by their commitment to *love, relief,* and *truth* as expressed as the five points of the society's symbolic star: (a) assisting a brother in his distress, (b) supporting him in his virtuous undertakings, (c) praying for his welfare, (d) keeping inviolate his secrets, and (e) vindicating his reputation as well in his absence as in his presence.

Masonry requires members to declare a belief in a supreme being, who is referred to in ritual as the Great Architect of the Universe. However, that being can be of whatever sort the candidate chooses—the Christian God, Muslim Allah, Hindu Brahman, or some other spiritual power, such as the Vodou Bondye.

Beginning in the early 18th century, the policies to which Freemasons committed themselves no longer required members to be of a particular religion. Instead, the guidelines set forth in 1723 opened the door to a far broader range of religious beliefs and forbid the insertion of personal political and religious convictions in the society's meetings—a policy marking Masonry until the present day. The "Old Charges" of 1723 explained that:

> In ancient times Masons were charged in every country to be of the religion of that country or nation, whatever it was, yet 'tis now thought more expedient only to oblige them to that religion in which all men agree, leaving their particular Opinions to themselves: that is, to be *good men and true* or Men of Honour and Honesty, by whatever Denominations or Persuasions they may be distinguished; whereby Masonry becomes the *Centre of Union* and the Means of conciliating true Friendship among Persons that must have remained at a perpetual Distance. (Masonry, 1912, 1992)

By the middle of the 18th century, Freemasonry had been introduced into Haiti by French colonists. A growing number of French/African mulattos joined the newly established Masonic lodges, which figured importantly in the revolution that, in 1804, changed Haiti from a French colony into an independent nation. The first president of the United and Free Haitian government was Jean Pierre Boyer, an important activist in the Masonic organization. In 1812, the New York Prince Hall Freemasons named their first lodge after Boyer.

> The idea of mystical fraternities appealed to Haitians whose ancestors had developed their own secret societies in Africa. After Independence, they joined Masonic lodges in great numbers and freely used fraternal

imagery in other sacred contexts. The [Masonic] all-seeing eye, pyramid, square and compass, skull and crossbones, pick, shovel, top hat, and other symbols are especially prevalent in imagery evoking the [Vodou] *Gedes* and *Bawon Samdi*. (Buta, 2010)

Throughout the next century, Masonic lodges in the United States, France, England, and Spain opened branches in Haiti. The Grand Orient of Haiti, founded in 1824, had 64 lodges by 1914.

Although Freemasonry in Haiti has been able to mesh compatibly with Vodou tradition over the decades, the same has not been true of the relationship between Masonry and Roman Catholicism. As described in the *Catholic Encyclopedia,*

The ultimate purpose of Freemasonry is "the overthrow of the whole religious, political, and social order based on Christian institutions and the establishment of a new state of things according to their own ideas and based in its principles and laws on pure Naturalism." In view of these several reasons, Catholics since 1738 are, under penalty of excommunication, strictly forbidden to enter or promote in any way Masonic societies. The [Roman Catholic] law now in force pronounces excommunication upon "those who enter Masonic or other sects of the same kind, which, openly or secretly, plot against the Church or in any way favor these sects or do not denounce their leaders and principal members." (Masonry, 1912, 1992)

Rationalizing Secret Societies within a Vodou/Christian Worldview

To explain why Vodou societies (*Biango, Sanpwel*), Catholic orders and sodalities, and Freemasonry might compatibly exist within a Vodou/Christian belief system, I appeal to three of the principles-of-accommodation proposed in Chapter 1—*in-name-only, nonconflicting-add-ons,* and *tolerance.*

In-Name-Only

All three traditions—Vodou (from its African forbears), Catholicism, and Freemasonry—are founded on a belief that invisible spirits exert a critical influence on people's lives. Furthermore, an all-powerful supreme spirit created the universe and continues to affect the fate of the world and its inhabitants. While Vodou and Catholicism assign a particular name to that spirit,

Freemasonry accepts any title that a person might prefer. Thus, in terms of the belief in spirits, and particularly in a supreme spirit, I propose that the difference among the three traditions is in name only, so they might live compatibly together.

Nonconflicting Add-Ons

Freemasonry is a brotherhood whose principal intent is mutual support among members in their life ventures. Although Masons view themselves as agents for bettering the fate of all humankind, they are forthright in declaring that their principal charge is to further the welfare of their fellow members. When there is a conflict between the interests of members and outsiders, fellow Masons' interests take precedence.

Although the primary announced purposes of such societies as Vodou's Bizango and Catholicism's Knights of Columbus do not include giving preference to fellow members' welfare, that aim is tacitly assumed. In such societies, members look after each other. That's what fraternal organizations are about. Therefore, the openly announced central goal of Freemasonry can be considered an implicit, nonconflicting add-on to the aims of Vodou and Catholic societies.

Tolerance

Official Catholic dogma, as issued from Rome, does not tolerate members of the Church subscribing to many of the beliefs and practices of Vodou or Freemasonry. However, the application of dogma in Haiti over the centuries has been notably lax. There apparently have been several reasons for Catholic clerics and laity alike condoning—or at least enduring—the intrusion of Vodou and Freemasonry convictions and behavior. In the early decades of colonialism, the slaves' rituals—dancing and chanting to drumbeats—were frequently conducted surreptitiously in a plantation's slave quarters. Or, if witnessed by the European colonialists, the rites were not recognized as religious in nature. Furthermore, the slaves obediently adopted the Christian beliefs and rituals that Catholic clerics pressed on them—although without abandoning their African roots. In addition, European operators of plantations and mines found it prudent to overlook the slaves' traditions so as to avoid unduly antagonizing the work force. And over the years, a growing number of individuals born of Euopean/African matings formed an educated social class between the Europeans and Africans—a mulatto elite—whose beliefs often merged Vodou and Catholic traditions.

Hence, a level of tolerance that accommodated a mixture of religious beliefs developed in Haiti across the decades. That tolerance, I believe, helps account for: (a) a merged Vodou/Christian faith being a reasonable belief system and (b) secret societies—Vodou, Catholic, Freemason—existing side by side rather compatibly.

CONCLUSION

The purpose of this chapter has been to trace the origins of important secret religious societies in modern-day Haiti, to identify their roles, and to propose why they have been able to exist together compatibly in the Vodou/Christian faith that has dominated the religious life of most Haitians.

PART III

Postscript

This final section consists of a single short chapter in which I estimate what can be expected in the years ahead for the Haitians' religious beliefs and practice.

CHAPTER 12

The Years Ahead

In this final brief chapter, I speculate about the future of religion in Haiti. I attempt the task by extending into the coming years the trajectory of trends over recent decades for religious beliefs and practices in general and for the components of religion that were the focus of Chapters 3 through 11 in this book.

GENERAL TRENDS

I estimate that the religious life of Haitians in the future will include the following three trends:

- An increasing number of Haitians who particularly venerate and valorize their African heritage will seek to eliminate Catholic elements from Haiti's traditional Vodou/Christian faith, thereby resulting in beliefs and practices limited to Haitian versions of African indigenous religions.

  This sort of re-Africanizing effort is happening in Vodou, where people want to get rid of the Roman Catholic saints. Even in Haiti, we now have priests wanting to remove the Roman Catholic prayers typically recited at the beginning of ceremonies. But I think that is denying history (Strongman, 2011).

- The Roman Catholic Church in Haiti will continue its past tradition of accepting, with little or no criticism, Vodou elements that church members include among their religious beliefs and practices.

- The proportion of Haitians who subscribe to the Vodou/Christian faith that has been the subject of this book will decline at an increasing rate, due chiefly to competition from Protestant fundamentalist denominations that aggressively recruit new adherents and forbid their followers from clinging to any vestiges of traditional African religions.

  In 1930, only 1.5 percent of the population of Haiti was Protestant. The population of Protestants tripled between 1930 and 1940, then doubled between 1940 and 1950. By 1977, 20 percent of the country had converted to Protestantism. It is currently estimated that about a third of Haiti is Protestant (Louis, 2010).

However, I suggest that in the 21st century, despite Protestant groups' prohibiting newly recruited Haitian followers from retaining any Vodou beliefs or practices, it is likely that many Haitians who have been drawn from the Vodou/Christian tradition into the Protestant fold will still furtively hold onto remnants of Vodouism. I base this estimate on so many examples throughout the world of the conversion of people from an established worldview into an imported belief system. Frequently, the transition from the old to the new is accompanied by elements of the old being retained by adherents who adopt the new. For instance, Bhardwaj (2011) noted that conversions to Christianity in India involved "a gradual process in which the large numbers of traditional traits continue with the new." Furthermore, Rambo's analysis of religious conversion led him to conclude that conversion is:

> a dynamic, multifaceted process of transformation. For some, that change is abrupt and radical; for others, it is gradual and very subtle in its effects upon a person's life. . . . Debates about whether conversion is sudden or gradual, total or partial, active or passive, internal or external, are useful only if we accept that conversion can occur anywhere between these poles. (Rambo, 1993)

Malik's study of Islam in South Asia led him to observe that conversion does not occur at a specific moment. It is "not mere syncretism, neither can conversion involve a simple and absolute break with a previous social life," but rather, conversion acts as a religious passage which is ongoing and partial (Malik, 2008).

According to Mathews, throughout the past four centuries, American Indians responded to the introduction of Christianity in much the same fashion as had Haiti's black population.

The Catholic faith was young compared with the time-honored and well-revered structure of Pueblo Indian religion, one that honored the two- and four-legged and winged creatures, the land, the sky, and the plant life that surrounded them, among much else. As they had for generations, Pueblo Indians adopted only the manifestations of the new spiritualism that fit into their understanding of the world. (Mathews, 2008)

Therefore, I suspect that such a pattern of retained beliefs will be true for numbers of former Vodou/Christian followers who are drawn into fundamentalist versions of Protestantism in Haiti.

TRENDS IN SELECTED AREAS

The chapters in Part II of this volume focused on nine facets of religion: (a) sources of belief, (b) organizational structure, (c) spirits, (d) creation, (e) causes and ceremonies, (f) maxims and tales, (g) symbols and sacred objects, (h) sacred sites, and (i) religious societies. In the following pages, I speculate about the condition that each of these of these elements may well assume in the years ahead.

Sources of Belief

In Chapter 3, I proposed that adherents of African and Christian religions derived their convictions through the same six channels—prayer, inspiration, dreams, visions, spirit possession, and instruction. Those six continued to be the media through which followers of the Vodou/Christian faith drew their beliefs and practices, and I would expect that tradition will continue into the future.

The Organization of Religion

Chapter 4 identified the structure of African and Catholic religions as well as the types of participants within those structures. African religions have been local organizations, limited in scope to a particular village or, at their greatest size, to a confined region. In contrast, Catholicism has been a worldwide religion, directed from its headquarters in Italy. Haiti's Vodou/Christian faith has continued this bifurcated tradition, with the Vodou elements varying from one houngan's or mambo's congregation to another and the Catholic portion being a Haitian version of the universal Catholic doctrine and structure.

I estimate that in the future, a major portion of the combined Vodou/
Christian faith will continue to reflect the traditional dual nature of that persuasion: (a) local versions of African traditions and (b) recognition of the
international form of Catholicism's hierarchy.

As noted in Chapter 2, Haiti's 1987 constitution, for the first time in the
nation's history, accorded Vodou the same official status that traditionally
had been given Christianity's Catholicism and Protestantism. Since that time,
Vodou has increasingly been celebrated in the open, with its practitioners
authorized to perform such civil ceremonies as marriages and baptisms that
traditionally were the exclusive province of the Christian clergy. I suggest that
this advance has encouraged a youthful segment of the Vodou community
to value and embrace their African religious heritage and reject the Catholic
vestiges of the traditional Vodou/Christian version, thereby forming one or
more Haitian forms of African beliefs and practices.

Spirits

Chapter 5 proposed that Vodou/Christian's invisible beings were derivatives
of both African and Catholic belief systems, with many of the spirits bearing
both African and Christian identities. I imagine that this dual nature of spirits
will be retained in the mainline Vodou/Christian faith of the future, whereas
more recent revisions of the faith that seek to eliminate Catholic saints from
a revised Haitian Vodou will limit spirits' identities to those of lwa derived
solely from African origins.

The Creation of the Universe

Although indigenous African religions abound with stories of the beginning of the world and its occupants, those tales apparently have not survived
in modern-day Haitian lore. In contrast, the Catholic biblical story of creation, as found in the opening pages of Genesis, is apparently well known
among Haitians, and therefore, the version that people are likely to recall.
As mentioned in Chapter 6, recent years have witnessed a change in Catholic
authorities' beliefs about the way humans have developed since their initial appearance on earth. Recently, rather than contending that the first two
people were Adam and Eve in their mature homo sapiens form, Pope Benedict XVI accepted a Darwinian version of evolution and credited God as the
creator of the process of evolution. It therefore seems likely that, in public
schools and in ones conducted by Catholic orders, the literal account of creation from the opening pages of the Bible will be replaced with Darwinian

evolution. Therefore, with the advancing years, adherents of the Vodou/Christian faith will increasingly prefer a Darwinian view to a biblical interpretation of human beginnings.

Causes and Ceremonies

Chapter 7 distinguished between two ways of interpreting the cause of events in the world—direct cause and mediated cause. People are assuming a direct cause when they propose that one event (the effect) is the obvious result of a previous event (the cause). For instance, the horse wandered away because the stable boy had failed to close the barn door. In contrast, people attribute an event (the effect) to a mediated cause when they see no obvious previous event (the cause) that seems sufficient to produce such an effect. In other words, the cause is a mystery. One way to resolve the mystery is to assume that there has been a mediator—an invisible spirit—between an initial event and a subsequent event. For example, (a) a mother failed to create an altar to honor a god, (b) so the god was angered, and (c) caused the mother's child to fall ill.

I suggest that the ceremonies, rites, and rituals observed in the Vodou/Christian faith serve as instruments of mediated cause. I imagine that in the future, adherents of the Vodou/Christian faith will continue to interpret many events in their lives as resulting from mediated cause. However, I also expect that, as more Vodouisants/Christians gain additional formal education, they will increasingly substitute direct for mediated causality in accounting for events that have scientific explanations.

Maxims and Tales

The wise sayings and stories that are associated with the Vodou/Christian faith have derived from three principal sources—African religions, the Christian Bible, and Haitians themselves.

The African tales were passed orally from one generation to the next, allowing for individual variations of the stories as introduced by each successive raconteur. Thus, in Haiti, the details of stories could change over the years from the form in which they were originally brought to the Caribbean by slaves in the 17th and 18th centuries. And over the decades, tales could be lost through neglect. Because the Bible stories were cast in print, they assumed a stable form across the centuries. Furthermore, Haitians themselves created tales relating to Vodou characters and incidents—a practice that continues today.

I expect that in the years ahead, both Haitians and foreign folklore enthusiasts will increasingly collect and publish Vodou maxims and stories. At the same time, new versions of old tales will appear in print, and new ones will be created by Haitians.

Symbols and Sacred Objects

Recent decades have witnessed a remarkable growth in the visual arts in Haiti, especially in paintings, sequined flags, dolls, metal work, and woodcarvings. The paintings, in particular, are notable for their naïve, primitive, folk style. Many of the creations include Vodou and Christian elements. I would expect this trend to continue in the years ahead, with Haitian art attracting increasing interest and respect internationally.

Sacred Sites

Devotees of Haiti's Vodou/Christian faith have traditionally visited sanctified locations to honor the spirits and gain solace, blessings, moral strength, and hope for the future. A frequently visited sight is the sacred waterfall of Saut D'Eau to honor the nation's most celebrated patron saint, Our Lady of Mount Carmel. According to legend, she appeared on a tree in 1847 in the palm grove in Saut d'Eau and was integrated into Haiti's Vodou culture as the goddess of love, Ezili Danto.

The number of devotees visiting such sites increases at times of great trial and trouble, such as in the days following the disastrous earthquake of 2010. I imagine that in the years ahead, these revered places will continue to attract their greatest number of visitors during times of disaster and widespread misery.

Religious Societies

Chapter 11 identified three types of secret societies in Haiti: (a) the Bizonga and Sanpwel that trace their ancestry to African vigilante societies, (b) Catholic religious orders and lay societies, and (c) Freemasonry.

I estimate that both the traditional African societies and the Catholic groups will continue in the future to assume a strong role in Haiti, particularly because Haitians, by 2014, continue to suffer from the devastation of the 2010 earthquake and the deep poverty that has plagued the island nation over recent decades. The Bizonga and Sanpwel can continue to be useful in maintaining order in local communities that are prone to suffer disorder and vandalism during economic crises. The Catholic orders and lay societies have continued over the decades to provide social services to the populace, and the need for such services could hardly be greater than in recent times. Thus, their aid in the years to come will probably continue to be vital.

However, the Masons are a different matter. Freemasonry worldwide has, in recent decades, been on the decline. For example, membership in the United States (from which Haiti's Masons have traditionally received support) in 1960 was 4,099,219, in 1980 was 3,251,528, in 2000 was 1,841,169, and in 2011 was 1,336,503—a decrease of 21 percent over the half century (U.S. Grand Lodges Membership, 2011). Therefore, I surmise that Freemasonry will have little effect on life in Haiti over the years ahead.

References

A treasure of 3,360 prayers. (2011). *Catholic doors ministry.* Retrieved October 3, 2011, from http://www.catholicdoors.com/prayers/.

Addo, P.E.A. (2011). The loss of African traditional religion in contemporary Africa. *African traditional religion.* Retrieved September 15, 2011, from http://afgen.com/desecration.html.

Adelowo, E. D. (1990). *Rituals, symbolism and symbols in Yoruba traditional religious thought.* Retrieved October 4, 2011, from http://obafemio .weebly.com/uploads/5/1/4/2/5142021/04-1_162.pdf.

A.D.H. (2012). Voudoun or Voodoo. *The Mystika.* Retrieved April 22, 2012, from www.themystica.org/mystica/articles/v/vodoun_also_voodoo.html.

African architecture. (2011). *Encyclopedia Britannica.* Retrieved December 22, 2011, from http://www.britannica.com/EBchecked/topic/ 756980/African-architecture/57114/Palaces-and-shrines.

African legend of Ananse. (2012). *Spider yarns.* Retrieved November 1, 2012, from http://www.spiderroom.info/spideryarns/myths.html.

African religions. (2009). *Encarta.* Retrieved January 4, 2009, from http:// encarta.msn.com/encyclopedia_761589488_3/African_Religions.html.

African religions. (2011). *Academic Room.* Retrieved June 3, 2012, from http://www.academicroom.com/topics/african-religions.

African shapes of the sacred: Yoruba religious art. (2007). *Everson Museum of Art.* Retrieved November 24, 2011, from http://www.everson.org/_ pdf/_teacher_packets/Yoruba%20Lessons.pdf.

African shrines, altars, and ancestors. (2011). *Spirit houses, shrines, and altars.* Retrieved December 4, 2011, from http://spirithouses-shrines .ucdavis.edu/content/lessons/readings/african.html.

African Studies Center. (2011). Kenya—Ethnic groups. *East Africa living encyclopedia.* Retrieved September 8, 2011, from http://www.africa .upenn.edu/NEH/kethnic.htm.

Aldama, A. M, et al. (1982). *Formula of the institute.* Rome: Centrum Igna tianum Spiritualitatis.

All About Saints. (2006). Retrieved December 9, 2006, from http://www .catholic.org/saints/faq.php.

Anansi legend. (2012). *Spider yarns: myths and legends.* Retrieved October 31, 2012, from http://www.spiderroom.info/spideryarns/myths .html.

Anderson, A. (2001). African religions. *Encyclopedia of death and dying.* Retrieved December 20, 2011, from http://www.deathreference .com/A-Bi/African-Religions.html#b.

Anderson/Sankofa, D. A. (1991). *The origin of life on earth: An African creation myth.* Mt. Airy, MD: Sights Productions.

Arsenault, N., & Rose C. (2006, March). Slavery in Haiti. *Africa enslaved.* Retrieved May 26, 2008 from http://www.utexas.edu/cola/orgs/ hemispheres/resources/africa/noformat/resources/PDF/africa/Slav ery_in_Haiti.pdf.

Asson sacred rattle. (2012). *13 Moons.* Retrieved May 20, 2012, from http:// www.13moons.com/index.php?main_page=product_info&products_ id=13578&zenid=221943c7284b4cc485d1449b1da44271.

At a glance: Haiti. (2008). Retrieved December 18, 2008, from http:// www.unicef.org/infobycountry/haiti.html.

Atlantic slave trade. (2008). *Encarta.* Retrieved November 11, 2008 from http://encarta.msn.com/encyclopedia_761595721_2/Atlantic_Slave_ Trade.html.

Auld, M. (2012). *How Kweku Anansi became a spider.* Retrieved January 10, 2013, from http://www.anansistories.com/Anansi_Spider_Man.html.

Bancroft, M. (1998). *The history of psychology and spirit possession and exor-cism.* Retrieved January 10, 2013, from http://www.enspirepress.com/ writings_on_consciousness/spirit_possession_exorcism/spirit_posses sion_exorcism.html.

Bandele, K. (2009). *Slave trade and African-American ancestry.* Retrieved March 3, 2009 from http://wysinger.homestead.com/mapofafricadias pora.html.

Bandura, A. (1977). *Social learning theory.* Englewood Cliffs, NJ: Prentice-Hall.

Barbezat, S. (2014). Rosca de reyes. *About.com.* Retrieved January 23, 2014, from gomexico.about.com/od/christmas/g/rosca-de-reyes.htm.

Baron Samedi. (2012). *Planet Voodoo.* Retrieved January 12, 2013, from http://planetvoodoo.com/baron-samedi.htm.

Bastian, M. (2008). *Yoruba religion.* Retrieved May 16, 2008, from http://server1.fandm.edu/departments/Anthropology/Bastian/ANT269/Yrelig.html.

Basu, M. (2011, June 22). Haiti government in limbo as prime minister candidate rejected. *CNN.* Retrieved June 22, 2011, from http://edition.cnn.com/2011/WORLD/americas/06/22/haiti.government/.

Bellegarde-Smith, P. (2011, October 10). Interviewed by C. Michel in Santa Barbara, California.

Bellman, B. L. (1984). *The language of secrecy.* New Brunswick, NJ: Rutgers University Press.

Benin bronze altar head. (2006). *For African art gallery.* Retrieved December 4, 2011, from http://www.forafricanart.com/Benin_Bronze_Altar_Head.html.

Beyer, C. (2012a). Are voodoo dolls real? *Alternative religions.* Retrieved February 3, 2012, from http://altreligion.about.com/od/controversy misconception/f/Voodoo_dolls.htm.

Beyer, C. (2012b). Vodou, an introduction for beginners. *Alternative religions.* Retrieved February 3, 2012 from http://altreligion.about.com/od/alternativereligionsaz/p/vodou.htm.

Bhardwaj, P. R. (2011, August). Dynamics of religious conversion in Himachal Pradesh (HP) paradox of manufactured uncertainties. *International Journal of Sociology and Anthropology, 3* (8), 261–270. Retrieved August 21, 2012, from http://www.academicjournals.org/ijsa/PDF/pdf2011/Aug/Bhardwaj.pdf.

Biblioteca Pleyades. (2011). Creation myths in Africa. *Creation myths of civilizations.* Retrieved September 6, 2011, from http://www.bibliotecapleyades.net/mitos_creacion/esp_mitoscreacion_0.htm.

Biomba mask. (2011). *African masks.* Retrieved November 24, 2011, from http://www.artyfactory.com/africanmasks/masks/biombo.htm.

Bizango altar. (2012). *Universes in universe.* Retrieved January 11, 2013, from http://universes-in-universe.org/eng/specials/2010/vodou/tour/bizango/14.

Bloom, P. (2009, December 25). When we were gone astray. Retrieved November 14, 2011, from http://stmaryvalleybloom.org/homily forchrist mas09.html.

Boddy-Evans, A. (2009). *The trans-Atlantic slave trade.* Retrieved March 12, 2009, from http://africanhistory.about.com/od/slavery/tp/TransAtlantic001.htm.

Boudinhon, A. (1912, 1992). *The Catholic encyclopedia*. New York: Robert Appleton Company. Retrieved September 23, 2011, from *New Advent* http://www.Newadvent.org/cathen/12406a.htm.

Brictson, R. C. (2001). *Vodoo: Spirits in Haiti art*. Retrieved May 18, 2012, from http://www.webster.edu/~corbetre/haiti/voodoo/brictson.htm.

British Broadcasting Corporation. (2004, October 4). *An introduction to Vodou*. Retrieved September 28, 2011, from http://www.bbc.co.uk/dna/h2g2/ala baster/A1019666.

Brothers and sisters of Penance. (2012). Retrieved January 20, 2012, from http://www.bspenance.org/.

Buta, J. (2010, January 20). The Masonic importance of Haiti in the New World. *The Freemason Academy*. Retrieved February 7, 2012, from http://freemasonacademy.com/Blog/tabid/77/EntryId/19/The-Masonic-Importance-of-Haiti-in-the-New-World-by-Jack-Buta-P-M.aspx.

Buys, G. (2000). Competing worldviews in Africa. The search for an African Christian worldview, *REC Theological Forum*, 28 (3–4), 12–14.

Catechism of the Catholic Church. (1993). *Vatican: Libreria Editrice Vaticana, Citta del Vaticano*. Retrieved various dates in 2001, http://www.vatican.va/archive/ENG0015/_INDEX.HTM.

Catholic Biblical Association of Great Britain. (1966). *The Holy Bible*. London: Catholic Truth Society.

Catholic secret societies. (2011). *Liberals like Christ*. Retrieved December 28, 2011, from http://liberalslikechrist.org/Catholic/secretsocieties.html.

The Catholic Study Bible. (2006). New York: Oxford University Press (2nd ed.).

Censer, J., & Hunt, L. (2008). *Liberty, equality, and fraternity: Exploring the French Revolution*. Retrieved December 5, 2008, from http://chnm.gmu.edu/revolution/.

Ceramic arts. (2011). *National Museum of African Art*. Retrieved December 8, 2011, from http://africa.si.edu/exhibits/ceramics.htm.

Chalice. (2006). *New advent: The Catholic encyclopedia*. Retrieved October 29, 2012 from http://www.newadvent.org/cathen/03561a.htm.

Chef de la Patrie. (2010, April 19). *Bouki ak Ti-Malice*. Retrieved November 2, 2012, from http://www.haitixchange.com/index.php/forums/viewthread4845/.

Chery, D. (2011, February 24). *Tézin Nan Dlo*. Retrieved October 30, 2012, from http://www.dadychery.org/2011/02/24/tezin-nan-dlo/.

The Code Noir (The Black Code). (2008). Retrieved December 28, 2008, from http://chnm.gmu.edu/revolution/d/335/.

Colonization and emigration. (2008). Retrieved December 27, 2008, from http://www.inmotionaame.org/migrations/topic.cfm;jsessionid=f830 664201230 576864311?migration=4&topic=5&bhcp=1.

Columbus, C. (1962). *Diario de Colón; libro de la primera navegación y descubrimiento de las Indias.* Madrid, Spain: Graficas Yagues.

Constitution of Haiti 1987. (2005, November 22). Retrieved December 22, 2008, from http://pdba.georgetown.edu/constitutions/haiti/haiti1987.html.

Corb, J.M. (2011, September 14). *Haitian sculptures and paintings.* Retrieved May 20, 2012, from http://ezinearticles.com/?Haitian-Sculptures-and-Paintings&id=6559556.

Corbett, B. (1997, December 19). *Haitian art before and after 1994 and Dewitt Peters.* Retrieved May 20, 2012, from http://www.webster.edu/~corbetre/haiti/art/pre-1944.htm.

Corbett, B. (1983). *Haitian folktales and proverbs.* Retrieved May 30, 2012, from http://www.webster.edu/~corbetre/haiti/literature/folktale.htm.

Corbett, B. (1988, March). *Introduction to Voodoo in Haiti.* Retrieved December 29, 2008, from http://www.webster.edu/~corbetre/haiti/voodoo/overview.htm.

Corbett, B. (1990, Spring). Notes on central loa. *Haiti: List of central loa.* Retrieved May 14, 2012, from http://www.webster.edu/~corbetre/haiti/voodoo/listlwa.htm.

Courlander, H. (1964). *The Piece of Fire and Other Haitian Tales.* New York: Harcourt, Brace, & World.

Courlander, H. (Ed.). (2002). *A treasury of Afro-American folklore.* Cambridge, MA: Da Capo Press.

Creation. (2009). *Manual—Church of the Nazarene.* Retrieved September 8, 2011, from http://media.premierstudios.com/nazarene/docs/Manual2005_09.pdf.

Creation in African thought. (2011). *Afrikaworld.* Retrieved September 6, 2011, from http://afrikaworld.net/afrel/creation-in-atr.htm.

Creationism. (1912, 1992). *The Catholic encyclopedia.* New York: Robert Appleton Company. Retrieved September 23, 2011, from http://www.newadvent.org/cathen/04475a.htm.

Curia. (2007, May 5). *Society of Jesus.* Retrieved January 24, 2012, from http://www.sjweb.info/resources/searchShow.cfm?PubID=11802.

Dahomey mythology. (2009). *Absolute astronomy.* Retrieved January 20, 2009, from http://www.absoluteastronomy.com/topics/Dahomey_mythology.

Dakwar, E., & Wissink, T. (2004/2009). Lwa. *Voodoo therapy.* Retrieved May 13, 2012, from http://altmed.creighton.edu/voodoo/history.htm.

Damballah Wedo. (2012). *The mystic Voodoo.* Retrieved May 14, 2012, from http://www.mysticvoodoo.com/damballah_wedo.htm.

Dante Alighieri. (2014). Divine comedy-I: Inferno summary. *Gradesaver.* Retrieved January 23, 2014, from http://www.gradesaver.com/divine-comedyinferno/study-guide/short-summary/.

Davis, D. B. (1966). *The problem of slavery in western culture.* New York: Oxford University Press.

Davis, W. (2012). *Haiti & the truth about zombies.* Retrieved May 10, 2012, from http://www.umich.edu/~uncanny/zombies.html.

DebChris. (2007, November 10). Speaking in tongues. *Catholic answers forums.* Retrieved April 22, 2012, from http://forums.catholic.com/showthread.php?t=197568.

Deep look: The Spanish conquest. (2008). *Discover history.* Retrieved November 19, 2008, from http://www.discoverhaiti.com/history00_4_1.htm.

Delva, J. G. (2010, January 17). Haiti's voodoo priests object to mass burials. *Reuters.* Retrieved June 6, 2012, from http://www.reuters.com/article/2010/01/17/us-quake-haiti-voodoo-idUSTRE60G2DF20100117.

Desmangles, L. G. (1992). *The faces of the gods.* Chapel Hill: University of North Carolina Press.

Divination. (2008). *Catholic encyclopedia online.* Retrieved April 26, 2012, from http://www.newadvent.org/cathen/05048b.htm.

Divination bowl—Nigeria. (2011). *Science Museum.* Retrieved December 10, 2011, from http://www.sciencemuseum.org.uk/broughttolife/objects/disp lay.aspx?id=10710&keywords=divination+bowl.

Douglas, O. (2002). Masks and carvings. *Pitt Rivers Museum.* Retrieved November 24, 2011, from http://www.prm.ox.ac.uk/maskscarvings.html.

Drapo Vodou: Spirit flags. (2012). *Haitian Art Company.* Retrieved May 18, 2012, from http://www.haitian-art-co.com/flag2.html.

Drewel, M. G. (1992). *Yoruba ritual: Performers, play, agency.* Bloomington, IN: Indiana University Press.

Drucker, P. F. (1989, May 5). The divine flow chart. *New York Times.* Retrieved September 23, 2011, from http://www.nytimes.com/1989/05/28/books/the-divine-flow-chart.html.

Dumballah Wedo. (2012). *The mystic Voodoo.* Retrieved May 14, 2012, from http://www.mysticvoodoo.com/damballah_wedo.htm.

Ecstasy. (1912, 1992). *Catholic encyclopedia.* Retrieved November 22, 2008, from http://www.newadvent.org/cathen/07114a.htm.

Efik Creation Myth. (2011). *African fables and myths.* Retrieved August 14, 2011, from http://www.gateway-africa.com/stories/Efik_Creation_Myth.html.

Egwin. (2010). Haití: A drop of solidarity in a land of thirst. Retrieved Mary 30, 2012, from http://www.opusdei.ca/art.php?p=40456.

Ejizu, C. I. (2001). African traditional religions and the promotion of community-living in Africa. Retrieved September 2, 2011, from http://afri kaworld.net/afrel/community.htm.

Ellis, A. B. (1890/1970). *The Ewe-speaking peoples of the Slave Coast of West Africa*. Oosterhout, Netherlands: Anthropological Publications.

Encyclopedia of science and religion. Retrieved September 8, 2011, from http://www.encyclopedia.com/doc/1G2-3404200089.html.

Epiphany mass. (2011). *CatholicCulture.org*. Retrieved October 28, 2011, from http://www.catholicculture.org/culture/liturgicalyear/activities/view.cfm?id443.

Erzulie, Voodoo goddess of love. (2012). *The mystic Voodoo*. Retrieved May 14, 2012, from http://www.mysticvoodoo.com/erzulie.htm.

Eshu. (2011). *Myths encyclopedia*. Retrieved November 3, 2011, from http://www.Mythencyclopedia.com/Dr-Fi/Eshu.html.

Faculties of the soul. (1912, 1992). *Catholic encyclopedia*. Retrieved December 27, 2012, from http://www.newadvent.org/cathen/05749a.htm.

Farmer, P. (2003). *The uses of Haiti*. Monroe, ME: Common Courage Press.

Fleury, J. (2012, January 12). Haitian folk tales: The snake and the pauper. *Spare Change News*. Retrieved October 30, 2012, from http:/www.spare changenews.net/news/haitian-folk-tales-snake-and-pauper.

Forty-seven religious counted among Haitian casualties. (2010, February 2). *Zenit*. Retrieved January 22, 2012, from http://www.zenit.org/rss english-28232.

Fox News. (2010). *Fast facts: Haiti earthquake*. Retrieved June 22, 2011, from http://www.foxnews.com/world/2010/01/13/fast-facts-haiti-earthquake/.

Franciscan Order. (2012). *Catholic encyclopedia online*. Retrieved January 19, 2012, from http://www.catholic.org/encyclopedia/view.php?id=4838.

Frank, B. E. (2011). Field research and making objects speak. *Ceramic arts in Africa*. Retrieved December 8, 2011, from http://www.thefreelibrary.com/Ceramic+arts+in+Africa.-a0160331982.

Frederick-Malanson, L. (1998). Three African Trickster myths/tales—primary style. Retrieved November 2, 2011, from http://www.yale.edu/ynhti/curriculum/units/1998/2/98.02.04.x.html.

Glazier, S. D. (2001). *Encyclopedia of African and African-American religions*. New York: Taylor & Francis.

Glossary of Voodoo terms. (2011). *Voodoo authentica*. Retrieved November 19, 2011, from http://www.voodooshop.com/voodoo/glossary.html.

Grisso. (2011) Shamanism and African traditional religion. *The African*. Retrieved September 14, 2011, from http://www.theafrican.com/Magazine/shaman.html.

Guidelines for the order of Christian funerals. (2012). Retrieved June 7, 2012, from http://www.saintjohntheapostle.org/Updates/Guidelines_Rite_Christian_ Funerals.pdf.

Guyup, S. (2004, July 7). Haiti: Possessed by Voodoo. *National Geographic Channel*. Retrieved February 6, 2012, from http://news.nationalgeographic.com/news/2004/07/0707_040707_tvtaboovoodoo.html.

Haggerty, R. A. (Ed.). (1989). *Haiti: A country study*. Washington, DC: GPO for the Library of Congress. Retrieved November 20, 2008 from http://countrystudies.us/haiti/5.htm.

Haiti. (2012). *The world factbook*. Retrieved April 28, 2012, from www.cia.gov/library/publocations/the-world-factbook/geos/ha.htm.

Haiti economy 2008. (2008). *2008 World factbook*. Retrieved December 18, 2008, from http://www.theodora.com/wfbcurrent/haiti/haiti_economy.html.

Haiti earthquake: 70,000 buried in mass graves. (2010, January 18). *The Telegraph*. Retrieved June 6, 2012, from http://www.telegraph.co.uk/news/worldnews/centralamericaandthecaribbean/haiti/7014634/Haiti-earthquake-70000-buried-in-mass-graves.html.

Haiti Franciscans survive quake. (2010, January 20). *Spero News*. Retrieved January 23, 2012, from http://www.speroforum.com/a/25874/Haiti-Franci scans-survive-quake.

Haiti, mission history. (1912, 1992). *Catholic encyclopedia*. Retrieved November 22, 2008, from http://www.newadvent.org/cathen/07114a.htm.

Haitian Proverbs. (2004). Retrieved June 4, 2012, from http://www.haitian pro-verbs.com/.

Hale, T. A. (1998). *Griots and Griottes: Masters of words and music*. Bloomington, IN: Indiana University Press.

Ham, K. (2010, September 8). A sad day for the Assemblies of God denomination. *Around the world with Ken Ham*. Retrieved September 8, 2011, from http://blogs.answersingenesis.org/blogs/ken-ham/2010/09/08/a-sad-day-for-the-assemblies-of-god-denomination.

Hayashida, N. O. (1999). *Dreams in African literature*. Atlanta, GA: Rodopi.

Heaven. (2006). *New advent: Catholic encyclopedia*. Retrieved January 11, 2013, from http://www.newadvent.org/cathen/07170a.htm.

Heinl, R. (1966). *Written in blood: The history of the Haitian people.* Lantham, MD: University Press of America.

Hipple, A. S. (2008, Fall). Coming-of-age rituals in Africa: Tradition and change. *Prudence International Magazine,* 4 (1). Retrieved October 5, 2011, from http://www.annikahipple.com/writing-samples/coming-of-age-rituals-in-africa-traditi on-change/.

History of African textiles and fabrics. (2011, April 29). *Textiles and Fabric of Africa.* Retrieved December 5, 2011, from http://textilesandfabrico fafrica.com/textile_and_fabric_history.html.

History of Freemasonry. (2012). *Masonic Service Association.* Retrieved May 29, 2012, from http://www.msana.com/historyfm.asp.

History of Ghana's tribal groups. (2011). *Lotus masks.* Retrieved December 1, 2011, from http://www.lotusmasks.com/category/ghana-history-tribes-mask.html.

History of Haiti. (2006). *Nationsonline.* Retrieved January 23, 2014 from http://www.nationsonline.org/oneworld/History/Haiti-history.htm.

Horton, H. (1989). Yoruba religion and myth. *Postcolonial Web.* Retrieved May 26, 2008, from http://postcolonialweb.org/nigeria/yorubarel .html.

Hudson, E. (2011, November 21) Among the vodouisants. *The McGill Daily.* Retrieved April 26, 2012, from http://www.mcgilldaily.com/2011/11/among-the-vodouisants/.

Hunsu, F. (2011). *Zanbeto.* Upsala: Nordiska Afrikainstitutet. Retrieved January 14, 2012, from nai.diva-portal.org/smash/record.jsf?pid=diva2:419980.

Ibo religion. (2008). *Triipod.* Retrieved May 26, 2008, from http://members .tripod.com/ih8_tuxedos/index4.html.

Idizol, A. N. (2011). The Voodoo religion of Haiti. *Le Peristyle Haitian Sanctuary.* Retrieved April 21, 2012, from http://www.gromambo .com/voodoo.html.

Igbo religion. (2008). *Book rags.* Retrieved May 26, 2008, from http://www.bookrags.com/research/igbo-religion-eorl-07/.

Ikenga-Metuh, E. (1984, September 1). Essence and meaning of sacrifice among the Igbo of Nigeria. *Journal of Religious Thought, 41* (2), 19–34.

Immigration and Refugee Board of Canada. (2005, July 12). Nigeria: Ogboni Society. Retrieved January 6, 2012, from http://www.unhcr.org/ref world/country,QUERYRESPONSE,NGA,440ed73711,0.html.

Introduction to Vodou. (2004, October 9). *H2G2.* Retrieved December 14, 2011, from http://h2g2.com/dna/h2g2/alabaster/home.

Iwuama. (2000). Igbo religion summarized. *Igbo world forum.* Retrieved December 12, 2012, from http://groups.yahoo.com/group/IgboWorld Forum/message/45480.

James, C.L.R. (1990). *The black Jacobins.* New York: Vintage Books.

Jobarteh, S. (2008, October). Music and dance in African religions. *African Holocaust.* Retrieved October 20, 2011, from http://www.africanholo caust.net/html_ah/musicand danceinreligion.htm.

Kiigbo Kiigba and the helpful spirits. (2009). *Allfolktales.com.* Retrieved November 12, 2011, from http://allfolktales.com/wafrica/kiigbo_ kiigba.php.

Knights of Columbus—History. (2006). Retrieved May 29, 2012 from http://www.kofc.org/about/history/index.cfm.

Kopytoff, I. (2009). *Ancestors as elders in Africa.* Retrieved January 21, 2009, from http://lucy.ukc.ac.uk/ERA/Ancestors/kopytoff.html.

Kovach, L., & Robert, J. (2007). Burial customs. *CSI: Cemetery scene investigations.* Retrieved June 5, 2012, from http://connections.smsd.org/csi/burial%20customs.htm.

Kruszelnicki, K.S. (2004, December 4). Zombie. *ABC News.* Retrieved May 10, 2012, from http://www.abc.net.au/science/articles/2004/12/09/1260445.htm.

LaBorde, E. (2009, June 22). Voodoo's big days. *My New Orleans.* Retrieved April 17, 2012, from http://www.myneworleans.com/Blogs/The-Editors-Room/June-2009/Voodo-039s-big-days/.

Lacy, J. (2009, April 21). The legendary Madi rainmakers. *Yahoo! Contributor Network.* Retrieved September 19, 2011, from http://www.Associatedcontent. com/article/1630366/_legendary_madi_rain makers.html.

Lafuente, A. (2010, March 8). Haiti's disaster is the worst I have seen. *Opus Dei.* Retrieved May 30, 2012, from http://www.opusdei.org.sg/art .php?p=37667.

Lavenda, R.H., & Schultz, E.A. (2011). Secret societies in Western Africa. *Anthropology—What does it mean to be human?* Retrieved December 27, 2011, from http://www.oup.com/us/companion .websites/9780195189766/student_resources/Supp_chap_mats/ Chapt07/Secret_Soc_West_Africa/?view=usa.

Lay Marianists and the spiritual life. (2012). *Characteristics of Marianist Lay Communities.* Retrieved January 24, 2012, from http://www.Mari anist.com/files/2011/05/MLNNA-Brochure.pdf.

Leeming, D.A. (2010). Efik & Fang. *Creation myths of the world: An encyclopedia.* (Vol.1). Santa Barbara, CA: ABC-CLIO.

Lewis, J. R. (1995). *Encyclopedia of afterlife beliefs and phenomenon.* Detroit, MI: Visible Ink Press.

Lippy, C. H., & Williams, P. W. (Eds.). (2010). *Encyclopedia of religion in America.* Thousand Oaks, CA.: CQ Press.

Litany of the Saints. (2011). *EWTN.* Retrieved October 6, 2011, from http://www.ewtn.com/devotionals/litanies/saints.htm.

Literature. (2012). *Haiti lives.* Retrieved June 4, 2012, from http://haitilives .com/blog/?page_id=18.

Lot, J. (2002, May). Who holds your history? *Research—Penn State.* Retrieved September 15, 2011, from http://www.rps.psu.edu/0205/ keepers.html.

Louis, B. M., Jr. (2010). Haitian Protestant views of Vodou and the importance of karacte within a transnational social field. *Anthropology Publications and Other Works.* Retrieved August 17, 2012, fromhttp://trace .tennessee.edu/utk_anthpubs/3.

Louis, L. N. & Hay, F. J. (1999). *When night falls, kric! krac!—Haitian folktales.* Westport, CT: Greenwood.

Love your neighbor as yourself. (2011, October 23). *Catholic doors ministry.* Retrieved November 9, 2011, from http://www.catholicdoors .com/homilies/2011/1110 23.htm.

Luebering, C. (2011). Confirmation: A deepening of our Christian identify. *American Catholic.* Retrieved October 5, 2011, from http://www .americancatholic.org/Newsletters/CU/ac1095.asp.

Mabrey, V., & Sherwood, R. (2007, March 20). Speaking in tongues: Alternative voices in faith. *ABC News.* Retrieved April 22, 2012, from http://abcnews.go.com/Nightline/story?id=2935819&page=1# .T5W6ac01dMM.

MacDonald, J. (2007). West African wisdom: Adinkra symbols and meanings. Retrieved November 30, 2011, from http://www.adinkra.org/ htmls/adin kra_site.htm.

Malik, J. (2008). *Islam in South Asia: A short history.* Leiden: Brill.

Mambo Chita Tan. (2012). Maryaj lwa (spirit marriage). *Faith Web.* Retrieved June 10, 2012, from http://vodou.faithweb.com/maryaj.html.

Markham, I. S. (Ed.). (1996). *A world religions reader.* Cambridge, MA: Blackwell.

Masks of Ghana and Africa. (2009). *National Museum of Ghana.* Retrieved December 1, 2011, from http://ghana-net.com/National_Museum_ of_ Ghana_EXHIBITION_Masks_of_Ghana_and_Africa.aspx.

Masonry (Free Masonry). (1912, 1992). *The Catholic encyclopedia.* New York: Robert Appleton Company. Retrieved September 23, 2011, from *New Advent* http://www. Newadvent.org/cathen/12406a.htm.

Mathews, S. K. (2008). American Indians in the early west. Santa Barbara, CA: ABC-CLIO.

Mbiti, J. (1991). *Introduction to African religion.* Portsmouth, NH: Heinemann.

Mbiti, J. S. (1969/1999). *African religions and philosophy.* Oxford: Heinemann.

Mbiti, J. (1988) The role of women in African traditional religion. *Cahiers des Religions Africaines,* 22, 69–82. Retrieved September 5, 2011, from http://afrikaworld.net/afrel/atr-women.htm.

Mbiti, J. (2001). General manifestations of African religiosity. *Afrikaworld.* Retrieved January 3, 2012, from http://www.afrikaworld.net/afrel/mbiti.htm.

McAlister, E. A. (1995). A sorcerer's bottle: The art of magic in Haiti. In D. J. Consentino (Ed.), *Sacred arts of Haitian Vodou.* Los Angeles: UCLA Fowler Museum of Cultural History.

McAlister, E. A. (2012a). From slave revolt to a blood pact with Satan: The evangelical rewriting of Haitian history. *Studies in Religion/Sciences Religieuses,* 41, 187–215.

McAlister, E. A. (2012b). Vodou. *Encyclopædia Britannica Online.* Retrieved February 4, 2012, from http://www.britannica.com/EBchecked/topic/6328 19/Vodou.

Meier, J. (1912, 1992). The beginnings of the Catholic Church in the Caribbean (pp. 1–85). In *New advent Catholic encyclopedia..* Retrieved September 23, 2011, from http://www.newadvent.org/cathen/.

Michel, C. (2012). Introduction to Haitian Vodou. *Kosanba.* Retrieved June 4, 2012, from http://www.research.ucsb.edu/cbs/projects/haiti/kosanba/.

Miller, I. L. (2009). *The voice of the leopard: African secret societies in Cuba.* Jackson, MS: University Press of Mississippi.

Mizrach, S. (2014). Neurophysiological and psychological approaches to spirit possession in Haiti. *Florida International University.* Retrieved January 23, 2014 from http://www,=2,flu.edu/—mizrachs/spiritpos.html.

Monteiro-Ferreira, A. (2009). Dance and song. In M. K. Asante & A. Mazama (Eds.), *Encyclopedia of African religion.* Thousand Oaks, CA: Sage.

Morgan, R. (1997, April 22). Legba. *Encyclopedia Mythica.* Retrieved May 13, 2012, from http://www.pantheon.org/articles/l/legba.html.

Nicholls, D. (1970, September). Politics and religion in Haiti. *Canadian Journal of Political Science/Revue canadienne de science politique, 3* (3), 400–414.

Nosotro, R. (2009). *Animal sacrifice.* Retrieved January 12, 2009, from http://www.hyperhistory.net/apwh/essays/cot/t0w13sacrifice.htm.

Ohiomoba, C.O. (2009). The tortoise, the dog, and the farmer. *Allfolkttales.com.* Retrieved November 12, 2011, from http://allfolktales.com/wafrica/tortoise_dog_farmer.php.

Oliver, P. (1970). *Savannah syncopators.* London: Studio Vista.

Omowunmi. (2009). The tortoise goes to a feast in the sky. *All folk tales.* Retrieved November 6, from http://www.allfolktales.com/.

Onwu, E.N. (2002, November 4). Toward understanding of Igbo traditional religious life and philosophy. *IgboNet.com.* Retrieved September 13, 2011, from http://ahiajoku.igbonet.com/2002/.

Oracle Think Quest. (1998). Ethnic groups. *The living Africa.* Retrieved September 8, 2011, from http://library.thinkquest.org/16645/the_people/ethnic_groups.shtml.

Osun-Osogbo sacred grove. (2011). *UNESO World Heritage Centre.* Retrieved December 20, 2011, from http://whc.unesco.org/en/list/1118.

Papadimitropoulos, P. (2009). Psychedelic trance: Ritual, belief, and transcendental experience in modern raves, *Durham Anthropology Journal, 16* (2), 67–74. Retrieved October 20, 2011, from http://www.dur.ac.uk/anthropology.journal/vol16/iss2/papadimitropoulos.pdf.

Perfect obedience to the will of God. (2011, September 25). *Catholic doors ministry.* Retrieved November 9, 2011, from http://www.catholicdoors.com/homilies/2011/110925.htm.

Pew Forum. (2010, April 15). *Tolerance and tension: Islam and Christianity in Sub-Saharan Africa* (Chapter 3). Retrieved September 2, 2011, from http://pewforum.org/traditional-african-religious-beliefs-and-practices-islam-and-christianity-in-sub-saharan-africa.aspx.

Pope Benedict. (2011, January 6). God responsible for big bang and universe creation. *FoxNews.com.* Retrieved September 7, 2011, from http://www.foxnews.com/world/2011/01/06/god-responsible-big-bang-universe-creation-pope-says/.

Pope Benedict "believes in evolution." (2007). Retrieved January 23, 2024 from http://www.dailymail.co.uk/news/article-447930/Pope-Benedict-believes-evolution.html.

Prayers. (2011). *Catholic Online.* Retrieved October 3, 2011, from http://www.catholic.org/prayers/.

Prophecy. (2008). *Catholic Encyclopedia Online*. Retrieved April 26, 2012, from http://www.newadvent.org/cathen/12473a.htm.

Quotes from the saints. (2011). *Catholic Bible 101*. Retrieved November 10, 2011, from http://www.catholicbible101.com/quotesfromthesaints.htm.

Racine, M. (Kathy Grey). (1990). *A Visit to a Sanpwel Temple*. Retrieved May 26, 2012, from http://groups.yahoo.com/group/Carrefour/message/1074.

Racine, M. (Kathy Grey). (2012). *Sanpwel*. Retrieved May 26, 2012, from http://thelifeandtimesofanecclecticfreak.blogspot.com/2007/03/sanpwel.html.

Rael, A. (2011, August 2). The Knights of Columbus convene in Denver. *The Huffington Post*. Retrieved May 29, 2012, from http://www.huffington post.com/2011/08/02/the-knights-of-columbus-c_n_916125.html.

Rambo, L.R. (1993). *Understanding religious conversion*. New Haven, CT: Yale University Press.

Real brothers, real stories, real difference. (2012). *The Marist Brothers*. Retrieved January 24, 2012, from http://maristbr.com/.

Relics in Christianity. (2006). *Religion facts*. Retrieved October 29, 2012 from http://www.religionfacts.com/christianity/things/relics.htm#locations.

Religion—Africa—gods and spirits. (2009). *Science encyclopedia (Vol. 5, The history of ideas)*. Retrieved January 14, 2009, from http://science.jrank.org/pages/11038/Religion-Africa-Gods-And-Spirits.

Ribnek, D. (2010, March 8). A nurse in Haiti. *Opus Dei*. Retrieved May 30, 2012, from http://www.opusdei.us/art.php?p=37274.

Right for anointing of the sick. (2010). *Sancta Missa.org*. Retrieved October 29, 2011, from http://www.sanctamissa.org/en/resources/books-1962/rituale-romanum/33-the-sacrament-of-the-anointing-of-the-sick-rite.html.

The rite of committal. (2012). *Guides to Catholic Ceremonies*. Retrieved June 7, 2012, from http://www.archatl.com/offices/odw/ceremony/funeral/riteofcommittal.html.

Robinson, B.A. (2006). *The afterlife*. Available online: http://www.Religious tolerance.org/heav_hel2.htm.

Rock, M. (2004, October 9). An introduction to Voodoo—A traditional African religion. *Conversation Forum*. Retrieved May 16, 2012, from http://h2g2.com/dna/h2g2/alabaster/F120749?thread=413159&latest=1.

Rock, M. (2002, June 1). Haitian Vodou: Serving the spirits. *Pagan Traditions*. Retrieved February 4, 2012, from http://www.witchvox.com/va/dt_va.html?a=ustx&c=trads&id=6325.

Roman Catholic Church Hierarchy. (2007). *Infoplease*. Retrieved January 23, 2014 from http://www.infoplease.com/ipa/.

Roman Catholic homilies for holy days (2012). *Archives of Catholic doors ministry*. Retrieved October 29, from http://www.catholicdoors.com/homilies/archives.htm.

Rooke, A. (November 1980). Reincarnation in African traditional religion. *Sunrise Magazine*. Retrieved September 5, 2001, from http://www.Theosociety.org/pasadena/sunrise/30-80-1/af-rook2.htm.

Rudd, S. (2011). *The 3-tier hierarchy of the Roman Catholic Church*. Retrieved September 25, 2011, from http://www.bible.ca/catholic-church-hierarchy-organization.htm.

Russell, C. (2012). The genius of Georges Liautaud. *Haitian crafts—Metal*. Retrieved May 20, 2012, from http://www.haitianna.com/metal_crafts2.html.

Schmidt, H. (1995). *The United States occupation of Haiti, 1915–1934*. Brunswick: Rutgers University Press.

Schwartz, M. (2003, Fall). Rhythms without end: Haitian Vodou drum music. *World Percussion & Rhythm Magazine*. Retrieved Mary 20, 3012, from http://haitiforever.com/windowsonhaiti/rhythms.shtml.

The secret life of trance. (2003, January 7). *West African traditions*. Retrieved January 1, 2009, from http://fusionanomaly.net/secretlifeoftrance.html.

Shaw, E. (Ed.). (2009). General essay on the religions of Sub-Saharan Africa. *Overview of world religions*. Retrieved April 15, 2009, from http://philtar.ucsm.ac.uk/encyclopedia/sub/geness.html.

Shrines of Italy: Journeys of devotion to holy sites. (2006). Retrieved July 28, 2012, from http://www.mycatholictradition.com/italy.html.

Singh, S. K. M. (2008). *A brief history of Voodoo*. Retrieved December 27, 2008, from http://www.omplace.com/articles/Voodoo_History.html.

Sister Mary of St. Peter. (1843). *The golden arrow*. Retrieved October 3, 2011, from http://www.catholictradition.org.

Sky Flowers. (2011). *Fulani creation story*. Retrieved September 11, 2011, from http tumblr.ausetkmt.com/post/6152266643/sky-flowers-fulani-creation-story.

Smith, G. (2012). African traditional burial rites. *Blackethics*. Retrieved June 5, 2012, from http://blackethics.com/640/african-traditional-burial-rites/.

Smith, J. (2005, November 30). *African and Native American trickster folk tales.* Retrieved November 3, 2011, from http://www.associatedcontent.com/article/14919/african_and_native_american_trickster_pg2.html?cat=38.

Spiritual numerology. (2001). *Black spirituality religion.* Retrieved January 11, 2013, from http://destee.com/index.php?threads/spiritual-numerology.2882/.

St. Clare. (2012). *Catholic Online.* Retrieved January 19, 2012, from http://www.catholic.org/saints/saint.php?saint_id=215.

Stam, R. (1997). *Tropical multiculturalism.* Durham, NC: Duke University Press.

Stine, M. (2006). How to live in a rotten world. *Spreading light.* Retrieved June 12, 2008, from http://www.spreadinglight.com/sermons/m-r/rotten.html.

The story of Anansi. (2000, February 26). *Anansi-Web.com.* Retrieved November 4, 2011, from http://anansi-web.com/anansi.html.

Strongman, R. (2011, September 9). Interviewed by C. Michel in Santa Barbara, California.

Suranyl, A. (2008, August 30). *Short stories: Folk tales.* Retrieved January 11, 2013, from http://www.helium.com/items/1165454-haitian-folk-tale.

Tenneson, M., & Badger, S. (Spring, 2010). A brief overview of Pentecostal views on origins. *Enrichment Journal.* Retrieved September 8, 2011, from http://enrichmentjournal.ag.org/201002/ejonline_201002_origins.cfm.

Theisen, J. (2007, February 22). The Benedictines: An introduction. *The order of Saint Benedict.* Retrieved January 23, 2012, from http://www.osb.org/gen/benedictines.html.

Thomas, R. M. (2007). *Manitou and god—North American Indian religions and Christian culture.* Westport, CT: Praeger.

Timeline for the history of Judaism. (2011). Context of ancient Israelite religion. *Jewish Virtual Library.* Retrieved September 21, 2011, from http://www.jewishvirtuallibrary.org/jsource/History/context.html.

Top 10 secret societies. (2011). *Listserve.* Retrieved December 28, 2011, from http://listverse.com/2007/08/27/top-10-secret-societies/.

Traditional African elders. (2008, June 5). Questions about priests and devotees in traditional African religion (spirituality) Part 2. *Roots and rooted.* Retrieved September 15, 2011, from http://www.rootsandrooted.org/?p=97.

Traducianism. (1912, 1992). *New advent: Catholic encyclopedia.* Retrieved January 3, 2012, from http://www.newadvent.org/cathen/15014a.htm.

Trenton, D. (2011, June 3). US: Flaws in death toll report on Haiti quake. *Associated Press.* Retrieved June 22, 2011, from http://news.yahoo.com/s/ap/cb_haiti_earthquake.

Trivedi, T. P. (2004, April 9). Jesus' shroud? Recent findings renew authenticity debate. *National Geographic Channel.* Retrieved October 29, 2012 from http://news.nationalgeographic.com/news/2004/04/0409040409TVJes usshroud.html.

Turaki, Y. (2000). Africa traditional religious system as basis of understanding Christian spiritual warfare. *The Lausanne Movement.* Retrieved January 18, 2009, from http://www.lausanne.org/nairobi-2000/west-african-case-study.html.

Ụkaegbu, F. J. O. (2003). The kola nut: As an Igbo cultural and social symbol. *Igbonet.* Retrieved October 17, 2011, from http://kaleidoscope.igbonet.com/culture/kolanutseries/jukaegbu/.

Understanding Catholic funerals. (2012). *Catholic cemeteries.* Retrieved June 7, 2012, from http://www.rcancem.org/index.php?option=com_cont ent&view=article&id=103:understanding-catholic-funerals&catid=66.

U.S. Department of State. (2011, August 26). *Background note: Tanzania.* Retrieved September 8, 2011, from http://www.state.gov/r/pa/ei/bgn/2843.htm.

U.S. Grand Lodges Membership. (2011). *Masonic membership statistics.* Retrieved August 23, 201, from http://www.msana.com/msastats.asp.

The Vatican. (2007, July 25). Pope: Creation vs. evolution clash an "absurdity." *Msnbc.com News Services.* Retrieved September 7, 2011, from http://www.msnbc.msn.com/id/19956961/ns/world_news-europe/t/popecreation-vs-evolution-clash-absurdity/.

Ventura, C., & Gutek, A. (2011). *Beadworking in Western Cameroon, Africa.* Retrieved December 6, 2011, from http://iweb.tntech.edu/cventura/bead.htm.

Vodou. (2012). *The Louverture Project.* Retrieved February 4, 2012, from http://thelouvertureproject.org/index.php?title=Vodou.

Vodou: Art and cult from Haiti. (2010). *Universes in universe.* Retrieved May 18, 2012, from http://universes-in-universe.org/eng/specials/2010/vodou.

Vodun. (1988). In Lippy, C. H., & Williams, P. W. (Eds.), *Encyclopedia of the American religious experience, Vol. I.* Retrieved January 10, 2009, from http://userwww.sfsu.edu/~biella/santeria/doc18.html.

Voodoo, African spiritual religious systems. (2011). *African Holocaust.* Retrieved November 27, 2011, from http://www.africanholocaust.net/news_ah/vodoo.htm.

Voodoo history. (2008). Retrieved December 27, 2008, from http://www.templex.org/Voodoo/voodoo_history.htm.

Walker, B.M. (2010, November 25). Honoring the ancestors in religion. *OurWeekly.* Retrieved October 18, 2011, from http://www.ourweekly.com/spiritual-living/honoring-ancestors-religion.

Walker, S.S. (1972). *Ceremonial spirit possession in Africa and Afro-America.* Leiden: E. J. Brill.

Weekly African proverbs. (2004). *Afriprov.org.* Retrieved November 10, 2011, from http://www.afriprov.org/index.php/weekly-african-proverbs/250-2004-weekly-african-proverbs.html.

Welbourne, F.B. (1968). A diviner at work. *Atoms and ancestors.* Retrieved January 6, 2009, from http://www.ucalgary.ca/~nurelweb/books/atoms/CP5.html.

What is Opus Dei? (2006, June 9). *ODAN-Opus Dei Awareness Network.* Retrieved January 18, 2012, from http://www.odan.org/what_is_opus_dei.htm.

What is Opus Dei? (2012). *Opus Dei.* Retrieved January 18, 2012, from http://www.opusdei.us/art.php?p=10879.

Wicked and righteous commingled. (2007). *Gospel chapel ministries.* Retrieved January 10, 2013, from http://www.gospelchapel.com/Devotion/Genesis/28.htm.

Wickland, C.A. (1974) *30 Years among the dead.* First published in 1924. USA: Newcastle Publishing Co.

Williams, C.J. (2003, August 3). Haitians hail the "President of Voodoo." *African traditional religion.* Retrieved December 28, 2008, from http://afgen.com/voodoo_haiti.html.

Wyndham, J. (1921). *Myths of Ífè.* Retrieved September 26, 2011, from http://www.sacred-texts.com/afr/ife/index.htm.

Yohure mask. (2011). *African masks.* Retrieved January 11, 2013, from http://www.artyfactory.com/africanmasks/masks/yohure.htm.

Yong, A., & Elbert, P. (2003). Christianity, Pentecostalism, issues in science and religion. *E-Notes.* Retrieved December 21, 2011, from http://www.enotes.com/christianity-pentecostalism-issues-science-reference/Christianity-pentecostalism-issues-science.

Yoruba ancient art. (2006). *Yoruba traditional religion.* Retrieved November 30, 2011, from http://www.yorubareligion.org/_con/_rubric/index.php?rubric=yoruba+ancient+art.

Yoruba creation myth. (1997). *African fables & myths—African safari campfire stories.* Retrieved September 9, 2011, from http://www.gate way-africa.com/stories/YorubaCreation_Myth.html.

Zeiger, C. (2008, October 9). Secret society. *Colourlovers.* Retrieved December 27, 2011, from http://www.colourlovers.com/pattern/251240/ Secret_society.

Zinzincohoue, B. (1993). Traditional religion in Africa: The Vodun phenomenon in Benin. *Afrika World.* Retrieved May 26, 2008, from http:// www.afrikaworld.net/afrel/zinzindohoue.htm.

Index

About the Author

R. MURRAY THOMAS, PhD (Stanford University), is professor emeritus of educational psychology and international education at the University of California, Santa Barbara. His published books include *Manitou and God: North-American Indian Religions and Christian Culture; Religion in Schools: Controversies Around the World; Oriental Theories of Human Development (Hinduism, Buddhism, Confucianism, Shinto, Islam); God in the Classroom: Religion and America's Public Schools; An Integrated Theory of Moral Development;* and *What Wrongdoers Deserve.*